D0458465

"Tom Koulopoulos combines real world attitudes and thinking with thought-provoking challenges. *Smartsourcing* provides an instructive approach that integrates two fundamental initiatives: Cost reduction and innovation. Companies that can execute against this model will separate themselves from their competition and lead the charge in globalization."

William A. Burke, III
Group President, N. A. Tools
Newell Rubbermaid

"If you have read *The Earth is Flat,* then *Smartsourcing* is your next MUST READ—it is a wake-up call for twenty-first-century economic survival."

Roger Garriock
VP
DIcor®

"Movement from outsourcing to smartsourcing will drive corporate innovation in the future. Tom Koulopoulos describes both the terrain ahead and a framework to develop truly innovative, globalized organizatons."

Christopher H. Colecchi
Vice President
Partners HealthCare System, Inc.

"Moving beyond the often-used argument of cutting costs, *Smartsourcing* takes a fresh look at globalization and outsourcing. Providing practical insights based on in-depth research and corporate examples, Koulopoulos' new book is a must-read for any executive tasked with leading his or her organization into the Innovation Age economy."

Patricia Brown
Senior Executive Editor
Optimize *Magazine*

THE MOST PROFOUND IMPACT OF THE
TWENTIETH-CENTURY ENTERPRISE
WAS IN THE WAY WE MOVED
WORKERS TO WHERE THE WORK WAS.

THE MOST PROFOUND IMPACT OF THE
TWENTY-FIRST-CENTURY ENTERPRISE
WILL BE IN THE WAY WE MOVE WORK
TO WHERE THE WORKERS ARE.

SMARTSOURCING

Driving Innovation and Growth Through Outsourcing

THOMAS M. KOULOPOULOS, CEO AND FOUNDER OF THE DELPHI GROUP
AND TOM ROLOFF

PLATINUM
PRESS

ADAMS MEDIA
AVON, MASSACHUSETTS

Dedicated to James Champy
Friend, Mentor, and Muse

Copyright © 2006, Thomas M. Koulopoulos.
All rights reserved. This book, or parts thereof, may not be reproduced in
any form without permission from the publisher; exceptions are made for
brief excerpts used in published reviews.

Published by
Platinum Press, an imprint of Adams Media,
an F+W Publications Company
57 Littlefield Street
Avon, MA 02322
www.adamsmedia.com

Platinum Press is a trademark of F+W Publications, Inc.

ISBN: 1-59337-514-X

Printed in the United States of America.

J   I   H   G   F   E   D   C   B   A

Library of Congress Cataloging-in-Publication Data
Koulopoulos, Thomas M.
Smartsourcing : driving innovation and growth through outsourcing /
Thomas M. Koulopoulos and Tom Roloff.
p.   cm.
ISBN 1-59337-514-X
1. Contracting out. 2. Organizational change. 3. Globalization.
I. Roloff, Tom. II. Title.
HD2365.K68 2006
658.4'058—dc22
2005021886

This publication is designed to provide accurate and authoritative information
with regard to the subject matter covered. It is sold with the understanding that
the publisher is not engaged in rendering legal, accounting, or other professional advice. If legal advice or other expert assistance is required, the services
of a competent professional person should be sought.
—From a *Declaration of Principles* jointly adopted by a
Committee of the American Bar Association and
a Committee of Publishers and Associations

Many of the designations used by manufacturers and sellers to distinguish their
product are claimed as trademarks. Where those designations appear in this
book and Adams Media was aware of a trademark claim, the designations have
been printed with initial capital letters.

Image © www.istockphoto.com.

This book is available at quantity discounts for bulk purchases.
For information, please call 1-800-872-5627.

Contents

WORK MOVES AS GLOBAL MARKETS BECOME REAL

The forces of globalization have finally kicked in. For years, business has talked about being "global." But in truth, global often meant having a headquarters operation in London with distant branches elsewhere, and manufacturing products in countries with low labor costs.

Today, people, goods, and ideas move freely across the globe. The operations of headquarters are also scattered: the CEO sitting in New York; finance and accounting being performed in the Philippines; IT services delivered from Romania; and benefits programs administered from India. Material and product sourcing move between multiple countries as a function of price, quality, and speed. And customers are everywhere, expecting to be served with consistent quality and price, independent of location. The Internet has made markets global, even for the smallest company. In fact, information technology is the great enabler of these changes.

The migration to truly globalized operations has been occurring for some time. But three factors now require a new way of managing the movement of work: the scale of the geographical dispersion of work has increased dramatically; broad improvements in productivity have stepped-up the pressures of competitiveness as companies are driven to become more and more efficient; and the work that is moving—onshore as well as offshore—is increasingly intellectual, not just physical. Another way of describing the current condition is that the brains of an organization are now moving, not just the brawn.

But for many companies that have tried outsourcing or offshoring, the experience of moving work has not been good. Service quality has sometimes decreased, rather than being improved; and companies have become less agile in their ability to adapt to changing markets, rather than more agile.

There are multiple causes for the failures of outsourcing. Service relationships are often just focused on price, rather than on creating some new business value. Deal structures are made too rigid for too long a period of time. Service providers can lack process competency as well as scale. Relationships often lack transparency. Companies can also be unreasonable, unwilling to accept standard ways of doing simple processes, arguing that their needs are special, when, in fact, industry standards should be applied.

This book offers prescriptions about how to outsource and offshore intelligently. The term "smartsourcing" is an appropriate moniker for what companies must do. Work cannot simply be thrown over corporate walls, and it's not just processes that move. Competencies get outsourced, and competencies are a combination of processes, people, and attitudes.

So an intelligent outsourcing proposition must consider how a service partner will manage processes and people consistent with corporate needs and how the behavior of a service partner can be synchronized with the culture of a company that outsources. Once a decision on what to outsource has been made, being smart requires a cultural match.

Outsourcing and offshoring also require a high degree of transparency. Work across a value chain must be efficiently integrated, and transparency becomes critical in order to design cross-organizational processes that are in harmony—not conflict. Being smart doesn't mean being secretive. In fact, it's just the opposite that becomes important. Be prepared to open up to a service provider and also demand that a service provider be open about its costs and operations.

And to get the most value out of outsourcing, be prepared to use the resources and capabilities that sit within the network of your industry, from suppliers to customers. Know what is operationally unique to your company and be prepared to use the resources of your industry in the form of standard operating processes. There is no need to reinvent what others have done well—especially on the increasingly weak argument that what your company does is different. Yes, there must be differentiation to compete, but that differentiation need not be in all processes.

Open markets and information technology have made intellectual work movable. Work will naturally go to where it can be best done—in quality and price. Trying to prevent this movement will just result in protected and weak economies. The movement of work must be intelligently managed and intelligently replaced in an increasingly dispersed world.

Jim Champy
July 2005

ACKNOWLEDGMENTS

A journalist I worked with once said to me, "It is much better to have written than to be writing." Her point being that the real joy in writing is to have and see the final work. In most all cases that is true, but occasionally a project comes along that is so compelling as to draw you into the process of writing in an almost addictive way. Such was the case with this book. The topic was seductive in its appeal, taking us as authors through a fascinating journey, challenging what we knew and introducing us to ideas we had barely considered at the outset.

It was an ambitious undertaking to consider the ways in which globalization would change so much of what we have taken for granted in the way organizations and societies operate. As we made our way along that journey, something happened that caused us to get even more excited by the project. Associates, friends and family were also drawn into the discussion, voicing their own opinions, ideas, and prognostications. Their input is found throughout this book, sometimes in profound contributions and at other times as subtle undercurrents, but in all cases as an essential part of the ideas we have put forward.

To take only a few pages to thank all of these individuals, whose contribution we feel is so great, seems patently unfair. Yet, these few pages may, at the end of the day, be the most important of this book as they truly embody the spirit of collaboration, creative thought, and innovation that we have tried to capture in the few hundred pages that follow.

To begin, we were inspired by the direction and mentoring of our long-time friend and colleague Jim Champy. Jim is one of a rare breed of very successful people who has maintained his ability to see beyond his own success and continue help those around him. His insights have been foundational in helping us to see through the complexity of the topic and to hopefully cuts to its core. We've dedicated this book to Jim for the tremendous impact he has had on not only our own thinking but also on the much broader contemporary ideas we all share about the evolution and engineering of enterprise.

Jim was also the person who introduced me to Peter Drucker many years ago. Sadly, Peter passed away as this book was being finalized. He was always an enormously kind and generous person, working with Delphi on a variety of our efforts and giving me the great privilege of working with him. Many of the ideas and opinions expressed in this book, especially those on the shift from ownership to strategy, had their origins in my many discussion with Peter. He was a brilliant and wonderfully entertaining man, but more importantly, a caring mentor.

I have to thank my parents for my own introduction to globalization, which began as a child going back and forth to Europe. I was fascinated as I watched firsthand the narrowing disparity between countries separated by so much distance. My father, who traveled extensively throughout the globe, brought home tales of other cultures that fed my curiosity and created an appreciation for the fertile ground in which the seeds of smartsourcing were planted. His stories of glowing praise for Asia, vivid descriptions of India, China, and Japan, at a time when these were still exotic locations and developing economies, well outside of the mainstream of conversation, created a spark whose flames were quickly fanned by the growing popularity of the topic in later years.

The project would never have gotten beyond the bright idea stage were it not for my longtime literary agent John Willig.

John's guidance and encouragement was invaluable. As is the case with most authors, I am often approached by friends and associates who aspire to write a book. Their question is inevitably, "Where do I start?" Trying to write a book without a trusted agent is akin to climbing Everest without a Sherpa—getting 90% of the way to the summit just doesn't count.

Jill Alexander and the wonderful team at Adams Media saw the promise in this book and have worked hard and enthusiastically on the project. Jill has has been, without any doubt, the most astute and committed editor I have come across in my experience as an author. She took it upon herself to help develop the ideas and position of the book in a way that is far above the call of duty for many editors. Having her so fully dedicated to the project was inspiring. The marketing team at Adams Media, Gene Molter, Karen Cooper, and Steve Quinn, were very quick studies and immediately embraced the project. Behind the scenes, our copyeditor Heather Padgen did a magnificent job of not only making sure we were actually true to the English language but also checked our facts, quotes, and examples. Her work may be invisible to readers but we saw the changes and are grateful for her attention to every detail. (By the way, her work was outsourced!)

During the early stages of the book's development, Anupam Gosh joined us as an intern and helped with our first drafts. Slugging his way through what were, at the time, gaping holes in logic, grammar, and facts, he nonetheless provided us with a thorough review of the raw material and a ground-zero view of the outsourcing and offshoring.

General Stephen B. Croker was very kind to take the time to give us such an incredible and intimate view into the way changing military doctrine has influenced the structure and operations of the military and the formation of a joint forces approach to war and peace. It is rare to find someone who is so knowledgeable and yet also so incredibly articulate. So amazing was his recall and ability to talk about military doctrine off the cuff that the Q&A with him in Chapter 4 barely needed any editing. That interview gives you the clear sense that a highly structured organization can transform itself through adaptive methods and technologies and that the military continues to be an archetype for the way a modern enterprise should be run. Thanks go to Lt. Col. Jon Tigges who introduced me to General Croker.

The closing chapter of this book was perhaps the hardest to write. I had struggled with many versions for some time, and was just not able to hit the mark with any of them. Then, in a case of sudden serendipity, I was invited to join a group of some 25,000 youngsters at a global competition held at The University of Tennessee for a program called Destination Imagination (DI). DI is a global program that teaches kids in K-12 creative problem-solving skills. After returning from the competition, it took me about two hours to compose the outline for the book's closing. What became clear at that competition was that the world these kids would inhabit not only needed an entirely new set of skills but that there were places for them to go to get the necessary skills. DI is a magnificent program that is building a bridge to the future for the next generation of problem solvers. I am deeply grateful to a few key folks who brought me into the DI program: Dan Fague, Roger Garriock, Bob Purifico, Linda Wayne, Susan Nunemaker, Laura Barc, Dr. Donald Treffinger, and Dr. Edwin Shelby. I applaud the dedication of these individuals to our childrens' future.

Having been part of the talented team at Perot Systems has given us both a front-row view of the changes that globalization, outsourcing, and offshoring are bringing to organizations. More importantly, they have shown us firsthand how these factors, often disparaged by popular media, can be constructive and essential aspects of building a thriving economy, in the United States and across the globe. Being part of the vast industry transformations that are brought on by smartsourcing comes with a high calling in terms of integrity and trustworthiness. Perot Systems, and its associates, epitomize these values in their words and actions. We are indebted to this exceptional team for their support and contributions to our thinking.

For the past seventeen years, a core group of exceptionally committed and bright individuals have been at the center of my personal universe of thought leadership. They are the founders and partners of Delphi Group. Together, they form one of the most powerful and focused teams in the industry. Carl Frappaolo, Nick Koulopoulos, MaryAnn Koslowski, Nathaniel Palmer, Carlene Lanier, Dan Keldsen, Linda Wynott, Hadley Reynolds, Ralph Marto, Tom Reed, Susy Martins, and Rich DiLonardo have been my greatest allies. Many of their ideas have helped to shape markets and were the genesis for much of what is in this book, from Nathaniel's ideas on business process orchestration to Hadley's perspectives about On Demand, Carl's groundbreaking work in the area of knowledge management, and Dan's forward thinking on social networks. It is beyond rare to bring together such incredible talents, much less to keep them together for so long. I am honored to be a member of their team.

Finally, when all is said and done, those who ultimately provided both of us with the greatest inspiration and support were, of course, our families. Authors do not exist who have not thought about what it would mean to a member of their immediate family, a spouse, parent, or child to pick up their book and read it, while simultaneously thinking of the time it takes away from family to write a book. It seems small recompense to get a few lines in an acknowledgment in return for such a sacrifice. Debbie, Michelle, Mia, Adam, Jackson, and Alexandra, as grand as we may hope our ideas to be, they pale against the gratitude we have for your support, inspiration and love.

Thomas M. Koulopoulos
and Tom Roloff
Boston, December 2005

INTRODUCTION

And it ought to be remembered that there is nothing more difficult to take in hand, more perilous to conduct, or more uncertain in its success, than to take the lead in the introduction of a new order of things.

—Niccolò Machiavelli

A MILLENNIUM OF CHANGE

This book is about a journey that started long before the topic of globalization became popular. It is a journey through the evolution of the way we work and the structure of the places we work in. It is a winding journey that meanders and takes us through 500 years of change; and whose path will lead us into the next 500 years. A millennium of change packaged in a book that occupies only a few hundred pages. Overly ambitious? Yes, but the topic is far too complex and its outcome is far too important to trivialize by taking too narrow a path.

The thread of this story will take you to places you may never have considered going, from the changing role of education, to lessons on globalization, to detailed prescriptions and frameworks for deploying a global strategy and choosing global partners. There are no railroad tracks for this discussion. In many ways, this book reflects the reality and the challenge of blazing a new trail, creating a new vocabulary, and establishing a shared experience for the tough decisions ahead.

At the same time the premise of this book is simple; namely, that the mobility of work is propelling rates of disruption, discomfort, innovation, and opportunity for which it is difficult to find a historical comparison. While this book will cover much ground in describing the way this mobility has evolved, framing its impact and prescribing behaviors and methods to adapt to it, its components are found in three sections: mobilizing the power needed to do work, mobilizing the people who do the work, and mobilizing the work itself.

Many of the revolutions that have occurred in industry, commerce, and political and social institutions can be traced back to shifts in these three fundamentals. Today we are at the threshold of a base shift in mobility as globalization alters the way in which businesses make decisions about where work can and should be performed. Traditional notions about the workplace, competency, and innovation are being challenged and redrawn on a global canvas, with implications that we are only starting to understand.

This mobility in the work force, even though it is called by the new name of outsourcing, is hardly a new topic. In the late eighteenth century, the global economy was rocked by a series of propitiously timed innovations and events that together created not only the industrial revolution, but also a precedent for the mobility of work. James Watt's coal-fueled portable steam power altered nearly every aspect of the economies of the eighteenth and nineteenth centuries by mobilizing the power needed to run industry and transportation. Manufacturing, automation, and immigration were launched by this one innovation. No longer were workers or work local. People, raw materials, and knowledge could be brought to whatever place was best equipped to accept the commercial, social, and political opportunities offered.

Much has changed in the last few hundred years, but what we are experiencing today as businesses look to globalization in order to obtain lower cost alternatives for goods and services is hardly a new phenomenon. The current political and social debates about this age-old topic may gain greater visibility as the media itself gains greater power to transmit the images and implications of globalization. There is far more to the discussion than most of us have yet to fully appreciate. The topic of using outsourcing to cut costs, which has occupied the headlines so far, is only the smooth tip of the iceberg. The jagged edges and the greater challenges to our organizations lie just below the waterline and out of sight of most debates.

These more difficult and powerful forces are what this book labels as *smartsourcing*. These forces are the dynamics that will play out not only in the U.S. economy, but also throughout all of the world's economies as we start to make the gradual but determined global shift to metrics that are based fundamentally on innovation, rather than manufacturing and services.

Smartsourcing is the rule book for this new global economy—an economy that is based fundamentally on mobility, innovation, and the creation of a new set of attitudes about how we measure the value of our organizations and our people. It presents us with the final bridge we need to cross from the industrial to the innovation age economy.

This book will offer insights on how to build that bridge.

Part I explores the basic ingredients of smartsourcing. It frames the forces that have defined organizations to the present day—and discusses what will define them in this next era. The concepts of *core competency, economies of scale,* and *work mobility* are addressed, as are the roles of innovation and risk transference, and the impact of uncertainty in decision-making.

Part II delves into the nuts and bolts of the business of smartsourcing. You'll learn how to make sourcing decisions, as well as what defines the value of the smartsourcing approach—

beyond simple cost reduction. The challenges to smartsourcing and how to manage the resulting firm are also addressed. Our objective is to go beyond the philosophy of globalization and provide you with the frameworks you need to embark on a smartsourcing initiative with confidence and competency.

Part III discusses the impact of smartsourcing on the structure of organizations. It explores how products and services will be created and delivered in the future, as well as some of the key technologies that will enable the creation of extended enterprises. Most importantly, we will look at the do's and don'ts of winning in this new environment. This section concludes with a look at how smartsourcing will change many basic institutions and notions of the organization—and offers some predictions about the legacy of globalization. The objective is to provide a context for the developments to come that will accelerate and mature the precepts of globalization—and reinforce the assertion that smartsourcing will be one of the defining trends of our age.

Make no mistake, progress here will not come easy. Consider that half of all organizations have yet to even consider using outsourcing, while 75 percent have yet to consider its global counterpart, offshoring. The reluctance with which many organizations and managers are approaching smartsourcing stems from their already high level of resistance to simply outsourcing core aspects of their business. Such resistance is not surprising given the real high-stakes obstacles to outsourcing—and the recent public outcry about jobs being shipped overseas. Backlash against outsourcing is the political issue du jour and public debate on its pros and cons will most likely rage on for the next several years.

With this kind of attitude toward the most basic component of smartsourcing, how can we be so antithetically optimistic about its impact? In short, because the current prevailing public sentiment is overly risk averse. It is steeped in antiquated thinking about what can be sourced through partners and, until only recently, heavily biased by the lack of technologies and methods available for outsourcing sophisticated processes. Nevertheless, a watershed is approaching. And its impact will be greatest on those who are most firmly set against change.

While today's hard-dollar savings are appealing for all of the obvious reasons, the soft-dollar contributions that drive the numerator of most business models are much more crucial in transforming industries. One has only to look at the incredible track record of innovation over the course of the last fifty years to understand that the greatest changes, those that drive industries to new heights, consistently come from those outside the mainstream, with the least amount vested in the current way of doing business and most willing to adopt new approaches.

The shelves of stores are packed with products that should never have made it if surveys and focus groups had scripted the future. Markets do not shape innovation as much as markets are shaped by innovation. New innovations redefine the way we experience the world, which in turn change our behaviors. After all, what would a citizen of the 1950s have thought of the sight of millions of people wandering the streets of any major metropolis in relative oblivion while earphones attached to MP3 players, cell phones, and PDAs link them to a virtual network connected to any point on the globe?

Similarly, what would we make of a world in which employment hinges on an economy of pure innovation, where work moves freely from point to point? What will that world look like and how will its inhabitants manage the pace of change and invention necessary to sustain growth and prosperity? These are tough questions that can only begin to be answered in the pages that follow. Nevertheless, it is a journey that business has already embarked upon.

PART I

INVISIBLE FORCES

"Vision is the art of seeing the invisible."

—*Jonathan Swift*

Chapter 1

Global Vista Ahead

"We are not in the middle but at the beginning of a transition with the high probability of a long period of dramatic changes. So how does one manage in a period of great uncertainty and very rapid change such as we quite obviously face at the present?"

—Peter Drucker

Picture a map of the world. What do you see? Is the image in your mind that of the classic Mercator projection that hangs in nearly every grade school classroom? What are the physical features of the globe? Do you see the great oceans and waterways that separate landmasses? Can you picture the national boundaries—those that were and those that are? Do you see the earth illuminated in the darkness by the bright lights of its largest cities glowing in clusters of commerce and technology?

Whatever your image of the world is, keep it firmly in mind. Now, where are the information superhighways that connect us to the world and the world to our desktops? Where are the networks that link us? Where are the myriad connections of power, wealth, intelligence, innovation, poverty, and terror that define our time?

Probably missing.

Our collective view of the world still lacks the most fundamental dimension of our lives and the promise of our future—the invisible conduits that connect us. *Apollo 14* crew member Edgar Mitchell once recounted his memories of looking back at a world without borders. "It's impossible," said Mitchell, "to come around from the dark side of the moon and see Earth floating out there in this vast sea of blackness and not have it affect you in a profound way."

From the instant that billions of us first saw that same image, globalization began to form as a collective vision and a realization of our fragile, interconnected, and isolated existence. The plain but striking image of a globe without manmade boundaries forever changed the way people regard the planet and view their place on it.

Today, every industry is experiencing a similar transformation as our definition of enterprise radically changes from an isolated collection of tasks to one that cuts across all dimensions of an organization's structure and geography. With the ability to capture, store, retrieve, and distribute vast amounts of information across the globe, we are pushing the limits of existing technology infrastructures and challenging current models of enterprise. We are faced with a fundamental challenge and a basic question: What will best define us, the factors that separate us or those that connect us?

Three days after September 11, 2001, we were scheduled to give a talk to a group of graduate students at a local Boston university. These were ambitious, driven people from around the world who had spent the last two to four years of their lives preparing to enter what had been one of the most prosperous periods in global economic history.

By September 14 the window of prosperity had been nearly welded shut. Uncertainty was lurking around every corner and a roomful of graduate students was waiting to hear a reason, any reason, for why they should be excited by the prospects of what was to come.

What would you have told them about the world and the job market they were entering? One colleague we sat on a board of directors with suggested, "Tell them to simply be patient; this too will blow over soon enough." Wishful, but naive, counsel.

The fact is that we have not entered a cyclical arrhythmia in the economy. While the vivid pain and tragic memory of a single event may well dim with the passage of time, the context of our experience is not defined by any single event. We are in a period of profound and prolonged uncertainty, risk, and volatility. There will be fluctuations and periods of stability, but the context of uncertainty will not subside.

We are in for a long transition that will redefine our attitudes toward, and our abilities to cope with, this new image of the world—an image of connectedness that both causes and counters uncertainty and where small, loosely connected networks of people can have tremendous impact for better or worse.

Each age that humanity has passed through has been the result of unfathomable changes in society, economics, and technology, but the common thread among all of these transformations has been the move toward integration of global disparity. The path has not been a direct one. The most recent difficulties in creating a common European market, the continuing conflicts in the Middle East, the rise of terror networks, speak to the slow and uncertain nature of this process. Still, it is clear that the direction of humankind has been consistently toward increased global communications and economic interreliance. It appears that this need is something that is a vital and intuitive aspect of human nature. We strive to bridge the gap between individuals, work groups, organizations, societies, and nations in order to accelerate the process of progress.

However, global reliance also creates cascading effects. Troubles in one economy can quickly disrupt economies in other parts of the globe. Mutual reliance requires mutual reliability.

The political and social rifts that will surround this new age are already at full throttle. Globalization is a nemesis to as many as it is a savior. But our opinion here, in the pages of this book, will be clear. Globalization is evolution, it is survival, and it is the necessary counterbalance to the power of disruption now vested in the networks we are building civilization upon. Globalization creates mutual reliance, security, tolerance, and prosperity. It promotes values that dignify humanity through greater access to economic resources.

But it does none of this of its own accord. The technology of connectedness is without moral dimension. There is work to do, much work. It is the work of these newly minted MBAs as much as it is for any of us.

For you as a leader, businessperson, technologist, or student, that work begins by creating organizations that understand the basic tenets of this new age, that can navigate in these new dimensions, and whose image of the world is as radically different from the maps of Gerardus Mercator as Copernicus's universe was from Ptolemy's.

SEEING THE INVISIBLE

Smartsourcing raises difficult questions about an organization's core values and competencies. It forces dialogue that can be disruptive and uncomfortable for the status quo. It peels back layers of protective procedures to uncover the essential elements of innovation, and it makes apparent the presence, or lack of, the true differentiators of an organization, its products and services. In short, it makes visible much of what has been deeply hidden inside the organization's legacy.

As children many of us played the game "lights on, lights off," where one player removes an object from a familiar but darkened setting and another player tries to figure out what was removed once the lights come back on. The more familiar the setting the harder it is to figure out what is missing. We simply ignore the commonplace and accept it as simultaneously immutable and invisible. Put another way, nothing is easier to ignore than that which you see day in, day out.

The same often applies to our organizations as part of what we call the *execution gap*. You may not be able to see the execution gap, but it is there. It is a gaping hole in most organizations into which they collectively funnel billions of dollars each year, money that could otherwise be invested in new innovations, great discoveries, and the advancement of every industry.

It is a gap between strategy and execution, governance and accountability, planning and uncertainty. It is a gap that stifles partnership on what does *well enough* and distracts organizations from focusing on what they do *best*.

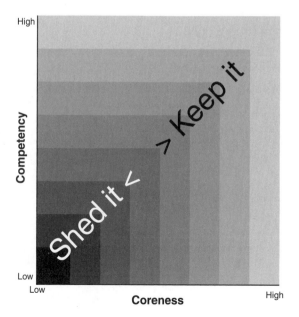

FIGURE 1.1
KEEP IT OR
SHED IT?

Smartsourcing begins with a straightforward question: What is your core competency as an organization? Once you have answered that deceptively simple question, you can start to shed everything else that takes you away from your core competency.

Even if an organization can define the areas that constitute its high-performance core competencies and those that make up its low-performing noncore activities, and then figure out how to partner effectively to bolster the latter, the remaining gray area between what an organization does well and what it does poorly becomes a gap. Unfortunately that gap often becomes a cost of doing business. Smartsourcing is about bridging that gap in order to finally shed the industrial age model of vertical integration.

At its core, smartsourcing provides a lens by which you can look at the spectrum of your organization's capabilities in order to determine how to best achieve the highest level of performance, cost, and innovation in each. But defining what it *is* may be easier to do by first defining what it *is not*.

Smartsourcing is not about economies of scale;
   it is about economies of scope.
Smartsourcing is not just about technology;
   it is about competency.
Smartsourcing is not about ownership;
   it is about partnership.
Smartsourcing is not just about cost cutting;
   it is about innovation.
Smartsourcing is not about cheap labor;
   it is about smart, educated workers.
Smartsourcing is not episodic;
   it is here to stay.
Smartsourcing is not just about outsourcing;
   outsourcing is only one facet.

Most importantly, smartsourcing is not a theory. It is practiced today by many organizations in reaction to the pressure to lower costs without sacrificing process excellence, innovation, or agility. These organizations recognize the opportunity smartsourcing offers to close the gap.

The unfortunate reality is that in a climate of uncertainty and cost scrutiny the natural tendency of most people and businesses is to adopt an overly conservative attitude toward all decisions. Additional time is spent evaluating alternatives and overscrutinizing investments. In short, every decision gets dragged out. The irony is that uncertainty actually decreases the window of opportunity within which to make decisions. Innovation suffers at a time when it most needs to shine.

As uncertainty and market opportunity accelerate, the time to react shrinks dramatically. Information systems and management methods must reign in the tendency toward conservative decision-making by synchronizing the time to react with the window of opportunity (what we will describe further as the *uncertainty principle* in Chapter 4).

Accelerating innovation and increasing agility requires management and business systems that keep pace with the velocity of uncertainty. This can only be done if an organization forces itself to focus its bandwidth on its core areas.

Lastly, smartsourcing is the process through which an entire economy evolves and matures by creating more productive and innovative networks of partnerships that can react to smaller windows of opportunity. In the same way that standardization in manufacturing created opportunities for the evolution of global supply chains, smartsourcing opens the door to a new era of integration for knowledge work.

WHY CALL IT SMARTSOURCING?

One of the reactions to the term *smartsourcing* may be to ask, "As opposed to what, dumbsourcing?" At the risk of sounding trite our response would be, yes, exactly! The streets are littered with the remnants of sourcing deals that have not performed as expected or that have simply gone bad. These are decisions that were poorly thought out, for which both parties were ill prepared and from which collateral damage resulted, thus souring other companies on the sourcing process and its potential benefits.

Objective success estimates for sourcing are not easy to come by because the culprit in most of these cases is that an initial baseline and success metrics were never well established. After several years into the relationship sponsors are bound to ask what the payback and performance metrics are. Without a baseline from which to measure these and a set of service level performance criteria in place, all that remains is the cost of the engagement to consider when evaluating its success. Inevitably the steep costs involved in any sourcing arrangement lead to increased scrutiny, which few of these arrangements will stand up to without a well thought out and agreed upon framework and a corresponding set of metrics in place to objectively assess results.

In addition, there are many cases where the external economies of outsourcing have given way to internal economies of scale. In banking alone a number of large organizations have brought sourcing arrangements back in-house. For example, in the financial community, JPMorgan Chase, Citigroup, MBNA, Bank of America, and Capital One have all taken their credit card processing back as an in-house operation. While this seems to contradict the trend, it is no more peculiar than any other case where the scale of an organization may cause it to assume more of the risk for a particular process if the costs are lower or the performance is better in-house.

Take, for example, the case of large organizations that self-insure their employees rather than rely on third-party insurers. Even these organizations will use a third party to administer the insurance payments and health care process. This combination of accepting risk in one area (self-insurance) but shedding it in another closely related area (administration of the insurance) is an ideal example of smartsourcing where both internal and external economies of scale are maximized.

Smartsourcing is about establishing this balance of risk and putting in place methods by which to understand and manage risk. The frameworks we will present to help you strike that balance are simple but essential in establishing a constitution for the governance, measurement, and objectives of not only your sourcing relationship but also the relationship that you have with the risk inherent in all of your organization's processes.

To call anything less than this degree of due diligence and scrutiny of your risk *dumb* is to be kind in the extreme.

The second reaction that people have to the term *smartsourcing* is to question whether we are using it as a description or a prescription. The answer is both. Smartsourcing is as much a description of what you do as it is a set of recommendations for how your organization should work. In its simplest form, smartsourcing is the next logical step in the progression of work mobility; and this will occur no matter what we call it. But beyond the immediate trends of contracting, outsourcing, nearsourcing, and offshoring, smartsourcing looks at how an organization identifies the best way to coordinate its processes and resources in order to focus on what it does best—its core competencies.

HOW IS SMARTSOURCING DIFFERENT FROM OUTSOURCING?

The greatest risk in traditional outsourcing is focusing exclusively on costs and ignoring a concurrent innovation initiative—this is simply being shortsighted. While outsourcing will often deliver reduced costs, the focus of outsourcing is too often replicating the status quo. Improving process excellence and promoting innovation are not prime objectives of the outsourcing process, although we will admit that a good partnership may yield dramatic improvements. Smartsourcing, on the other hand, is accompanied by a renewed attention on excellence and innovation among the organization's core process initiatives. This sort of partnership not only achieves cost savings, but it also establishes pre-eminence and differentiation. The combination of these capabilities is central in the shift from outsourcing to smartsourcing and will be the driving force in shaping the most competitive organizations.

While outsourcing's focus is on cost cutting, smartsourcing refocuses managers on building innovative capacity within organizations and ultimately within a global economic web of commerce.

Many organizations that pursue an outsourcing relationship operate under the premise that there are a core group of distinct and separate processes (shown in **FIGURE 1.2** in dark gray) that are candidates for outsourcing. While this can result in dramatic cost savings, it limits the ability of an organization to fully focus on its core competencies, as much of its time

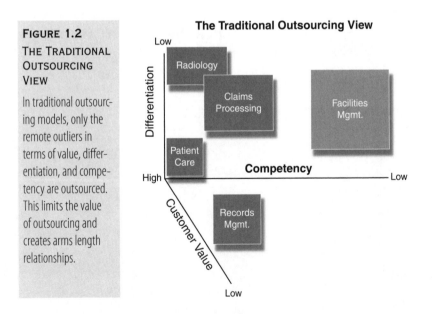

FIGURE 1.2

THE TRADITIONAL OUTSOURCING VIEW

In traditional outsourcing models, only the remote outliers in terms of value, differentiation, and competency are outsourced. This limits the value of outsourcing and creates arms length relationships.

and effort is still expended on peripheral processes that do not add high customer value or differentiate the organization in its industry. For example, in **FIGURE 1.2,** the health care provider should focus on the core competency of patient care. However, they are likely to be spending much more time and money on the many peripheral activities where their differentiation, competency, and customer value are relatively low. When sourcing or service partnerships are created, the relationship with the service partner is fairly isolated and the handoffs few and well defined.

A smartsourcing strategy creates a much more intimate relationship between the organization and its service partner. Smartsourcing increases innovation throughout the range of process from core to noncore, allowing organizations to focus on their most critical areas of differentiation and customer value, while also achieving high levels of innovation in non-core operations. In the example shown in **FIGURE 1.3,** this means increasing the differentiation, competency, and customer value

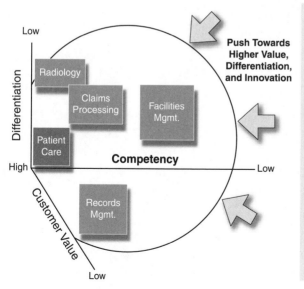

FIGURE 1.3

THE SMART-SOURCING VIEW

In a smartsourcing model, organizations consider partnering on everything other than their core competencies. This requires high intimacy, trust, and collaboration, but also delivers far higher returns and increased innovative capacity.

across the spectrum of activities involved in delivering patient care. This is the precise opposite of the commodity label that is often placed on outsourcing services.

And it all starts by answering some simple questions.

First, do you know what your core competencies are so that you can focus and prioritize your energies on them? Second, can you define your processes and your work so that you can transport them easily to partners? Third, are you able to measure innovation and its impact in all aspects of your business?

The answers we have found in working with organizations as we researched this book are frightening:

- 70 percent of organizations believe that their core competencies *are* their products. Products are not core competencies.
- 26 percent of all organizations claim they cannot define their noncritical processes well enough to source them to a partner. As the saying goes, "When you don't know where you're going, any road will take you there."
- Only 10 percent of organizations have innovation management programs in place. Most of the others openly admit that innovation is a matter of extreme redundancy, waste, and serendipity. The impact and effectiveness of innovation is simply *not* measured.

While most of us acknowledge that we are entering a new era of globalization and partnership, few of us have a road map for navigating in this new era, much less a sense for the implications that it will have on the way our economies operate.

Take for example the simple illustration of the shift in focus from tactical to strategic utilization of resources. As the number of opportunities presented to an organization increase, the rate at which the organization needs to respond also increases. Bandwidth is at a premium, as is the need to focus.

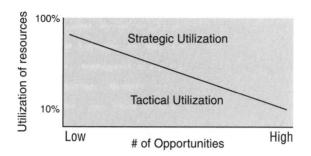

FIGURE 1.4

UTILIZATION OF RESOURCES

As the number of market opportunities for an organization increases, a target rich environment is created that requires a shift from a tactical to a more strategic utilization of resources in order to pick and chose those opportunities best suited to the core competencies of the organization.

Although **FIGURE 1.4** is true in concept, it is difficult to predict what it will look like in real life and what impact it will have on the structure of our organizations and work forces over time. What will the bird's eye view of this new economic landscape look like? If we were to ask what an agricultural, manufacturing, or even a service-based economy looked like, most people would have an image in mind of farmland, factories, or skyscrapers. They would have some sense for the economics and the social structures that support it. The role of workers, educators, the middle class, the distribution of wealth, all of these would be somewhat understood. But what does an innovation-based economic landscape look like? If smartsourcing organizations shed all but the very core innovations that differentiate them, what are we left with?

Over time the inevitability of this transition will make the answer self-evident. But for now we need a rulebook. Smartsourcing is the road map and the framework. It is the rulebook for understanding how to make the shift into this new period of global uncertainty, alliance, strategy, and competition. It defines the fundamental behaviors, attitudes, and practices that organizations in every industry will need to adopt in order to compete. It is the most basic tenet of how we will structure and manage our organizations. And it is the overriding principle by which stockholders and stakeholders will measure value and performance.

Still, we will be the first to admit that smartsourcing is tough. It is without abundant precedent and it is certainly not without risk. But it is not optional. For individuals, organizations, and the global economy to prosper we have to build the bridge and cross the gap.

CHAPTER 2

AN ECONOMY OF SCOPE

"We consistently fail to grasp how many ideas remain to be discovered. The difficulty is the same one we have with compounding. Possibilities do not add up. They multiply."

—Paul Romer

At its heart, smartsourcing is fundamentally about creating a new type of enterprise that focuses obsessively on its core competencies and sheds everything except the most essential and innovative aspects of its business. Organizations that utilize smartsourcing are able to delegate their nonessential activities to partners across a global network. The organization's intellectual resources are maximized because they are not distracted by nonessential work—nor does the organization waste resources trying to strengthen a weakness they can only marginally improve. Thus, costs decrease and the rate of innovation accelerates.

Organizations that smartsource also shift from internal economies of scale to external economies of scale in their information systems, human resources, financial systems, customer support, engineering, and even research and development. They define new rules for success and competition by drilling deep into the bedrock of their intellectual capital to set a pace for innovation that is unencumbered by the distractions and costs of peripheral activities.

Consider that at the start of the twentieth century more than 98 percent of all factories were powered by water wheels or steam. The other 2 percent were just starting to experiment with a radically new form of power—electricity. These new factories were hardly role models at the time. Electric power was dangerous, complicated, and unreliable. It required the retooling of factories and it created vast changes in the behaviors and economics of manufacturing. Today it seems absurd that a utility so simple to use, so prevalent in our lives, and so fundamental to our businesses was once so radical.

Most radical new technologies follow a similar adoption curve. As reliance on them begins to scale, they rapidly go from a simple concept to a mad rush of innovation and incompatible approaches. To maximize the competitive differentiation that a new technology delivers, organizations end up building deep competencies in a technology, making it proprietary and fragmenting it even further. Over time complexity and investment mounts, causing internal economies of scale to emerge as a small number of organizations develop de facto standards for their internal business units and private networks of partners.

Ultimately, however, the reliance on the new technology is so widespread, the threat of incompatibility such a stifling factor in the marketplace, and the risk of obsolete investment so great that broad-based standards emerge and consolidation occurs. Less than twenty years ago, for example, you would send a fax by going to your local FedEx office to use Zap-Mail—a proprietary precursor to commodity faxing. It is estimated that FedEx lost upward of $300 million on ZapMail as the fax market standardized and took off. It is at this point in a market that internal economies of scale give way to external economies of scale.

An economy of scope comes from the ability to derive greater value from one large external entity than a collection of smaller internal ones. The example we will use later is that of an electric utility as opposed to a generator. Simply put, in the long run it is almost always less expensive and more reliable to work with an economy of scope for standard business practices.

An economy of scope is the first cornerstone of smartsourcing. It results from being able to perform many business functions through a single shared service rather than differently in many parts of one or more businesses. The most familiar example is the use of outside providers, such as ADP, to process payroll for many small to medium-sized businesses. In effect, an economy of scope is nothing more than an internal economy of scale that has been shifted to outside the organization. The shift reduces risk, increases performance and reliability, and opens the door to rapid innovation for both the technology and the remaining elements of the organizations that have used and devoted precious resources to support the technology.

Electric power, for example, was initially justified as an internal economy of scale; it was most economic when provided in-house by the same factories using it. But this created

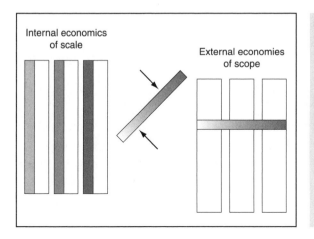

Internal economics of scale

External economies of scope

FIGURE 2.1
ECONOMIES OF SCOPE

An external economy of scope comes from the ability to derive greater value from one large external entity rather than from a collection of smaller internal ones.

countless standards for the dynamos, motors, wiring, voltages, amperages, and machinery. As electric power became pervasive the costs incurred by trying to resolve these problems started to approach and eventually exceeded the savings of internal economies of scale. In fact, many factories began to sell power to local shopkeepers and municipalities in an attempt to shore up an eroding financial proposition.

Although we often compress the history that follows, from the first large-scale power plants in 1891 at Telluride, Colorado, and then in 1895 at Niagara Falls, it took decades for electrical grids to take shape across the globe. In fact, the European power grid would likely have been in a state of disarray for the better part of the twentieth century were it not for the decimation of regional and factory-based power plants during World War II, which made reconstruction of interconnected and centralized power less expensive than rebuilding the hodgepodge of proprietary power plants and power sources in place before the war.

The problem was also not just limited to electric power. In fact much of London was powered by 150 miles of underground hydraulic power by the London Hydraulic Power Company, which finally closed its doors in 1977!

However, the more interesting story is not about electricity but what happened to the factories that used it. As power utilities came on line during the 1900s, factories, for the first time in history, did not have to worry about generating and managing power. They could instead focus on the things that really mattered—what they built.

The competitive landscape shifted drastically. It is no coincidence that manufacturing experienced a surge of innovation in the early part of the twentieth century. With the increasing ability to focus on their core processes and products, factories developed a far more sophisticated approach to manufacturing. The impact was felt across all industries, from moving assembly lines in automobile manufacturing to farming and agriculture.

What is most striking about this shift to external power generation, however, is that it happened over such a prolonged period of time. In 1905 there were 50,000 individual power plants in the United States. Today there are approximately 2,300! The reinvestment in infrastructure to replace this first wave of proprietary innovation was so great as to be daunting, if not outright impossible, to cost justify for most organizations. It's the same reason that postal systems, railroads, highways, and telecommunications networks have all required massive investment or intervention and policy on the part of government in order to bridge the pain of replacing outdated infrastructure and offer some protection for new investments. Amazingly, even today there are many factories that still generate their own electricity, accounting for a whopping 200 billion kilowatt hours, or 13 percent of all electricity consumed in manufacturing.

Today we are once again at the crossroads of such a shift as organizations struggle under the weight, costs, and volatility of information and business systems that are relentless in their rush to obsolescence, often incompatible with each other, and progressively less critical to the competitive differentiation of organizations.

Smartsourcing is not just about technology; it is about how businesses are run. That is why smartsourcing is counterintuitive for many who have grown up with traditional notions of business such as economies of scale, vertical integration, command and control organizational hierarchy, lack of transparency, and closed, sterile corporate environments.

Smartsourcing turns all of these traditional tenets inside out. Scale gives way to scope. Vertical integration within a single organization takes a back seat to horizontal coordination across myriad smaller organizations. Federation replaces command and control hierarchy. Closed, black box systems and processes transform into transparent open systems. Smartsourcing is a radical departure in behavior, vernacular, and structure from what most managers and organizations have grown up with and know so well—possibly as radical and frightening as the idea of relying on someone else to power your loom must have been to those in an 1800s textile mill.

FROM OWNERSHIP TO STRATEGY

The shift from an internal economy of scale to an external one is most noticeable in the way work is managed from the standpoint of ownership. The fundamental reason that vertical integration, economies of scale, and hierarchy worked so well in the past was that without them there was no ability to control costs and coordinate the activities and exceptions involved in the myriad handoffs of work within a process. This was the case with our analogy about electric power. While this philosophy has worked well for the better part of the industrial era, during which ownership and proprietary products defined the dominant model of organization, today few organizations produce proprietary products and fewer still can produce a product entirely on their own. Instead, even the most trivial products are built, sold, and differentiated as services with extensive networks of suppliers.

Take for example the trend to deliver custom-fitted clothing and apparel by retailers such as Levi's, the Gap, and Lands' End. In the case of Lands' End, consumers even have the ability to create a virtual model of themselves online and design custom-fit pants that are cut to order for each individual in an offshore factory. The complexity of this sort of mass customization should not be underestimated and is quickly finding its way into many consumer products. Service-based approaches of this sort include high levels of information and content. Products are malleable and instantly customizable. Organizations that provide them are constantly responsive to their markets and thus have the competitive advantage. Therefore the organizations are held together more by shared strategy among its partners than through ownership of any single organization.

The shift from ownership to strategy and products to services represents the second cornerstone for the move to smartsourcing. As supply chains increase in their complexity, the ownership of the work that makes up any given product or service is also accordingly more distributed among an everbroadening number of organizations. The ownership that typifies vertical integration provides the alignment, incentives, and management controls to coordinate how and when work is done. But today companies must rely on strategy and communication across multiple organizations and processes in order to provide alignment. This is already happening without smartsourcing but it will certainly be accelerated as the result of further globalization and fragmentation of processes that used to be well contained in one enterprise.

At the same time the agility of these supply chains is delivering products that are increasingly more personalized for each buyer, thus creating an expectation in consumers that they can have nearly endless variety and products customized to their every need, from jeans to watches to automobiles.

This shift has moved organizations from the neat and tidy lower left-hand quadrant of **FIGURE 2.2** (on the following page) to the chaotic and ever-accelerating demands of the upper right-hand quadrant of this figure.

Smartsourcing provides the tools by which organizations can thrive in this new framework by creating excellence not just in each process but, more importantly, in how they coordinate the white space between processes—in other words, the many processes and roles that nobody has ever taken the time to define and document. As you will see later in Chapter 9, managing the business processes that allow companies to create

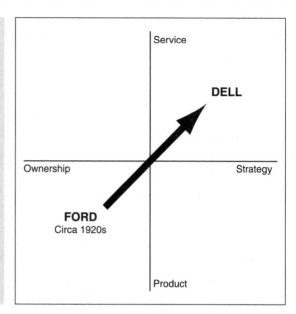

FIGURE 2.2
THE SHIFT FROM OWNERSHIP TO STRATEGY

During the early part of the twentieth century, organizations were built around the fundamentals of ownership and products. Today's organizations are built around the principles of strategy and service. This puts a much greater value on alignment and coordination among partners and innovation.

these extended strategy-driven organizations is a core aspect of smartsourcing.

While the promise of smartsourcing to revolutionize the way in which organizations work and partner is great, it will not be realized without passage through a period of pain.

There will be displacement and unrest as greater accountability is put on workers to build and rebuild their own skills and capabilities. This is not a new phenomenon. Unrest has accompanied every significant shift in the work force and more specifically those shifts that increase the mobility of work.

However, at the outset we want to advise some caution. When we raise the specter of work mobility, the first thing that most people think of is outsourcing. Smartsourcing is not synonymous with outsourcing. Outsourcing is only one part of smartsourcing. Outsourcing is meant primarily to reduce costs and transfer the risk of a defined process to a third party. In our own surveys we found that 61 percent of all organizations that

Outsourcing	Smartsourcing
CUT COSTS: Focuses on cutting costs	CUT COST+INCREASE INNOVATION: Combines cost cutting with increased innovation
STREAMLINE OPERATIONS: Focuses on operational areas	STREAMLINE THE VALUE CHAIN: Considers the entire value chain
PARTNER ON WHAT YOU KNOW: Works well with defined processes	PARTNER TO DEFINE WHAT YOU DON'T KNOW: Helps to define all processes from major to obscure
COMMODITIZE: Creates homogeneous processes that lack differentiation	DIFFERENTIATE: Innovates processes to increase differentiation
TACTICAL IMPROVEMENT: Used when markets are predictable	STRATEGIC EXCELLENCE: Used to align with shifting markets
DISCONTINUOUS: Changes in technologies and architecture are disruptive to the business process	CONTINUOUS: Thoughtful leadership combined with constant innovation buffer the business process from technology change
ARM'S LENGTH PARTNERSHIP: Creates yet another enterprise silo	TRUST-BASED PARTNERSHIP: Engenders trust and collaboration leading to greater value

undertook an outsourcing initiative did so for only cost reduction objectives (**FIGURE 2.3** on the following page).

The term most often used to describe this sort of outsourcing is *lift and shift*—meaning that an existing process is lifted out of its current organization and simply shifted over to a third party. The third party may achieve economies of scope through shared services, international wage arbitrage, or more sophisticated technology, but such an outsourcing relationship will never lead to substantially higher levels of innovation.

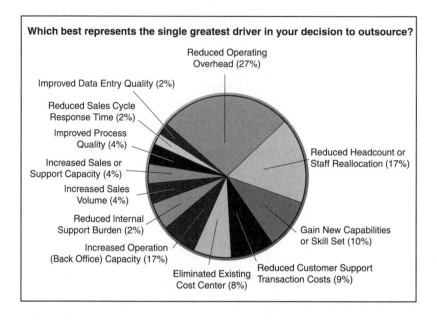

Which best represents the single greatest driver in your decision to outsource?

Reduced Operating Overhead (27%)

Improved Data Entry Quality (2%)

Reduced Sales Cycle Response Time (2%)

Improved Process Quality (4%)

Increased Sales or Support Capacity (4%)

Increased Sales Volume (4%)

Reduced Internal Support Burden (2%)

Increased Operation (Back Office) Capacity (17%)

Reduced Headcount or Staff Reallocation (17%)

Gain New Capabilities or Skill Set (10%)

Eliminated Existing Cost Center (8%)

Reduced Customer Support Transaction Costs (9%)

FIGURE 2.3

Sixty-one percent of all outsourcing decisions are still based primarily on cost cutting—or what is commonly referred to as a "lift and shift" approach.

In addition, our findings show that at least half of all organizations are still reticent to attempt outsourcing. And only 7 percent have used offshoring.

The problem is that outsourcing often does not address the critical issue of managing the gap that was discussed in the introduction—that is, the procedures and processes that govern how work between defined processes is accomplished (or the lack of these). Moving work from partner to partner without having this capability is like assembling a jet plane from pieces without any plan for how those pieces are ultimately going to work together. This is the third cornerstone of smartsourcing, the move from work that is location dependent to work that is free to move at will—or what we refer to as *placeless work* in the next chapter.

The Cornerstones of Smartsourcing:

■ Movement to external economies of scale
■ Shift from ownership to strategy
■ The evolution of the placeless job

If this comes across as too radical a leap from where you are today it may simply be helpful to think of smartsourcing as outsourcing version 2.0. Smartsourcing is the evolution of outsourcing to a more sophisticated and effective model of working with all of your partners and processes—not just those that are most easily transported to an outside party.

This becomes especially important when looking at one particular form of outsourcing, offshoring. Offshoring moves work to partners in other countries in order to take advantage of wage arbitrage opportunities. It is the tip of the globalization iceberg, and to many its menace is a fitting tribute to that description.

While the sort of offshoring we are most concerned about in this book is related to services, most people are already familiar with the sort of offshoring referred to as *production offshoring.* Production outsourcing is represented by the wave that swept through businesses during the second half of the twentieth century when China and Japan began to pursue a vigorous national agenda to build out their infrastructure and labor force for manufacturing. The now familiar "Made in China/Taiwan/Japan" label found its way onto nearly every consumer product, ultimately invading the very heart of U.S. manufacturing when Japan took on the automotive industry.

However, the sort of offshoring that is currently gaining much attention is services offshoring; that is, the transference of intellectual or knowledge work. The trend has been spreading for some time via a number of geographies including India, the Philippines, China, Vietnam, Russia, Eastern Europe, Africa, Latin and South America, Israel, and Ireland where an impressive infrastructure is being built to provide a pool of skilled workers to man call centers, software development operations, and other intellectually demanding work. However, offshoring is increasingly not limited to any particular country or economic region.

Offshoring has created an especially charged political debate as many of the high-paying jobs that only recently replaced production offshored work are now themselves being shipped offshore. The void is striking chords of fear in a work force that has already had to retool itself. Add to this the general groundswell of antipathy toward free trade and one is left to wonder if any sort of sourcing, much less offshoring, can possibly be a good thing.

There are already numerous bills in front of the U.S. Congress to provide for training and income assistance to service workers whose jobs are shipped overseas—something currently reserved only for manufacturing workers. And a handful of U.S. state governors have proposed or enacted executive directives to prohibit outsourcing of state-funded work.

All of this concern should not be surprising. When you total the production and services capacity of any organization you are hard-pressed to find a remainder. In other words, what's left after you offshore all of a company's production and services? The popular fear is that the United States will become a jobless consumer economy. Although we consider such claims to be hyperbolic, and most often driven by political agendas, we do not want to just brush this issue aside. The United States, perhaps more than any other nation, needs to pay close attention to the smartsourcing prescription. The reason is simply that more of our economy is already based on services than any other.

We are already an economy of knowledge workers. With the loss of even small percentages of these jobs we are put into a precarious economic situation that could rapidly spiral downward. We need to prepare ourselves not just to survive this shift but to leverage it and lead the globe in defining the tenets of an innovation-based economy.

If we can do that, then in the same way that an economy can survive without relying principally on manufacturing, it can also thrive without relying principally on services. And the bold answer to the question "What remains?" becomes, "not much, but that which matters most—innovation."

Smartsourcing is about intelligently shedding noncore production and services while taking the innovative capacity that remains and leveraging it in a way that would simply have been impossible under the burden of noncore activities.

Underestimating the impact this can have is shortsighted at best. In the case of General Electric's offshoring efforts, which we will discuss later in the book, approximately 100,000 jobs have been created overseas in the past decade. Yet GE's U.S. based operations have continued to increase in size and employment as GE has stepped up its ability to innovate and bring new products to market. Many would assert that GE's ability to offshore is precisely why it is able to keep innovating at such an impressive rate.

This shift in focus to innovative capacity is a key differentiator between pure outsourcing or offshoring and smartsourcing. The other closely related difference is that smartsourcing also looks at more than cost cutting. Smartsourcing should be intended to increase the total innovative capacity of an organization by focusing it on its core competency, while also enabling it to partner intimately with other organizations that are similarly focused on their core competencies. Think again of our framework, at the start of this chapter, depicting the move toward strategy and service. The result of working in the upper right-hand quadrant of this framework is much like an athletic all-star team where each player is world class at their respective positions. This is where our electric power analogy begins to break down.

If electric power had followed a smartsourcing model, then not only would the ability to move power production have shifted outside of the factory, but the actual work of producing the products would have been just as easy to move across the electric cables that linked the factory to the power plant. If only moving work were that easy. The movement of work requires us to transport not only the raw materials, which are used to create a product or service, but also the rules, judgment, and intellect that are necessary—and these do not travel well over any network.

In addition to the cornerstones we've already described, smartsourcing is also driven by some other important shifts in how businesses operate. While one can debate the merits, political implications, and challenges of smartsourcing it is difficult to argue or stem these underlying shifts:

- The increasing prevalence of risk and uncertainty
- The continued pressure to cut costs
- Transparency and governance
- Work force education
- Process automation
- Industry consolidation

Risk and uncertainty are increasingly prevalent in our economy.

As uncertainty increases the window of opportunity the time frame in which to take action decreases—what we will call the *uncertainty principle*. Moving in these smaller windows of opportunity means achieving greater focus on our core skills and competencies and better, faster coordination with our entire value chain of partners and customers.

There is unyielding pressure to cut costs.

Cost cutting is not an episodic phenomenon. While we may well have triggered renewed attention on the topic through the difficult economic cycle of the early 2000s, the pressure to run efficient and lean operations will continue to increase as global pressure and competition also increase. Cost cutting is like an arms race in which there is always a better weapon system over the next horizon.

We have entered a vicious global cycle of cost cutting that will not end soon—even as we proceed through the innovation and investment side of the economic cycle.

Transparency exists in operations, performance, and governance.

The mandate to create transparency plays a critical role in forcing organizations to better define and then shed their noncore activities. In a recent study we conducted we were amazed to find that the vast majority of organizations do not outsource due primarily to the fact that they do not believe they adequately understand their processes! Transparency requires a better understanding of processes. As this occurs the ease of partnering on otherwise black box activities will only increase.

Work force education is progressing at double-digit rates worldwide.

The number of universities in the developing countries of the globe is increasing at an astounding rate. For example, India today has nearly 300 universities and more than 10,000 colleges, a ten-fold increase since the 1950s. Across the globe these trends are reflected in a growing pool of talented and capable workers.

Process automation is maturing rapidly and fast becoming a component of managing the unpredictable nature of many cross-enterprise tasks.

In the classic example of Dell computer, the ability to coordinate activities in an orchestrated fashion has evolved from the traditional model of structured processes (as in an assembly line) to a timely model for orchestrating tasks in conditions of high volatility. As these tools create greater adaptability for business processes automation, we will see an even greater ability to link suppliers, partners, and customers in astoundingly responsive supply chains.

The final shift toward industry consolidation is here.

While especially pronounced in several key industries, such as financial services and banking, health care, and software, the increasing merger and acquisition activity across nearly all industries is creating a mandate to boost efficiencies in how companies merge and connect business processes. The payback is so great that it may well be the single greatest return of smartsourcing in the near term.

These shifts will be explored in more detail later in the book, but for now imagine that these underlying trends are similar to the fault lines on which many of the world's largest cities have been built. It is not an option to move the city or ignore the geography. Instead the cities must be built to withstand earthquakes.

CHAPTER 3

A DEFINING MOMENT

"Most of our assumptions have outlived their uselessness."
—Marshall McLuhan

C onsider the following question: "What basic force will
drive the greatest achievements of the twenty-first century?" If you are like most people your temptation will be to
answer in terms of advances in science, technology, or perhaps medicine. Certainly these are areas where we expect to
see enormous change and progress. But what will fuel these
advances? What is the underlying force that will drive the next
100 years of innovation and human progress?

It's a daunting question. Who among us has the ability to
see so far ahead as to understand the forces and events that will
shape the world 100 years hence? Perhaps an easier question
would be to look back and ask, what were the forces that drove
humankind's greatest achievements over the past 200 years?

Although there was no dearth of innovation during the
nineteenth and twentieth centuries, it is still difficult to single
out one underlying driver for all of them. Yet in each of these
periods there was one fundamental shift that propelled commercial, social, and political growth. It is a subtle shift that

we often pay little attention to except when it directly affects us—the shift in how we move work.

We are not speaking about just moving resources, tools, ideas, and people to where a product or service needs to be built and delivered. Electronic communications, a mobile work force, and rapid global transportation have made the movement of raw materials, goods, machinery, ideas, and people an everyday task. Despite that, however, we are only just learning how to actually package and transport the coordination of work through these same electronic networks.

The difference here may appear to be subtle—it is not.

Henry Ford understood the power of this concept nearly 100 years ago. Ford did not create new technology or even radically change existing technologies. Rather, his genius lay in a simple change in the movement of work.

In contrast to what most of us are taught in grade school, Ford's innovation was not mass production, nor the principle of interchangeable parts. Both had been in use for at least 100 years prior to the invention of the Tin Lizzie. In fact, Ford did not even create the assembly line. Ransom Eli Olds and the Cadillac Motor Company were already using complex interchangeable parts and assembly lines in their manufacturing processes.

Ford's innovation was so simple as to be overlooked in most history books. His assembly lines moved—work was transported to the worker, not the other way around.

The cornerstone principle of the twenty-first-century organization will be that the work, and all of the tools needed to do the work, can be moved to workers—wherever they are.

This is not a revolutionary concept when applied on a small scale, but when considered in the context of today's global, information-based economy it directly challenges what is perhaps the most salient feature of modern capitalism and the cornerstone of industrialism: the growth of the centralized enterprise, in which workers came to the work.

The impact this is having is just starting to register. Today the percentage of work being shipped offshore is light, representing less than 2 to 5 percent of all work in the United States, across industries, predicted to be offshore in the next decade. But even if the trend in this remains linear (we believe an accelerated trend is far more likely), we will see tumultuous change in employment over the next fifty years that will eclipse the sorts of social and economic upheavals of similar shifts in the work force over the past 500 years.

Business, political, and social leaders cannot sit idly by on the sidelines as this change occurs. We need to understand its roots and its implications intimately if we are to build better organizations, social institutions, and ultimately a higher quality of life for workers at home and around the globe.

Admittedly the challenge is not entirely new. The increasing mobility of work has a long history of great progress preceded by great resistance and often turmoil in the face of new technologies.

England's early-nineteenth-century Luddites took sledgehammers to the promise of the future. And in their time many followed. Their beef was not only with the technology but also with the purpose for which it was intended—to replace people. The democratization of work has consistently been met with antipathy—focused mainly toward the use of technology to displace workers. Whether it be Watt's steam engine, Ford's moving assembly line, factory automation, or outsourcing of factory jobs, the sentiment is initially always against increasing the mobility of work.

This makes any discussion on the topic emotional because it threatens to infringe upon the sanctity of work as something that we as individuals own. Whether it is an unskilled craftsman or a Ph.D. in biopharmacology, individuals tend to feel a strong sense of proprietary ownership over their work. Most workers regard their work as a personal asset. If you increase

work mobility you increase the risk associated with the ownership of this precious asset.

This very real threat causes us to consistently underestimate the benefits of work mobility and its ability to create new
opportunities and increased employment. In the United States,
for example, unemployment has held steady at less than 5 percent during the last 100 years. We have certainly experienced
economic cycles during that time, with unemployment at or
above 20 percent during the Great Depression and as high as
25 percent during 1933, but we have quickly rebounded from
each of these cycles to create more jobs, growing the work
force fourfold in that same period of time!

Still, while employment has steadily increased over the last
200 years, and despite all of the progress in more than 500 years
of technological achievement, the way in which most people
around the world work has barely been affected.

Despite the overwhelming proliferation of communications technology, the majority of the world lives well outside
of the work paradigm we so casually talk about. Consider that
the majority of the world's inhabitants have yet to use a phone,
and 85 percent have yet to use the Internet.

Perhaps more to the point is the fact that Asia has the
highest number of Internet users by major geography, with
300,000,000 users. Yet Asia has one of the lowest percent-of-
population usage rates at 8.4 percent! The untapped potential
is beyond mind-boggling.

How great is the opportunity to mobilize work within this
vast resource?

The question raises social issues of unprecedented magnitude, but it also challenges us to provide some sort of answer.
While national interests and personal welfare are often much
closer to our hearts, what we fail to realize, and what smartsourcing is already demonstrating, is that global and national
interests are far from competitive and are, in fact, symbiotic.

Globalization, outsourcing, offshoring, and the evolution of the core competency corporation will open up the doors to incredible opportunity that redefines the relationships between not only businesses but also among nations—leading us to a scope and scale of work mobility that would look as foreign to us today as air travel would have to the passengers of the *Mayflower.*

Although we are still far from it, by all measures, we are approaching a point when place will be one of the least important aspects of work.

THE PLACELESS JOB

The irony is that you don't need to go far to find out how unimportant place is becoming. If you find yourself in Norwood, Massachusetts, you might want to pull into the McDonald's drive-through and get a taste of a placeless job. The order taker you hear through the loudspeaker is seated in a call center two time zones removed, in Colorado Springs!

The call center is the brainchild of McDonald's franchisee Steven Bigari. As reported by Michael Fitzgerald in the July 18, 2004 edition of the *New York Times,* while limited in its application so far, Bigari has found that using a call center dramatically improves the quality and reliability of drive-through orders. The approach has been so successful that Bigari is even using it inside his restaurants as an alternative to counter service. Tabletop phones and card readers can be used to place an order in the call center, which is then delivered by local restaurant workers directly to the tabletop.

This sort of nonintuitive shift is at the center of the cultural change that will occur with the rise in prominence of placeless jobs—that is, jobs that do not have any inherent attachment or limits (other than cultural legacy) in terms of geography. This is central to the concept of work mobility. But work mobility also involves moving the rule and knowledge needed to perform work. The idea of moving rules and knowledge may be harder to grasp than that of moving work, but this is essential to the flow of information-based work. When we talk about moving rules and knowledge we are referring to the instructions and context needed to perform a task. In the case of Bigari's call center, those rules and knowledge may be limited to the choice between a regular or supersized order, but in many cases the complexity of the rules and the intimacy of understanding required are essential to getting the job done. Historically these issues have been addressed through location-based solutions that involved physical proximity to expertise; in other words, the customer support representative that you spoke with was probably not far, in distance or time zones, from access to a knowledgeable developer or engineer. This is clearly changing.

The most intimate aspect of work, from the individual's vantage point, is the workplace. If you look at how and why the idea of a workplace has changed over the past 300 years, you start to gain an appreciation for the dynamics driving some of the most basic changes in work mobility today. The workplace is the optimal location for an organization to have work done. Mind you that historically this has had little if anything to do with the optimal place to do work as far as the individual is concerned.

There is nothing uniquely nineteenth, twentieth, or twenty-first century about the idea of a workplace. If we wanted to we could apply the concept to activities that go back to the pyramids of Egypt. Formal settings for work have been a standard feature of all but the most nomadic of early societies. But the creation of formalized places to work for the majority of workers did not fully evolve until well into the eighteenth century.

Since the first water-driven looms of the industrial revolution, workers have started to troop off to foundries, mills, mines, and offices. The trend was driven in large part by the advent of scalable water, steam, and eventually fossil fuel power sources that allowed large factories to begin sprouting up en masse. Consider that in 1900 only 5 percent of all U.S. factories used electricity to power their operations. Where these factories were was intimately tied to their source of power. While raw material and finished goods needed to be moved, work mobility was virtually nonexistent for workers. The factory was bound to the concept of going to work. Work soon became a place to go, not a thing to do. Today the idea of the factory, its massive scale and economic clout, looms large in the collective consciousness and the history of the industrialized world. The idea provides the foundation not only for manufacturing but also for some of the most basic building blocks of commerce and society.

Whether it be transportation, communications, or industrialization, every innovation we live with today was somehow spurred by our ability to work in the large factory organization. From the rise of manufacturing and mass production to the advent of robotics and mass customization, no other single structure is more prominent on the landscape of twentieth-century organizations and more often associated with progress.

Factories defined the analog and the role model for not only how we did our work but also how we built our cities, transportation systems, and communications infrastructure. They were the role model for every modern organization, from manufacturers to research laboratories to social institutions. Factories have been the cauldron and the engine for innovation and commerce for 300 years, and, as we will see later, the factory concept has also been an anchor, creating enormously closed systems whose objective often became preservation of the factory organization above all else. Work mobility in these organizations was not only limited but also seen as a competitive disadvantage. If work were mobile, it could easily be taken away from the factory, used by competitors, and turned into a liability.

As manufacturing evolved and its economic prominence in many countries was replaced by information and service-based work, the factory metaphor remained as a guiding light and the organizing principle of work. In 1985, Harvard Business School professor Michael Porter cemented its place in our collective business consciousness when he introduced the conceptual framework of the value chain. The value chain elegantly simplified and described all of the internal and external activities that are part of producing and delivering a product or service to the market.

Porter's premise was simple: By maximizing the efficiency of a value chain, costs go down and differentiation goes up, and from this movement competitive advantage is created. Porter's work was rooted in the study of transaction cost economics, which looked at organizations as a series of activities and sought to assess the relative costs of performing and coordinating these activities. Porter's work followed that of earlier economists, such as R. H. Coase and later Oliver Williamson, who focused heavily on the costs of performing activities internally versus partnering or outsourcing them. In their time, information technology was in its infancy and as a result the transaction costs involved in the coordination of a value chain's externalities were much higher than they are today. Their conclusion was, in almost every case, to perform these tasks in-house. Although the value chain might have been interpreted by some as a manifesto to increase work mobility and allow greater sharing among businesses, it instead only increased the paranoia of most organizations that were already starting to lose control over their processes and the rules that made their work unique.

While Porter surely did not intend for this outcome, it is nonetheless the type of thinking that leads to the broad appeal of vertical integration, where competitive advantage comes from total control over every aspect of the value chain. Again, think of Henry Ford with his vision of the factory village where iron ore would enter one end and a complete automobile would come out the other. It is this model of vertical integration that has defined the economies of the nineteenth century and the better part of the twentieth century—where everything fit on one balance sheet, from the sheep that produced the wool to fill car seats, to the steel foundries that created raw metal, to the stamping machines that formed it into car parts.

Other examples from the early twentieth century abound. For instance, the oil industry was built on a model where everything from exploration to retail delivery of oil products was controlled by large integrated suppliers, from J. D. Rockefeller's Standard Oil Company to present-day behemoths such as Chevron, Shell, and ExxonMobil. Even industries such as information technology have, at least early on, relied heavily on a model of vertical integration. Think of the IBM Mainframe, where every aspect of design and production was controlled and owned by IBM, from the internal components to the software that ran on it. Early competitors such as Honeywell, Unisys, and General Dynamics promoted the same Byzantine models, governed by the notion that "not invented here" was anathema.

However, something started to change radically in this equation toward the end of the twentieth century. Advances in global communications, network bandwidth, and global economic infrastructure started to make the cost of maintaining vertically integrated infrastructure greater than the cost of coordinating external value chains. As a result, the notion of value chain integration has been eroding at an accelerating rate.

Today, in virtually every industry, partnering across the value chain has become the objective. In the oil industry, large players such as Chevron now buy the majority of their oil from other sources and distribute the majority of their gasoline through third-party retail outlets. Our example of Dell applies to the entire computer industry, which now relies heavily on third parties for software, electronic components, and services. In fact, today it is likely that behemoths such as IBM receive the majority of their revenue through external value chain activities.

Advances in information technology have drastically reduced the transaction costs that result from partnering, making integration a much more financially appealing proposition. Do not lose sight of just how important this point is. As transaction costs move toward zero, the traditional notion of the corporation becomes far less relevant and the trident of success becomes that of partnership, core competency, and skillful sourcing.

To look at this another way, today the costs that an organization can control represent a minority of its total cost base for any product or service that is fully under the direct control of that organization. Consider for example that in the automobile industry nearly 75 percent of the cost in manufacturing and selling an automobile is cost that resides in the supply and demand chains of the organization, namely suppliers and dealers. What is most striking about this analysis, however, is that even in industries where the costs may be under greater control of the product or service provider, an even smaller fraction of the costs for producing the product or service are attributable to the core competencies of the provider. In health care less than 15 percent of the cost to care for a patient is the cost of the *health care,* while the rest is attributable to managing the services required to administer and pay for the health care, in the form of insurance, administration, facilities, and myriad other services.

The result, as illustrated in **FIGURE 3.1**, is that over time we see a narrowing band within which organizations will be able to control their own costs for their own core competencies. While these core competencies may ultimately be the only area where an organization can fully control the level of cost and service, we do not regard this as a prognosis for higher costs.

The point to be stressed is that in the absence of a smart-sourcing approach, costs will rise (even though they may temporarily fall due to an opportunistic move to outsource), quality will suffer, and buyer satisfaction will drop. In many ways

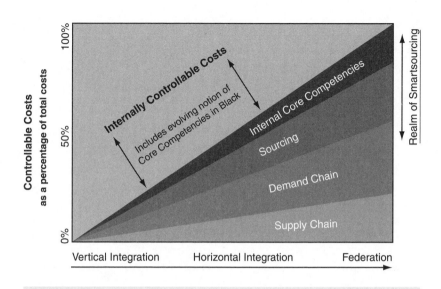

FIGURE 3.1

CONTROLLABLE COSTS

Increasingly, the costs that can be controlled internally are decreasing as a percentage of overall costs.

we believe this is a foundational problem that we are already experiencing in the health care industry. Without the development of greater skills in how these organizations manage their relationships with partners, make the determinations as to what they should keep in-house, and navigate efficiently through the sourcing maze, they will be unable to reduce their cost base in a way that permits them to remain competitive.

Part III of this book will take a closer look at the evolution of what we have labeled as the *federated organizational model* that this shift is causing. But for now we want to continue looking at how this movement in cost has already had profound implications on how we think about the economics of organizing work and workers.

During the first half of this century, the notion of "economy of scale," which was introduced in Chapter 2, dominated thinking on competitive advantage. The degree of competitiveness was measured in terms of how vertically integrated an organization could be and the degree of top-down control it could exert over individual value-creating activities. Recall that, in simple terms, an economy of scale is the ability to derive greater value from one large entity rather than a collection of smaller ones. This notion drove the design of value chains, and, in many cases, organizations themselves.

Nowhere is this more apparent than in the automobile industry, where organizations such as GM became the twentieth-century benchmark for what a vertical organization should be—or certainly what it should have been! It would have been inconceivable for anyone who grew up with the GM standard to imagine how an internal economy of scale could ever have made way for external economies of scale that would be more efficient. This continues to be a difficult leap for us to make today. But while most businesspeople still acknowledge the value of vertical integration in many industries, they also appreciate the value of horizontal integration across the value chain in ways that would have seemed absurd at the apex of the automobile industry in the mid-1900s.

What happened in the automobile industry to finally bring it to terms with vertical disintegration was half a world removed from Detroit, and it is perhaps the greatest lesson in how global economic forces and the concerted efforts of government can alter the shape of organizations and value chains. It is also one of the best illustrations of a concept that is central to many smartsourcing strategies, that of the *shared service*.

ZAIBATSU

The genesis of this change began in the pre–World War II era with the Japanese zaibatsu. Zaibatsu were large family-owned conglomerates that held enormous wealth and power over the Japanese market. For all intents they were sanctioned monopolies. In the aftermath of World War II, the zaibatsu were disbanded in an effort to foster democratization and free trade within Japan. However, with increasing pressure on the United States to rebuild Japan and simultaneously fight the Korean War and the Cold War, restrictions on Japan's ability to impose anti–free-market policy relaxed and the zaibatsu morphed into what is today commonly referred to as a keiretsu.

While the term *keiretsu* has become a popular euphemism for partnership across horizontal structures, inside and outside of an organization, the original keiretsu were hardly exemplary of the way we use the term today.

Keiretsu were a way to create analogues to the zaibatsu that incorporated horizontal integration within large conglomerates with a central holding company. They epitomized the concept of shared services while also maintaining high levels of independence in their operations. By owning stock in each other's companies and by defining certain core services that would be provided through a central holding company, and in some cases through each other, they developed a very sophisticated manner of partnership that included both interreliance and interoperability.

But the model was far from a free-market poster child. A total of six conglomerates controlled large parts of the Japanese economy—what have popularly come to be known as the commanding heights of an economy—and were spurred by national policy against imports to Japan that might undermine their markets. Over time, these keiretsu took on one of the world's most successful and powerful industries, the U.S. automobile manufacturers. And Japan's government, by using its own national buyers to subsidize low-cost imports to the United States, made it a priority to establish itself as the low-cost provider in the market.

With a foothold in the U.S. market, the keiretsu began to accelerate their ability to respond to U.S. market requirements well beyond what Detroit was able to achieve. Ultimately, however, it was not the low-cost appeal of the Japanese manufacturers but rather the nimbleness of their keiretsu that won the market. By using this nimbleness, Japanese manufacturers were able to compress their time to market within whatever category they chose to compete.

While we could attribute their initial success to poor trade policy on the part of the United States and even poorer enforcement of the Potsdam principles that were at the heart of the postwar democratization of Japan, this would be a purely academic discussion. The reality is that the idea of keiretsu partnerships, coreliance on intimate alliances, shared services, a focus on core competency, and horizontal integration have had a profound impact on our thinking about partnership.

Today, instead of thinking in terms of keiretsu as large conglomerates or small networks of alliances, we would suggest that you consider for a moment the notion of any size business not as a vertically integrated organization, but instead as an infinitely malleable and instantly responsive constellation of independently operating small businesses. While there may be a central or highly visible source of overall strategy, each of these businesses focuses on its own area of core competency and spends all its resources on producing value in this same area in the most expedient manner possible, and expends very little effort in dealing with the politics and byzantine organizational structure of a large organization. Now imagine the ability to address each opportunity by assembling the right combination of these small businesses and instantly being able to communicate, coordinate, and respond to the market appropriately. This is the vision we have of a smartsourced enterprise.

In this sort of organization, the workplace is constructed on demand, where and when the best competencies are most readily and inexpensively available. Conquering the challenges to the mobility of work, how the rules, knowledge, and nuances of work are coordinated (the white space of an organization) becomes the central challenge.

For companies such as Intel and Dell, the challenge has already been addressed. Intel already does more than 30 percent of its manufacturing offshore in countries such as Israel and Ireland, while the majority of Dell's manufacturing is done offshore.

Not only would these companies be out of business if they had not reduced their cost base but many would assert that they would have also been far less innovative in their products and marketing if they had not shed a significant piece of the production burden.

These are the types of organizations that smartsourcing is creating. They are organizations that can instantly adapt to their environments even in times of high uncertainty and market turmoil. They are organizations for which working in crisis mode is not the exception but the norm.

While the economic and political events of the early 2000s may have focused many people's attention on the importance of dealing with uncertainty, it is a phenomenon that has been steadily mounting as business has shifted subtly from the "economy of scale" to the "economy of speed" and from local to global economies. Simply put, the number of variables involved in any single transaction, from supply chains to customer interactions, has multiplied steadily and coordinating these in real time is the greatest competency and competitive mandate of any organization today and in the future.

THE NUMERATOR EFFECT

It is important to look at one last factor in the equation that was raised at the beginning of the book, and which in many experts' opinion is the most often (foolishly) ignored in the United States and in many of the developed economies of the world.

We call this the *numerator effect* because of the pronounced impact it will have on the way in which globalization will push organizations to new heights in their ability to innovate and to grow their businesses. More so than any other factor it is the accelerant behind the movement toward not just smartsourcing but, more importantly, the rate of innovation and the changing landscape of organizations and work. If you are thinking ahead, be forewarned that we are not referring to technology, which is what most people regard as the catalyst for globalization.

The advent of global business, outsourcing, and smartsourcing may coincide with the advent of the computer and information technology, but don't be misled into seeing this as purely a technology-enabled behavior. Technology has played a role in setting the stage for globalization, and it will undoubtedly be instrumental in its evolution, but the trend we are referring to is far more compelling.

We are, of course, speaking about education. And to understand its impact we need to look back at the conditions of not only employment and technology but also of education at the turn of the twentieth century. It is striking to plot global college enrollments worldwide in 1900 against college enrollments in 2000. No scale can do justice to the enormity of change in higher education during that time period. This is not an isolated geographic phenomenon. While it is certainly prominent in the United States, it is most pronounced in areas of the world where today much of the attention for technology development, outsourcing, and offshoring is being focused, namely Asia.

The roots of this change are many and nearly impossible to ascribe to any one social, political, or economic factor. But there are some milestones worth recounting. Closest to home, the GI Bill of 1944 created one of the greatest influxes of college enrollees worldwide. In fact, during 1947, 40 percent of college admissions in the United States were veterans!

Globally, higher education gained increasing prominence on the social agenda in the twentieth century and most notably in the post–World War II era as the result of retooling and social engineering efforts in many of the countries that took on massive rebuilding efforts after the war. For example, at the turn of the century, enrollments in Japanese universities rose from less than 1 percent of the population between the ages of 18 and 25 to 4 percent at midcentury, to nearly 25 percent by the year 2000. This same trend can be observed in most every developing nation during the last 100 years. Yet many are surprised to find out that India now has the second largest post–secondary education system in the world.

While the greatest investment of the twenty-first century will be in the movement of work, its foundation is the higher-education system that provides the skills for a capable global work force that is increasingly distributed geographically. This is fundamental to the evolution of smartsourcing and it is a trend that cannot be stemmed. Global higher education will continue to provide the opportunity for skilled workers in developing economies. In many ways it is the arms race of the twenty-first century. Our ability to move work, without regard to bandwidth, location, or cultural barriers, will only further this movement.

We can only speculate where this will take us. The shifts will certainly be profound and painful. The results will just as assuredly exceed any expectations.

However, the clues we have already explored will start the journey for us in understanding this new world of work. Clearly, the movement of work is a long-term trend; from Henry Ford moving work closer to the worker, to Michael Porter's thoughts about the value chain and its subsequent "dis-integration," to the placeless job at McDonald's in Norwood, Massachusetts, work is like water: It seeks a natural place, it flows along the path of least resistance, ultimately finding its path by wearing away at every obstacle in its way. And so it will be with smart-sourcing. We may be able to find 1,000 reasons why it is not politically, economically, or technically possible, but each of these will soon yield to the pressure and persistence of work to find its natural place.

The recent changes in our communications infrastructure, the rise in global higher education, and the willingness of the capital markets to punish those who do not fully utilize the levers available to them will force us to continue to ask ourselves where work should get done. Interestingly, it is leading us to ask not only where (physically) the work should get done, but also who (what firm) should do it. If I can move work to Prague or to Bangalore, why not think about moving it to the best provider I can find anywhere else in the world? This will eventually bring us to ask ourselves what we—in our company, our industry, even our country—really do best.

Smartsourcing provides the framework and the focus you need to achieve this pre-eminence. But just in case you are not yet convinced of the ties between core competency, innovation, trusted partnerships, and smartsourcing, let us add one more piece to the equation. In a world of increasing uncertainty—where your time to respond is rapidly decreasing—ask yourself a simple question: How could you hope to manage all the moving pieces by yourself? In the next chapter, we will suggest that you cannot; increasing uncertainty will force you and your firm to allocate all of its scarce resources to your core competencies, and to find trusted partners who will help you manage the noncore tasks.

CHAPTER 4

HARNESSING THE WINDS OF CHANGE

"You don't need a weather man to know which way the wind blows."
—Bob Dylan

S martsourcing is not a fad born of fancy. It has grown out of the long-term global progression toward greater complexity in both our organizations and our markets. To talk about smartsourcing outside of the economic context is a bit like a pilot filing a flight plan without first checking the weather report. Uncertainty demands high levels of our bandwidth. It prolongs the time needed to make decisions, and puts a company's strategic capabilities into overdrive. Without a means by which to shed at least some of the noncore aspects of a business, whether to increase strategic bandwidth or strategic capabilities through the right partnerships, uncertainty will undermine an organization's ability to innovate.

Like any system of increasing complexity, there are periods during which breakthroughs are needed in the way the increasingly sophisticated rules and dynamics that influence that system or organization are organized and managed. For example, it would be impossible for a modern-day jet pilot to fly the plane without the assistance of numerous self-adjusting mechanisms that react to environmental factors more quickly than any human being possibly could. While this does not obviate the need for a pilot's judgment and abilities, it does allow the pilot to focus on the issues most critical to flying the plane.

This is especially true for pilots of modern fighter aircraft. Why? Because such aircraft must be highly responsive and maneuverable; however, the more nimble it is in its maneuverability, the more unpredictable it becomes. An aircraft that responds to the slightest touch of the pilot will concurrently be the most susceptible to instability. A fighter pilot needs to make hundreds of tiny corrections and adjustments to the aircraft every minute. Even if the pilot were physically able to do that, he or she would have no time left over to focus on strategy, combat tactics, or mission objectives.

The concept is no different for organizations. Most small early stage organizations or start-up companies are also inherently unstable. They turn on a dime and confound their larger competitors, as well as their market! But as such organizations grow, they adopt rigid processes by which to govern their actions and responses that concurrently create higher levels of stability—and thus decrease agility. Yet uncertainty within the marketplace has not subsided. It has instead increased. Inherent instability is an asset in times of high environmental uncertainty but only if the ability is there to handle all of the additional controls and responses that an organization must take in order to maneuver with greater agility.

There are two things to consider when discussing how smartsourcing can help in this sort of a climate. The first has to do with the ability to coordinate an ever-increasing number of cooperative and interdependent systems in shorter durations of time. This is called *moving toward the singularity*. The second is the increased dependence on indirectly related but necessary systems. We will refer to this as *the move to open systems*.

The move toward the singularity is a cornerstone for smartsourcing. It is heavily dependent on the evolution of component-based systems and standards that will allow organizations to seamlessly bring together the many pieces of technology, partners, and resources that they need to react to the marketplace. Consider, for example, a fighter pilot who relies on not only all of his onboard computers to constantly adjust his aircraft but also on network links to satellite, AWACS, ground intelligence, and remote battlefield control operations in order to make a single critical decision.

The move toward open systems is an even more fascinating aspect of smartsourcing. In closed systems, organizations develop rigid and often unchallenged behaviors. Their success becomes an anchor that ties them to the past. A severe "not invented here" syndrome impedes new innovation and partnership. Creating organizations that are truly open systems is much easier to talk about than to achieve. Yet, if one of the basic precepts of smartsourcing is that partnering leads to higher total innovative capacity, then organizations have to create the sort of permeability that is necessary to allow uncertainty to become a point of leverage for new ideas and innovations, rather than thinking of it as a nemesis that must be locked out at all costs.

COUNTERING UNCERTAINTY

April 19, 1775, a crisp spring New England day. Rows of British soldiers in bright red coats line the rolling green of Lexington, Massachusetts. In their mind, there is nothing foolish or unstrategic in so openly and predictably approaching a rendezvous with their enemy. Their order and discipline is intended to intimidate the opposing colonists. Lines of well-armed British soldiers will precisely fall into sequence and unleash a fury of musket fire across the battlefield, the equivalent of a wall of lead, decimating the opposing side.

Yet the order of the moment is exactly what the ill-equipped band of colonists need to demonstrate the value of uncertainty. Scattered among the trees and bushes is a ragtag team of what can only in the loosest use of the term be called an army. The colonists follow no rules other than to be fully opportunistic in their approach to battle. As they crouch behind trees, rocks, and tall grass, the colonists pick off the brightly garbed Brits one by one.

At the time, such tactics were criticized as anathema. They were considered a disgrace to the culture and tradition of modern warfare . . . and they worked. Today an imposing bronze statue stands on Lexington Common memorializing uncertainty as an edge and an opportunity in the face of insurmountable order and precision. The ragtag colonists very name speaks volumes as to how uncertainty is intimately tied to time—the minuteman.

Despite the disparaging and often negative views applied to uncertainty, uncertainty itself is *not* the enemy. Rather, history bears out that a climate of uncertainty creates some of the greatest opportunities and periods of innovation, which are quickly followed by periods of high prosperity. Often it takes a crisis of extreme proportions to bring us to the brink of breakthrough opportunity. Ironically, uncertainty often brings a clarity that is impossible to find in times of prosperity. It is a human condition that we do not feel the hunger of innovation as keenly when our bellies and wallets are full.

To describe this phenomenon we will co-opt a term that was first coined in the early part of the twentieth century to describe the new world of quantum mechanics: *the uncertainty principle.* Then, its meaning was applied to the mechanics of subatomic particles. Our use of it here is in the context of enterprise risk and opportunity. However, the principle is fundamentally similar and elegantly self-evident to any businessperson: *As uncertainty with the economy, geopolitical events, and society increases, the effective time to react to opportunity decreases.*

At the core of the uncertainty principle is an essential framework (**FIGURE 4.1**) that illustrates what we refer to as the *decision curve*. The decision curve represents the optimal time to react given the velocity of opportunity in a specific situation. The greater the velocity of opportunity and the level of uncertainty, the faster organizations need to react. Though this sounds simple, it is counterintuitive. When uncertainty increases organizations want to slow down, thereby inflating their decision curve. The reason for this is that most people want to take more time to consider their options in times of uncertainty rather than act rashly in haste. The irony, as we alluded in the discussion about inherent instability, is that external chaos demands internal chaos. The question, of course, is how to manage that internal chaos.

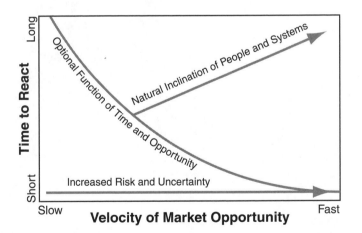

FIGURE 4.1

THE UNCERTAINTY PRINCIPLE

As uncertainty and the velocity of market opportunity increase, the time available to react to any given opportunity decreases.

It's easy to say that higher uncertainty requires higher innovation, but as is shown in **FIGURE 4.2** there is not only the risk of too little innovation, there is also such a thing as too much innovation. Innovation has to be paced with the degree of uncertainty. If a company invests too heavily in new products and services, it can easily overbuild its offerings. Early entrants into a new market are often prone to doing this. In the current climate, staying in the narrowing band where innovation and uncertainty are well matched is becoming a high-wire act; invest too little or too much and you will under- or overshoot the market.

The key, as we see it, is to buy latitude by staying as close to the point of certainty as is possible through focusing on what your organization does best, in terms of both capabilities and market savvy.

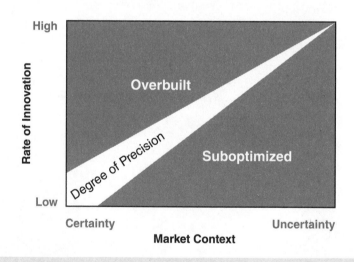

FIGURE 4.2

OVERBUILT VS. SUB-OPTIMIZED

Over time, the tolerable margin of error between a process that is overbuilt and one that is sub-optimized is narrowing. A simple example is that of the airline industry, which has been squeezed to limit the number of flights and equipment (reduce overbuilt capacity) while at the same time being expected to deliver better on-time service, fewer cancellations, and greater choices for travelers (increase optimization).

Our objective in this chapter is to look at a set of fundamental principles, which, if understood and applied correctly within a smartsourcing solution, can be used to turn the chaos of uncertainty into opportunity for growth and prosperity.

These principles can be distilled into a few quick observations that will guide our thinking throughout our discussion of uncertainty:

- Uncertainty creates opportunity.
- Uncertainty increases as the volume of information increases.
- Times of uncertainty require stronger bonds of trust to navigate.
- Uncertainty requires that we have rapid access to tacit rather than explicit knowledge.
- Uncertainty creates a greater need for radical thought, creativity, and innovation.
- Uncertainty demands patient, committed leadership and a long view to see beyond the near-term turmoil to the opportunities that will evolve.

Uncertainty creates opportunity.

One of the most basic responses to an uncertain situation is the marked increase in the time utilized to make a decision. Simply put, the increased risk of an uncertain climate causes us to be far more conservative in our actions. The irony is that uncertainty requires decisiveness because the volatility of the environment (economic or otherwise) decreases the duration of each opportunity and the time available to act on it.

Think of the simple but extreme example of timing within the stock market. When the market was certain for prolonged durations everyone thought they were a day-trading genius.

Today, the risk of uncertainty has agitated a sustained mass-market exodus. Yet the rewards of economic opportunity are still there, albeit in myriad rapid market fluctuations.

Similarly, if you look at periods of high innovation that have resulted in products and services of sustained value, these periods have almost certainly begun in times of high economic and geopolitical uncertainty. Consider some simple and obvious examples such as the space race against the backdrop of the Cold War or the enormous post–World War II boom in technology innovation. There is clearly something about uncertainty that causes organizations and society to dig deep into their collective capacity for innovation.

It is why we are so bullish on the idea of smartsourcing as a means to not only counter uncertainty but also, and more importantly, to benefit from the opportunity it creates to establish new ways to work together in extended global enterprises.

Uncertainty increases as the volume of information increases.

Intuition tells us that the more we know about something, the more certain we should be about it. In practice, things are usually much more complicated and the inverse is most often true. As we learn more, our certainty is often challenged. In the realm of quantum physics, scientists have long struggled with the dilemma of certainty. Although at a macroscopic level, physical events have unwavering certainty in following predictable behaviors, at a microscopic, subatomic level certainty is relatively nonexistent.

The situation most leaders and executives find themselves in is that as they gain more information about the details of their business and markets, they need an equally greater amount of time to reach decisions. The nagging question for any astute businessperson is not how much information can be gathered, but rather what information is needed to support effective conclusions in the necessary window of opportunity.

Times of uncertainty require stronger bonds of trust to navigate.

At a very base human level uncertainty creates an elevated need for kinship and trust. In times of heightened uncertainty, individuals seek out relationships and sources of trusted advice, counsel, and partnership. These provide a sort of haven and also allow people to exercise some modicum of control over what is otherwise an uncontrollable situation.

This trust can take many forms from very personal mentoring relationships to commercial ventures that require higher levels of transparency, disclosure, and information sharing. In all cases, however, they are essential elements of rebuilding what environmental uncertainty has taken away, namely the reliability and predictability of the future.

Perhaps the best historical example here is the evolution of contracts and common law, which together were primary forces in moving civilization out of the Dark Ages and into the modern commercial world. Although contracts are often dismissed as a necessary evil, red tape, or a way to justify administrative overhead, they do form a foundation of reliability in free-market economies. Peruvian economist Fernando de Soto has written extensively on the critical role that the indisputable nature of property rights plays in the formation of capitalist economies and the way the lack of these rights in developing countries undermines prosperity and commerce. In the same way, contracts provide a security in the future that offer a certainty in outcomes and allows us to plan with the assurance of certain events and resources. All of this speaks to the role of trust.

We believe firmly in the ability of smartsourcing to provide a greater base of global trust and reliance that crosses all manner of borders and barriers—from cultural and national to organizational and industrial. Whatever the mechanism, trust, at its most primal level, provides a higher level of certainty and confidence in our ability to make decisions and to take action.

Uncertainty requires rapid access to tacit rather than explicit knowledge.

For example, in a moment of crisis we are much more likely to seek out an expert in the situation than to refer to a policies and procedures manual.

Explicit knowledge of the sort contained inside information repositories is relatively easy to integrate and retrieve. Integration of this information has been the rallying cry of information technology for decades. However, tacit knowledge in its raw state is not particularly well integrated (if at all) into most information systems. To further exacerbate the situation, tacit knowledge of the sort that is gained through experiential learning is especially difficult to obtain in volatile markets. Namely, people are far less likely to take the time to engage in what are considered superfluous activities such as educating, mentoring, and sharing in volatile climates where the focus is on survival. If organizations do not increase their reliance on trusted relationships built on such knowledge, they eventually weaken the foundation of their business to support partnership.

This is especially critical in smartsourcing partnerships where this knowledge has to be shared across vast geographies. The challenge is hardly limited to technology. While information can be stored, scanned, and transmitted instantaneously to virtually any point on the globe we cannot capture and transmit experience and people. Until the Star Trek teleporter is here we will need to rely on tighter communities of practice and in some cases simply accept that there are many aspects of what an organization does that must be kept in-house.

Uncertainty creates a greater need for radical thought, creativity, and innovation.

Nineteenth-century satirist Ambrose Bierce said accountability is "the mother of caution." In a climate of fear, organizations tend to be insistent on tests and peer-driven standards of measure. This creates a vicious cycle, where organizations become increasingly risk-averse and closed to the acceptance of economic potential. They shy away from open systems, distrust the promise of smartsourcing, and generally limit their risks.

Taking risk, however, is precisely what is needed in times of uncertainty. Risk is ultimately the only avenue to innovation. And the demand for innovation in the current fast-paced, global, and technologically advanced economy is a given constant. Continual innovation is needed with respect to both product and process.

Instead, uncertainty often begets retreat and a move toward tightening of budgets and strategic investments. The attitude is one of making sure that no mistake is made. Although this may be ascribed to the pendulum swing from irrational exuberance to irrational despondence, the fact remains that the answers to uncertainty will not be found by relying on accountants to bury our heads further into the denominator of our businesses. Smartsourcing has to focus on the numerator. Organizations need to find new ways to grow themselves while enhancing their revenues, markets, and labor forces. These objectives are only fostered through innovation and creativity that transcends organizational and market boundaries, rather than retreating behind them.

Uncertainty demands a long view.

In many ways the ultimate calling and responsibility of leadership is to absorb uncertainty and provide a safe and focused haven for innovation and execution. The greatest leaders are those who rise to this calling in times of heightened uncertainty. Although we may disagree with and even downright despise their actions, we are still drawn to their unwavering focus on a direction despite the winds of change that are constantly at work to blow them off course.

What is most important for leaders to understand in times of uncertainty is that their greatest challenge and accomplishment is not to pick the right course, but rather to gain agreement from those they lead that the path, once chosen, must be made right. Through the numerous corrections, refinements, and unforeseeable impediments, leadership must absorb the uncertainty of the moment and focus the organization on its successes and progress toward specific goals.

Through a considered smartsourcing approach, managers and leaders can focus on what is important in setting the course and on those areas where they have the highest levels of confidence in their organization's capabilities. Like our fighter pilot they can focus on their mission objective despite the inherent instability of their markets, economies, and organizations.

So, can uncertainty be turned into a point of leverage and an opportunity for you, your organization, and your smartsourcing initiative? The answer lies in your ability to accept the principles outlined here and to make the concepts they contain essential to how you view the world and the opportunity uncertainty holds.

But before we delve deeper into how smartsourcing can offer solutions in the context of uncertainty we are going to set smartsourcing aside for just a bit and look more carefully at uncertainty itself.

To do that you will take a deep look at four perspectives on uncertainty that in total offer a comprehensive education and some necessary background on how uncertainty factors into the way in which you will need to organize and respond to our markets and competitors. There are many facets to this discussion, but we will focus on four critical areas that offer the most essential context:

- The emotional impact of uncertainty
- The foundation of uncertainty in economics
- The origins and the scientific basis for the uncertainty principle
- The changing doctrine of organizing around uncertainty

When you total the bandwidth that is consumed by each of these changes in our behaviors toward uncertainty and the shift in our view of uncertainty's role in our decisions, it becomes much clearer that the job ahead is not to eliminate uncertainty but rather to understand how we can best operate inside it.

Often our efforts are directed at averting uncertainty or simply overpowering it. There is a saying among hard-nosed CEOs: "I may be right. I may be wrong. But I am *not* uncertain." The point is that any certainty is better than uncertainty. Uncertainty is tedious. It exacts a heavy toll on individuals and organizations as it buffets us, undermining our confidence in our ability to prepare for the future. Uncertainty is disorienting. It takes away our business visibility, the liquidity of our assets, and our organizational equilibrium, leaving us confused.

Certainty, good or bad, can be planned for; it can be priced into markets, it can be built into financial and behavioral models, and it can be anticipated. We can adapt our businesses, our institutions, and ourselves to virtually any sort of certainty, no matter how distressing. To regain certainty we will do almost anything. But what if the state of uncertainty is not a temporal phase of the current economic cycle? What if uncertainty is increasingly becoming more a part of the social, organizational, and economic landscape? Can uncertainty be factored into business planning? Can leaders and managers exact opportunity from uncertainty? Dare you try to plan for it?

Admittedly the answers are not easy to come by.

UNCERTAINTY GAMES: THE ONLY RULE IS THAT THERE ARE NONE

Consider for a minute what games you would associate with uncertainty. Chess is undoubtedly a game that readily comes to mind. After all, chess is a complex game with nearly incalculable strategies and counter-strategies for every move. Furthermore, chess is perhaps one of the most popular game analogies for business, especially in cases of negotiation and strategic decisions.

Chess, however, is not representative of uncertainty. Chess is a closed system; that is, it is a system of measurable, and mostly predeterminable, alternatives and risks. For every game piece on the chessboard there is a finite set of possible moves. The bishop cannot suddenly decide to jump over a pawn and move vertically across the length of the chessboard. No matter how complex the combination of moves may be, each move is clearly detailed in a predetermined and agreed-upon set of rules.

Using such a context, think about a game that would be governed by the forces of uncertainty. Poker? Again, the rules are clear. There is an element of chance or risk involved with the cards you draw or discard, as well as the way you play your hand. You can bluff and force your opponent to operate based on a fear of the unknown. But there are only four aces in the deck and if you have all four there is *no chance* that your opponent will pull a pair of aces. Your risk can be calculated and your wager gauged accordingly.

Poker and chess are not examples of uncertainty but risk. Risk is critical to making good decisions, but it is not the same as uncertainty. Uncertainty results from doubt, mistrust, and a lack of confidence in observable phenomenon. Uncertainty is not calculable, arithmetic, predictable, and probabilistic. Uncertainty defies what you know.

Consider poker again. What would happen if your opponent did draw the same cards you had? You would have several choices of reaction:

- Confront him as a cheat, casting doubt on his integrity.
- Lose trust in the deck itself (were there fifty-two cards?).
- Question your own judgment and double-check your observations (did I really have four aces in my hand—does he really have two?).

Concurrently you would undoubtedly experience a rush of adrenaline. Uncertainty cannot be divorced from emotion; it is fundamentally an emotional, not a logical, state of mind.

Uncertainty results in loss of control, adoption of a defensive stature, and the inevitable ascription of blame.

It is this lack of a defined road map that causes the frustration associated with uncertainty. If there is one attribute shared by all living organisms it is a defined purpose of being. From amoebas to complex human beings, all living organisms are programmed to deal with the known. Evolution, genetics, and instinct have all worked to incorporate lessons from our environment into our behaviors. When these lessons no longer apply, when the environment so radically changes as to no longer map to our responses, we cross into the panic zone of uncertainty.

But make no mistake; this is not a hopeless situation. Nature has dealt with uncertainty in evolution and has demonstrated that resilience is possible. In fact, it could be asserted that because nature has no way to calculate the probability, risk, and potential outcomes of any wager, it is constantly dealing with uncertainty but has nonetheless succeeded through evolution.

So what game would best characterize the forces and dynamics of uncertainty?

There are none. No matter what game you choose there are rules that have to be followed. By definition a game is "a competitive activity or sport in which players contend with each other according to a set of *rules*." Therein lies the problem. Uncertainty is not marketable. Nobody wants it. Can you imagine trying to sell a game where a player could arbitrarily change the rules on a whim? Who would buy it? People play games because they want to believe that they can out-skill or outwit their opponents. Play monopoly with a five-year-old and you'll soon find out why a game with subjective rules would not get too far. Yet this is the essence of uncertainty. It is thrust upon us and our immediate response is to thrust back, to say under our breath, "Damn it—play by the rules!"

But while the example is a good illustration, the frustration is not about board games; it is about the very real implications of uncertainty in the most fundamental aspects of our lives and organizations. And surprisingly it is not a new topic. For the better part of the twentieth century, every discipline from physics to economics to military doctrine has been dealing with the increasing prevalence of uncertainty—with some startling revelations and lessons.

FRANK KNIGHT AND THE CHICAGO SCHOOL

"It is a world of change in which we live, and a world of uncertainty."
—Frank Knight, 1921

Although you might expect uncertainty and economics to be a combination of topics that is a much more recent discussion, its roots go back to nearly the start of the twentieth century and an obscure economist.

The year 1921 was a period of profound global change. World War I had exacted a heavy price from the industrialized nations of the time. Yet it had also provided one of the greatest periods of change, prosperity, and innovation in modern history. It was the beginning of a boom bubble market.

Now, nearly 100 years removed from these events, we identify the period in simplistic terms, with a few cornerstone events. But these mask the great sense of transition that was being experienced. While we may romanticize the period of the Roaring Twenties and the wistful lives of its Gatsbyesque socialites, there was much to lose sleep over.

Uncertainty was looming large for these early-twentieth-century citizens. Consider that this was a time when organized crime became rampant due to Prohibition. Women had just been given the right to vote. The first radio station had taken to the airwaves. It was a time of irrational jubilation, which in many ways led to the great crash of 1929, the Great Depression, and finally culminated in the global conflict of World War II.

Onto this stage walked Frank Knight. Knight was a contemporary of another influential economist of that day whose name is much better known: John Maynard Keynes. Both Keynes and Knight focused much of their time on the issue of uncertainty. But while Keynes was busy detailing the mathematics of economics, Knight was attacking the subject from an entirely different perspective, looking at the behaviors that define our interaction with the world of risk, uncertainty, and profit.

In 1914, Knight wrote a doctoral thesis at Cornell that later became one of the cornerstone books of the Chicago school of economics, *Risk, Uncertainty, and Profit*. The work was hardly noticed at the time, and will probably not strike a chord of familiarity unless you are a die-hard student of economics; and even then the recollection may be faint. Yet his observations are foundational to the discussion of uncertainty.

Knight's approach to economics was unorthodox, but his premise was profoundly simple: Uncertainty is the absence of future knowledge. From this, Knight constructed a complex view of the many ways in which uncertainty is factored into our lives, going so far as to state that the very role of consciousness is to give living beings "knowledge" of the future.

Today the term *Knightsian economics* is often associated with the description of situations where no amount of information can create greater certainty about an event. This is perhaps the most counterintuitive aspect of Knight's work.

After all, if uncertainty is the absence of knowledge about the future, shouldn't there be some amount of information that would rectify the situation? In a Knightsian scenario, such knowledge can only be gained by experiencing the event, but not beforehand. In fact, more information in such a situation only leads to delayed decision-making and lost opportunity. We should point out that Knight is careful to differentiate between the probabilities inherent in risk and uncertainty. Risk can be assessed through either knowledge of similar past events or the known probabilities of a set of possible events.

If you are rolling dice, the probability of any one of the six sides of each individual die coming up is identical. We can therefore assess the likelihood of rolling a number without any actual experience. This is what Knight called *a priori* probability. On the other hand, actuaries know from experience what the likelihood is of a person living to a particular age, or a house burning down. Knight called this *statistical probability*. Most economics will factor one of these two approaches into attempts to model an economic behavior.

However, although you can buy an insurance policy on a building, you cannot predict when or if that particular building will burn down. No amount of information will provide that knowledge. To put it in a sentence, risk results in an insurance company's profitability. Uncertainty results in its downfall.

To Knight this sort of irresolvable uncertainty was the essential ingredient in all forms of commerce, without which competition, entrepreneurship, and free enterprise would not be possible. According to Knight in *Risk, Uncertainty, and Profit,* published in book form in 1921, "The more important task is to follow out the consequences of that higher form of uncertainty not susceptible to measurement and hence to elimination. It is this *true uncertainty* which by preventing the theoretically perfect outworking of the tendencies of competition gives the characteristic form of 'enterprise' to economic organization as a whole and accounts for the peculiar income of the entrepreneur."

You can probably see why Knight's work never made it into the mainstream. This is hardly the prose that bestsellers are made of. But while Knight may have been less than accessible to the average reader, a group of even more radically inclined young Turks were about to cement the place uncertainty held in our lives with a series of experiments and theories that would make Knight's work look like child's play.

BUILDING OPEN SYSTEMS: HEISENBERG AND THE UNCERTAINTY RAT PACK

Uncertainty can't be discussed without at least briefly delving into some of the legacy behind the *uncertainty principle,* namely, quantum mechanics.

Fear not, our purpose here isn't to explain physics, but rather to tie a final loose thread into our discussion, and, in the process, briefly illustrate how the sort of open-systems thinking that smartsourcing leads us to is fundamentally more efficient and reliable than the sort of closed-systems thinking that you and your organization have probably been raised with.

Some of the most ingenious scientists of our time have applied the principles of uncertainty to the realm of the physical world, where common sense would indicate that certainty plays the greatest role. It was this bedrock of certainty in a set of irrefutable natural laws that was shattered at the beginning of the twentieth century by a cadre of young physicists with names such as Bohr, Heisenberg, and Schrödinger. What they suggested created a schism for the scientific community not unlike what resulted in the early 1500s when Copernicus asserted that Earth was not the center of the solar system, as had been thought for 1,400 years.

So what did these young Turks of physics suggest to cause such a sea change? Simply put, that at a subatomic level there was no certainty in the behavior of the physical world. Or, put another way, the closer one gets to reality, the less certain it becomes that there is an *objective* reality. To explain this concept, we can draw upon the earlier example of the poker game in which your opponent draws some of the same cards you thought you had in your hand: Bohr, Heisenberg, and Schrodinger proposed that it is not the cards but the way you look at them that matters. In fact, the cards do not even exist until and unless you look at them!

So, what is quantum uncertainty and how does it tie into our discussion of the greater uncertainty that challenges us in the world of business, and for which we're proposing smartsourcing as an antidote?

The story begins in 1900 when a young physicist named Max Planck discovered that light energy is transmitted in what he called *quanta*—what we today call a *photon*. Quanta are discrete packets of energy that cannot be subdivided. In other words, you can't have half of a quanta or two-thirds of a quanta. It's all or nothing. This is where the term *quantum leap* comes from. A quanta does not travel from one energy state (or, as we will soon see, one position to another). Instead it is either in one state or another. Imagine, for example, your car going from 0 to 60 miles per hour not by accelerating through each intermediate speed (1, 2, 3, 4, 5, 6 . . . 58, 59, 60 mph), but rather by simply being at 0 or 60, with no lapse in time.

What was even more peculiar about quanta was that they behaved differently depending on how you looked at them. If you looked at them as particles, they behaved as particles. However, if you looked at them as waves of energy, they behaved as waves. Such results confounded scientists. After all, particles had mass and followed the rules of particle physics. Waves had no mass and followed the rules of electromagnetic energy. They shouldn't be interchangeable.

However, light had always been the wild card in the field of physics. After all, it couldn't be touched or contained in the concrete way that matter could. Thus, it was okay for light to be a bit quirky in how it behaved. But in 1913, another physicist, Niels Bohr, took this quirkiness and applied it to all matter by suggesting that the principle of quanta could be applied to electrons (the tiny objects that orbit around the nucleus of an atom). In an instant everything that was considered real was uncertain at its most basic level.

Bohr's findings had many implications because they applied to everything tangible. However, it was Werner Heisenberg's unveiling of the original uncertainty principle that made the most significant impact.

In its simplest form, Heisenberg's uncertainty principle stated that you could not simultaneously know both the position and the mass of a quantum object. In this way the observer is more important than what is being observed. By the same token, you cannot know the precise energy of a quantum system over a precise period of time. As the time interval gets smaller, the uncertainty increases.

It is this simple premise that you will hear echoed in the most basic principles of this book: that the decreasing interval of time within which to react is the greatest nemesis of vertically integrated monolithic enterprises.

By the 1920s Heisenberg and his colleagues had shattered and rebuilt physics from the ground floor up. Less than two decades hence, in 1939, the seeds they planted would take horrifying form in an explosion over Hiroshima. Uncertainty had claimed its place in history.

What has become abundantly clear is that uncertainty is an integral part of the very fabric of the universe. Yet, order and predictability can exist despite this and even uncertainty itself can be leveraged if understood. To appreciate this in the business context of smartsourcing, a few ground rules for how uncertainty can be handled need to be established:

- Not all systems are uncertain.
- Uncertainty does not equal risk.
- The half-life of what we know is decreasing.

First, not all systems are uncertain. There are many cases where an outcome can be predicted with high certainty based on a variety of factors ranging from experience, to probabilities, to anticipated behaviors. We call these cases *closed* systems as opposed to *open* systems, which are inherently uncertain. An *open* system is one that is influenced by factors that are both unknown and unknowable. In other words no amount of time or information will increase certainty. Of course, the disturbing aspect of quantum uncertainty is that you would consider subatomic particles to be closed systems, bringing into question just how many of what we consider to be closed systems really are.

Still, we will yield on this point and accept that for practical purposes many systems that we work with are closed and can be adequately dealt with through probability, while also making the point that in the future fewer and fewer systems will be closed—and therefore more subject to uncertainty. The reason for the increase in open systems stems from what we will call *technology entanglement,* which is the increasing capacity of networking technologies to integrate otherwise disparate and separate systems.

Second, uncertainty does not equate to risk. While we can say, in a colloquial sense, that these two are the same, the differences are important to understand in dealing with each. Risk presents us with probabilities that are finite. The coin will land heads or tails. The die will come up with a number of dots from one to six. There are no intermediate or out-of-the-box possibilities in these cases. Again, they are all closed systems. Uncertainty, however, presents outcomes that could not have been bet on in any probabilistic sense. This is simply the definition of dealing with the unknown.

Third, although our experiences are constantly generating new knowledge of how both open and closed systems behave, increasing our confidence in what we know, the half-life of what we know is increasingly getting shorter. Another way to look at this is that what we know is increasing rapidly as measured in terms of volume (i.e., number of books, pages of research, Web sites, etc.), but it is increasingly a smaller percentage of what we need to know to deal with the ultimate open system of the marketplace.

By appreciating the differences between open and closed systems and the way these differ in terms of risk and uncertainty we can begin to develop expectations and behaviors that allow us to create what General Tommy Franks, who commanded the coalition in the Iraqi War, called a "plan *for* action." This anticipates and accommodates the presence of uncertainty— unlike a "plan *of* action," which hopes to encounter a much higher degree of certainty. It is a dramatic shift in not only our tactics but also our attitude and the very doctrine we adopt to counterbalance uncertainty.

A New Doctrine Emerges

If there is one place where uncertainty takes its greatest toll it is in the military. It is also the military that provides the role model for many of our industrial organizations. The problem is that the model is outdated. The strategies, role of command and control, and planning methods for the military have changed dramatically over the past fifty years. While we may have built our businesses around military doctrine, military doctrine has been reinvented to acknowledge new types of enemies, unconventional warfare, terrorism, and global coalitions. The result has been a far leaner and more agile military that puts a higher premium on risk assessment and real-time mobility. Assets on a battlefield are now tracked with amazing precision and an individual soldier is equipped to deal with unprecedented levels of information access, communications, and situational awareness—in the words of the recruiting tag line, a literal *Army of One.*

But the "Army of One" moniker is a double-entendre. While the individual is much more powerful, the coordination among the many resources involved in a theater has also increased tremendously, creating a truly unified military from what were once isolated and separate organizations. In fact, it was not that long ago that any one branch of the military conducting mock battlefield exercises had to make its own set of assumptions about how the other branches would behave, rather than actually involving the other branches as part of the exercise.

In writing this book we conducted an interview with General John Croker, one of only five senior mentors in the U.S. Air Force tasked with training three- and four-star generals on military doctrine. We looked closely at how the military's attitudes toward uncertainty have changed and considered the analogous shift that must also occur in organizations that are adopting smartsourcing and globalization against the backdrop of heightened uncertainty.

There has probably never been a global organization of the scope and scale that formed during World War II, and certainly none as critical in its mission and outcome. The creation of a massive military machine; the confluence of myriad new technologies for warfare, communication, and intelligence; and the challenge of dealing with simultaneous global conflicts in multiple theaters and a network of global allies all presented a daunting scenario of coordination and control.

It is difficult to fully appreciate the magnitude of this challenge today, but walking through the Cabinet War Rooms of London, the underground bunkers that Churchill and his cabinet used during the bombing raids on London, you get a much better sense for the absurd proportions of the task. The tools and techniques that the allies used to coordinate and communicate are amazingly primitive by today's standards. It seems unthinkable, for instance, that a military organization of any scale, much less that involved in World War II, could have been run by tracking planes, tanks, and troops on a wall map with pins and thread. Yet the nerve center of Churchill's war room was just that, a primitive process prone to enormous misinformation, delays, and error.

In its own experience the United States reeled from the devastating attack on Pearl Harbor, which by many accounts was the result of a lack of coordination and communication among the various sources of intelligence already available.

If we today shudder at how the allies and the free world survived and succeeded in World War II given the lack of sophistication and technology available, we should take pause. Our memory of recent terrorist attacks in the United States and around the globe are warning again that we need to raise the bar for how we deal with a new level of uncertainty.

One very visible aspect of this is found in how the military is changing to react to increased complexity in global communication and coordination. Here, too, we are not dealing with a new phenomenon. Not unlike the crisis of communication that spurred the formation of the Department of Homeland Security in the aftermath of the terrorist attacks on the United States in 2001, there was a similar crisis of communication that needed to be addressed after the end of World War II. The result was an effort to consolidate the services under one command and to create military and civilian intelligence agencies that would collaborate and share information in order to increase the effectiveness of the military. In many ways the modern military had its origins in this moment of retrospection and the National Security Act (NSA) of 1947.

While very broad in its impact, the NSA of 1947 is most often credited with the establishment of the Department of Defense, the Joint Chiefs of Staff, and the Central Intelligence Agency (CIA), which grew out of the Office of Strategic Services and small postwar intelligence organizations. The CIA served as the primary civilian intelligence-gathering organization in the government. Later, the Defense Intelligence Agency became the main military intelligence body.

But more importantly the 1947 law also caused far-reaching changes in the military establishment. The War Department and Navy Department merged into a single Department of Defense under the secretary of defense, who also directed the newly created Department of the Air Force. However, each of the three branches maintained their own service secretaries. In 1949 the act was amended to give the secretary of defense more power over the individual services and their secretaries.

Still, the U.S. armed forces had the equivalent of four separate corporations that operated independently, each with its own budget program activity and its own administration and support. In the battlefield the same mentality applied. The assumption was that the cumulative impact of those efforts would produce some net worth for the national security policy of the United States. Although the NSA of 1947 was an attempt to consolidate, it took decades for even its most basic aspects to take hold while many fought against its radical premise to merge the individual services into a joint forces military. Ultimately the act did create a greater level of cohesion than had been available in the past, but the lines of demarcation between the armed services and perhaps more critically between civilian and military intelligence gathering continued to exist.

In the post-9/11 era we are now trying to refocus on joint activities and processes that cut across military and civilian intelligence, thus effectively creating one company linked by common processes that work across company and service lines.

The military and intelligence establishments are shifting from the industrial model of a vertical hierarchical structure for each service to more of an integrated structure across the Department of Defense and Homeland Security. Such will allow each service and intelligence agency to make contributions to joint activity and unified objectives; the assumption being that the cumulative result will be more beneficial for the organization as a whole.

Creating the common processes and platforms on which to build this unification is a monumental task that will clearly take us into the next decade, but its precepts are at the heart of the principles and methods that private enterprise will also need to use in creating global processes and partnerships. For example, in the late 1990s the Air Force conducted a number of exercises in an attempt to figure out how to improve its processes so that when a sudden opportunity presented itself on the battlefield its response and decision-making was sufficient, allowing it to strike those targets in a hurry.

The Air Force always had a set of fixed targets that it could identify—buildings, runways, power plants, armory storage facilities, and other such strategic targets—but things that didn't seem important in prior planning could suddenly become important. For example, a bridge may not be strategic until an opposing force takes a course that was not anticipated. As we've already said, the challenge was that the opportunities might be many but the window of each opportunity was very short.

The Air Force conducted these exercises for a period of four years through a series of major experiments to identify and refine its processes. One result was that before the Iraqi War, the Air Force held a series of major tests at Nellis Air Force Base with all the participants that were going to be in the war—the equivalent of a live rehearsal.

Air Force, Army, reconnaissance, and Special Forces all practiced their procedures and refined them, so that when they got to the Iraqi War, they'd had about four years of dress rehearsals to get ready for it.

Up until that time, each military organization around the world had its own equipment, its own procedures, its own unique characteristics, and its own terminology. Yet as the armed forces had fewer people to support this sort of separateness, they needed to shift people back and forth between the services. As a result it became much more important that the military develop the use of a common concept of operations, common terminology, common equipment, common tactics, techniques, procedures, and common doctrine so that a single individual could go from one organization to the next and be effective without having a high start-up cost.

The same can be said today of organizations that are running lean and thereby creating the impetus and the environment to scrutinize processes across silos that otherwise could exist within their own realm, with their own language, solutions, and methods.

To offer a front-lines sense for how these changes are shaping the military and to uncover some lessons that we might also apply to our own organizations off of the battlefield we asked General Croker to describe some of the specific ways in which military doctrine is being recast to deal with uncertainty and globalization. While we could reword his thoughts and comments, they are best heard in their original context, in his own words.

Here is some of what he had to say:

AUTHORS: We are heading into a period of globalization and global alliances in every aspect of business, no less so in the military. What are some of the immediate challenges you see?

GENERAL CROKER: "In the future we're going to have to increasingly deal with coalitions and how we pass information and knowledge from one organization to another among allies.

"We have several fundamental problems. First of all, our national disclosure policy is fundamentally restricted. In other words, we don't share information with people unless there is an overwhelming reason to do it. I'm talking about sensitive military information. However, most other federal nations tend to operate on the reverse principle. They will share information unless there is a compelling reason not to. This creates as policy or philosophical difference about what type of information we will share and how we'll share it. That has caused us some frustrations that we haven't entirely worked our way through yet.

"We also have a technology gap in the information-sharing area. While we spend a lot of money on Command and Control and classified networks and casting information from one domain to another, most of our coalition partners and allies have not made similar early investments in technology, so there is relatively little in the way of coalition network equipment that we can provide to them that lets us share intelligence.

"Without that people tend to go off in different directions. So building trust and confidence with our coalition partners and our allies is facilitated to the degree that we can share sensitive information on a timely basis, and that continues to be a challenge."

AUTHORS: What has most changed that for the better?

GENERAL CROKER: "Within the United States one of the most startling advances has been in the area of collaborative tools. In the past, if you think of a military organization that's hierarchical, the senior organization would plan what it would want to do. Then it would task the lower organizations, who would take the mission and then task its components, and so on. So, it was a sequential, extended process. Increasingly nowadays, collaboration and visualization tools are being used. We can share slides, whiteboards, and maps, we can discourse, we can see each other visually and, in many cases, we are able to do both planning and execution collaboratively in a more parallel fashion and in a much more rapid manner.

"The danger to that, we have found, is the difference between thinking out loud and giving guidance or direction. When people get together collaboratively and they don't have good business rules and haven't been well trained, they tend to think through problems out loud and then bad information or inaccurate information gets distributed to a large group of people.

"The way we solve that is by starting to insist that people put out short written memorandum of agreements on what decisions were made during the course of a meeting. We found that if we interviewed ten different people who left and collaborated for a VTC [video teleconference] session, there were ten different ideas about what transpired in the meeting. So, now we are able to do planning together, build our facts in a common rapid fashion, and at the end of the meeting the commander will put out short written guidance that says, 'In this meeting, these are the decisions I've reached,' giving people a common view of what's been decided.

"We've also come up with a hybrid organizational structure where, although not a flat structure, we are no longer strictly a hierarchical structure but some sort of pyramid structure where there is a set of responsibilities for queuing certain events among the organization's levels. In Iraq, we were successful in allowing people at the operational level to carry out the strategic theater objectives without as much interference or misunderstanding from above. We were also able to give clear mission-type orders to the lower-level tactical groups without knowing how to carry out discrete tactical actions.

"That has allowed us to create simultaneous effects across the battlefield rather than working in area A and then in area B and then in area C. Or, as in the old days when we deployed our people in Desert Storm for six months, then fought an air war for our remaining days—flying thirty days, and then embarking on a ground offensive for 100 hours.

"In the 2003 Iraq War, we were simultaneously deploying people, employing people, and sustaining people over several major periods while we were working in the Western Desert, moving from Kuwait up to Baghdad and working in the north—all at the same time. And the objective there was to create enough uncertainty, enough confusion on the part of the Iraqis, that they couldn't handle it all.

"The next thing is that instead of building up forces and then deploying, we used what we call in the business world *just-in-time logistics*, where the forces arrived on the battlefield as they were needed. And you'll notice that several of the divisions got into the play, going there thirty days after the start of the conflict. So, we were able to move much more rapidly in this fight than we were in the past.

"We were also able to use much more dispersed forces instead of concentrated forces and use our precision weapons and our measuring techniques with global positioning satellites to make other weapons we have much more lethal with a much lower collateral damage. In other words, the last time we did a major campaign like this the fear was that we would take out their power structure—their roads, their utilities, and set back the country for some number of years.

"In the Iraqi campaign, we clearly devised a plan that let us be very discrete, achieving the effects we wanted to create, like destabilizing the regime without destroying the basic infrastructure. The ability to disperse forces and still be lethal with precision was very important.

"So, we were able to not just have new technologies but integrated technologies. All of that to try and gain decision superiority over the enemy. In other words, we're trying to make better decisions than the enemy and create a great number of effects—the cumulative impact of which you can't deal with.

"Now, all of that has meant a real price. The bottom line for me is that we've actually found that we can't create effects quicker than we can assess them.

"And one of the problems we had in the Iraqi War was that we were moving very rapidly over the ground. And so, in this sense, we were driving in front of our headlights."

AUTHORS: That's a great analogy to what we term visibility in business. Uncertainty limits visibility, making it difficult to project trends and performance with high confidence. Describe your view of that a bit more.

GENERAL CROKER: "We're driving on low beams and in the pitch black. In many cases the ground units actually had to close with the enemy to figure out exactly what we have done. And General Franks dealt with that by taking a lot of risks in certain areas and making assumptions and predictions about what we must have done to the enemy in the absence of certainty. By and large, in the first three phases of the campaign until we got to and secured Baghdad and major hostility ceased, we were able to achieve those objectives in the face of a lot of uncertainty and I think we managed that uncertainty a lot better than the Iraqis did. Now, that raises the question, 'What's going to happen when we have a world-class enemy who is very, very good at this and has some of the integrating technologies that we do and can either introduce some certainty onto us or deal with uncertainty as well as we deal with uncertainty?' And those are answers that I don't have yet. I would say that about four or five years ago we realized that the business model we were using and the way we were training and exercising people and the industrial-era processes that we were using just weren't allowing us to make much better decisions much faster with more austere forces moving more rapidly.

"And through a lot of concept development, through these major experimentations, through a lot of training and through the developing and refining of some common procedures and, most important, with the planning procedures we now have in place, we've made a lot of strides."

AUTHORS: But how do you get people to accept the higher propensity for failure needed to take these risks?

GENERAL CROKER: "First of all, the person who's making the predictions has to face a group of people to study this and anticipate and make predictions. And if they were not batting 100 percent you'd penalize them. So they learn to keep their mouth shut and they don't make predictions unless they have very high confidence they are right. They look in their rearview mirror to tell you what did happen rather than looking down the horizon beyond their windscreen to tell you what's going to happen.

"So, you have to train people and their supervisors to accept that people are going to make errors, and then what you want them to do is not make errors but learn from the errors they make so that they refine or improve their ability to make predictions based on experience. You can do that in the real world and you can also do that through exercises and simulations.

But both the leader and a predictor have to come to understand that it is safe and rewarding to make predictions. And it is desirable to learn from the errors in those predictions so that you gradually bring the bell-shaped curve closer to the x-axis. Or move the whole x-axis out to the right if you want to use that analogy, so that everybody on the bell-shaped curve is better at it than they were before.

"Mark McGwire gets $34 million to bat .295. Yet, we're expecting people to be at 995 or 1,000 instead, and so when they make mistakes they either get fired or let go or hammered. So that's number one.

"Number two is the thing I've tried to talk about upfront. I think that you can plan for uncertainty. I think we in the military do a very good job of it.

"Now remember, I said don't fall in love with the plan. Fall in love with the process of planning, because then you get a shared understanding of where the boss and the corporation are trying to go. I also said that the boss does planning at the same time as the staff is planning. Then, in the absence of him being there and leaning over your shoulder, when one of these anticipated circumstances arrives you have an idea of how to deal with it because you have balanced, equal planning to know what's next.

"George Patton once said something along the lines of, 'I don't want a brilliant or a perfect plan. But what I want is a reasonably good plan that's well-rehearsed that everyone understands.'

"So when the enemy makes a move or another corporation or competitor makes a move and you see you're at a decision point, you have already planned for that eventuality. Maybe not perfectly, but you've anticipated that that outcome could happen.

"A lot of people don't use the planning process methodically. Even though it's uncertain, you can narrow down the range of uncertainty. Try to stick to a number of different outcomes, pick a number. Then do some planning for each of those various outcomes in advance.

"If the outcome happens or if something suggests the outcome is about to happen, then you've already got a rough plan in place and the boss's guidance to help you deal with it. In the military, we have done a wonderful job at that—although perhaps less so in the first case of not killing the messenger—we're still learning on that one.

"It's also important to point out that there's a difference between uncertainty and zero knowledge. Pick a range of alternatives and plan for those. Plan different budget lines and different actions and different marketing strategies. When these eventualities come to pass or start to, you have an action plan in mind for how to deal with it.

"The third thing we've done is experiments and exercises where we developed some concept of how we're going to deal with the future and roughed it out to see how well it works out in our war game or our simulations. Then we refine the concept based on the mistakes we've made. So, once again, we've been planning for a war like Iraq for four to six years in the Air Force.

"When it came and we had these unanticipated opportunities, like the first night in Baghdad, we already had a process in place to deal with them. We didn't know what building Saddam was going to be in or what bunker he was going to be at, but we knew there's a high likelihood we may find him. So we not only have planned for that specific eventuality, we've developed the tools and processes to drive down our timelines and to help us respond to opportunity in a rapid fashion.

"So, it's not something you can fix overnight, but I think the single most important ingredient in my view, or at least from the military's perspective, is planning for uncertainty using branch plans and sequel planning and setting up small planning organizations, setting up a team for competitors or the enemy and trying to anticipate what they're about and what their game plan is."

AUTHORS: This really shifts this whole notion of situational awareness. It puts a distinctive process orientation into our situational awareness. Doesn't it?

GENERAL CROKER: "Right. Process, process, process, process. We tell our operational commanders that they should spend between 5 and 10 percent of their time in current operations and 90 and 95 percent of their time on future operations and future plans. They add value not by fighting today's fight. Our bottom line is you, as an operational commander, add value by setting the conditions for your components to succeed. I would say that the percentage of time that the senior operational people devote to the future is absolutely critical. And that has been an important part of our training."

AUTHORS: What about uncertainty and training? Many would claim that this is a bit of an oxymoron. How do we prepare ourselves, our people, for something we can't predict?

Let me bring it back. You mentioned the need for a new language in the face of uncertainty.

GENERAL CROKER: "One of the things that is critical in being agile enough to deal with uncertainty in overcoming some of the very deeply rooted cultural issues that you often find within a single organization much less across multiple organizations. You began by describing the different armed forces and how they had been uncoordinated and that coordination and collaboration provides a much more effective, much more responsive military organization.

"I first became a Joint Force Air Component Commander in 1996. I had an exercise and I simulated the Army, simulated the Navy, simulated the Marine Corps, simulated the Special Forces, simulated my boss and ran my own little air operation. And remember what Mark Twain said, 'It ain't what you don't know that gets you into trouble. It's what you know for sure that just ain't so.' And what we were doing was learning a lot of things about ourselves and the other services that weren't valid. So, then when we moved from single-service experiments to joint experiments, from single-service exercises to joint exercises, from single-service training to joint training, we started to learn about cultural and language differences. And as people began to train together and exercise together, they started to develop more trust and confidence in one another. We went through these realistic exercises and they said, 'Now I understand why they're doing this,' or, 'Now I understand that they have this capability that I never knew about.'

"The key is that we're training people together across the whole organization rather than in stovepipes. Each service has its basic combat skills and they're absolutely essential. Guys still have to know how to fly airplanes, drive ships, drop bombs, shoot guns, change clips—we're not trying to do away with that tactical training. But at the operational level, we are now trying to train all the services together jointly in collaborative processes so that they start to understand each other's language and culture.

"In the end you're speaking a common language and have trust and confidence in one another. And we found that the biggest impediment to joint war fighting was a lack of trust and confidence, the lack of common language and culture, the thing that General Franks was so successful with. He built a team over five or six years so that by the time the war came, those guys had all worked together for a long time at a common language, and a common sense of purpose, understood the bosses, guidance, and intent, and had trust and confidence in one another. But we go a lot of places in the world where we have ad hoc organizations, you know, temporary organizations where that trust and common view do not exist; we haven't broken the code everywhere in the whole world."

AUTHORS: One last question. Give us an example of a game that we play for fun that would epitomize uncertainty.

GENERAL CROKER: "The important ingredient is not the game. In my view, the most important ingredient is the mentor, if I have given the person who's going through the game feedback on his performance. In other words, we feel like you'll perform much better the next time, based on having informed feedback from your last experience.

"Have you ever bowled through a canvass awning? If you bowl through a canvass awning, you can't see the pins. You hear the noise, 'clatter, clatter, clatter, clatter, clatter' and the ball—about thirty seconds later your ball rolls back. So then, you roll a second time. And you hear nothing, or one pin falls. You don't have any idea if you've got a gutter ball or a seven-pin split, a strike, then you'd quit after five or ten minutes I mean, bowling would be no fun, because it would be a meaningless exercise of just rolling the stupid ball under the awning with no feedback.

"What we do with most of our people is we put them in a situation and say, 'You'll know when you're doing bad because I'll tell you.' We just sort of let him go off and learn.

"We find that the most dangerous thing is that people learn things that aren't so. You should have a senior mentor or trainers that are knowledgeable in this subject and observe these people and give them feedback as they proceed, as they are being trained. I don't care which organization we deal with. Every organization comes out of that training a lot better equipped to deal with it than they went in because of the performance feedback.

"My view is I don't care what the game is—bowling, golf, chess—you can give me any game you want and we'll put one guy by himself and let him play the game differently, maybe not even understanding the rules, and put another guy with a senior mentor or trainer or an observer who is knowledgeable and gives him feedback on his performance. I guarantee you the guy with feedback will perform better every single time."

The lessons to take away from this discussion with General Croker are several:

1. *Organizational structure has to allow for flexibility and rapid agility but this also can create the risk of "driving in front of your head-lights," where an organization is operating with near-zero visibility.* To operate in this way, organizations and leaders must accept a new level of risk and experimentation and put in place quick response mechanisms in order to instantly redirect resources. Much of this will depend on how well established and sophisticated the process methods and infrastructure you have in place are for the opportunity or challenge at hand. In a global setting, as on the battlefield, the challenge is compounded by the application of these processes outside of localized, well-controlled environments.

2. *We need to train our people and our managers to accept that people are going to make more errors as they enter realms of higher uncertainty and lower visibility.* We need to put in place tools by which they can quickly learn from these errors so that they refine or improve their ability to make predictions based on experience, from the vantage of an organization.

3. *Don't fall in love with the plan.* Fall in love with the process of planning, and do this across all levels of the organizations. In this way when uncertainty strikes and the hierarchy is not there, the team in the field can take initiative and respond. In a global organization this is especially critical because the nature of separateness and disconnection is an inherent part of how teams will need to work. Remember George Patton's quote, "I don't want a brilliant or a perfect plan. What I want is a reasonably good plan that's well-rehearsed that everyone understands."

4. *As a leader, spend between 5 and 10 percent of your time in current operations and 90 to 95 percent of your time on future operations and future plans.* Your value is not in fighting today's fight. Leaders add value by setting the conditions for success. As uncertainty rises, we need to make sure that our focus on future operations also increases.

5. *Make sure that "you're speaking a common language and have trust and confidence in one another."* For global partnerships there can be no greater call to action than this. Establishing a level of confidence and trust within extended teams is foundational to mutual reliability, shared expectations, and peak performance.

6. *Performance feedback is essential to building processes that are agile.* The alternative is that processes become stale and new partners learn outdated behaviors. Remember what Mark Twain said, "It ain't what you don't know that gets you into trouble. It's what you know for sure that just ain't so." Use senior mentors or trainers that are knowledgeable in this subject and observe people and give them feedback as they proceed, as they are being trained and as new partnerships are being created.

General Croker's observations on uncertainty may have had their origin in the military, but their application is clearly well beyond the scope of the battlefield. They speak directly to the ways in which all our organizations will need to reform themselves in order to counterbalance the heavy weight of uncertainty.

We have in the course of 100 years come from thinking we knew everything there was to know about the world, from feeling we would soon be able to predict the most minute implications of our actions, technologies, and organizations, to an ironic appreciation for the intimate role the unknown plays in our success.

Part II

The Business of Smartsourcing

"The significant problems we face cannot be solved at the same level of thinking we were at when we created them."

—*Albert Einstein*

CHAPTER 5

WHAT WILL MAKE
YOU GREAT?

"We know more than we can tell."
—Michael Polanyi

The first task of any organization interested in smartsourcing is defining its core competencies. Amazingly, few individuals understand this concept well enough to apply it to their own business. When asked to define their firm's core competency, most people respond with the name of a product or service. Very few will reply with a deep-rooted and sustained capability that underlies their success across products and product lines. In this chapter we will take a look at the essential ingredients of core competency and the ways in which exceptional organizations have translated an obsessive focus on core competency into long-term success.

CHALLENGING COMPETENCY

A core competency is best described as a set of skills and capabilities that create unique value in the marketplace. While *unique* may seem to be too powerful a word given that competitive forces in a free market will always offer alternatives to any single product or service, note that we did not equate a core competency to a specific product or service. In fact, if you were to chart the relationship of core competency against products and services, we would position them as nearly opposites on a scale of velocity of change. Although products and services may frequently change, the core competencies on which they are based are foundational aspects of an organization, not unlike its culture and values—and no more subject to sudden change.

Think of a radar image of a hurricane where the items on the periphery of the storm move in large sweeping arcs while the closer you get to the center of the storm the more volatile and forceful the churn and turbulence. In this analogy the greatest volatility exists at the point of impact where the energy of the storm meets the ground, or in the case of an organization, where its products or services meet the market. The surrounding context and environment that shapes the storm is the equivalent of culture, values, and core competency. The track the storm takes is defined by strategy.

A core competency should provide long-term differentiation of an organization if it is properly understood and articulated within the organization and to its partners. By the same token, the touch point between organizations in sourcing or in any sort of intimate partnering arrangement should include the segment of our funnel that is above the line—in other words, from strategy up. However, the challenge often resides just in getting an organization to understand its own core competencies.

There is perhaps no better example of obsessive focus on core competency than GE and the figure most closely associated with GE's rise as a role model for the core competency organization, Jack Welch, former CEO and chairman of GE.

While the notion of moving work that is outside of the core may seem fraught with logistical, project management, and quality concerns, GE has been moving the "work to the

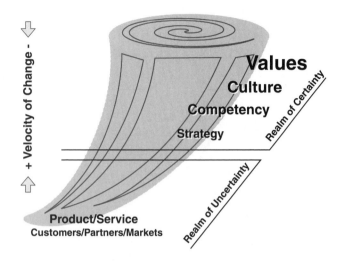

FIGURE 5.1

VELOCITY OF CHANGE

As the velocity of change increases, our products and services must become more responsive to the marketplace. However, this does not mean that everything in an organization changes as rapidly. In fact, high volatility creates an even deeper need for static values, culture, and competency since these will provide the context for many decisions that are made without a specific process or procedure in place. The critical link between these two realms is strategy, which must be constantly reevaluated in order to make sure that one is constantly aligning internal competencies with the marketplace.

worker" for over a decade. Welch had been quietly bullish on India since the late '80s. In the mid '90s he went so far as to declare that GE could wait no longer to leverage the lower costs and the seemingly endless supply of highly educated English-speaking labor India had to offer.

In characteristic Welch style, he is said to have declared the now famous 70:70:70 rule, whose most popular interpretation is that 70 percent of GE's back-office work would be outsourced, 70 percent of that work would be completed from offshore locations, and 70 percent of the offshore work would be performed from India.

At the time, that amounted to an incredibly overreaching ambition. Yet in November 2004, GE Capital International Services (GECIS) had over 17,000 employees who performed finance and accounting, supply chain management, customer relationship management, data modeling, analytics and IT services work for all eleven GE businesses. An amazing 12,000 of these employees were in India (don't bother with the math—it's 70 percent), 3,000 were in Mexico, 1,500 in China, and 500 in Hungary. GE has estimated its cost savings through offshoring of its back-office processes alone at over $300 million per year, or nearly $20,000 per GECIS employee!

But GE's interest in India has not been limited to saving cost in its back-office or IT processing. When it came time to think about where GE might best invest its scarce multidisciplinary research and development dollars to leverage its world-renowned Corporate R&D Center in Niskayuna, New York (located near the town of Schenectady, New York, where Thomas Edison founded GE in 1892), Welch once again chose India.

This is a cornerstone principle of smartsourcing. If you think of smartsourcing as simply a mechanism for reducing costs you may be right, but you are limiting your thinking. There is much more at play here: GE's foray is proof of it.

Inaugurated in September 2000 the JFWTC (John F. Welch Technology Center), in Bangalore, India, employs over 1,600 technologists and boasts the "highest IQ per square foot" in the world with 65 percent of its work force holding a Ph.D. or master's degree. By October 2003 scientists and engineers at JFWTC had already filed more than ninety-five patent applications.

WHY INDIA?

GE could have gone anywhere in the world to find the best R&D (research and development) talent (since 2000, they have also opened centers in Shanghai and in Munich), but GE chose Bangalore, India. Make no mistake, India has a low cost structure; but it is India's labor pool that gives it its greatest advantage. We think Jack Welch would have answered the question in the same manner. And Welch managed to take advantage of both India's cost structure lead (via GECIS) and India's labor pool advantage (via the JFWTC).

In 2004, GE sold 60 percent of GECIS for about $500 million, effectively recovering its entire investment in the venture while retaining a 40 percent equity stake and a long-term services contract. The financial return to GE—always a paramount issue for this paragon of capitalism—was considerable (and don't forget about the over $300 million per year GE believes it was saving by moving the work to India).

But there were incremental benefits to GE beyond cost or access to scarce labor. In this resides an important lesson about how smartsourcing can move organizations beyond the denominator effect of low-cost labor.

DEFINING THE PROCESS RULES

For starters, GE learned that in order to move the work at all, it had to better define the processes and work rules in its business. Without the ability to convert the tacit knowledge in its employees' heads into tangible business process maps, it was impossible to integrate the work done in India with the work left in the domestic locations, to train new employees, or to measure the cost, quality, or cycle time of the GECIS processes. Only after the work was documented—and it was understood by the domestic and the India-based GE employees who was doing what, how their work fit into a larger process, and how the output of their work would be measured—was it possible to effectively move the work.

CREATING PROCESS EXCELLENCE

Once documented and moved, the business process could be improved via another much emulated GE business discipline: six sigma process improvement. For those that have attempted to launch such programs in their own companies, you will know the value of the initial step of documenting the business process baseline. Without it, improvement efforts are not grounded. We do not think it a coincidence that GE's six sigma efforts and its offshoring efforts gained scale concurrently.

MANAGING THE COLLABORATIVE PROCESS

It turned out that GE's greatest challenge was not that of properly documenting and baselining the processes (that was tedious, but manageable), nor was it finding the talent or ensuring an acceptable quality of work—both of which are frequently cited concerns of firms considering offshoring for the first time. Instead the greatest challenge was GE's need for sophisticated remote project management technologies and procedures to take advantage of the ability of Indian associates to work while U.S. and European counterparts slept.

Remember, the work both GECIS and the staff at JFWTC did was off-cycle—by between six and eighteen hours—from the work of their U.S. and European counterparts. Software development efforts had to be handed off in midstream so that responsibility for key business process functions could be migrated back to U.S. or European locations when their workday began. For those processes that were moved entirely to India (of which there were more and more over time), access to India-based information and resources had to be as accessible to the domestic work force as it had been prior to offshoring the project.

The solution was to develop a sophisticated set of new business processes for this heightened level of collaboration. Experience has shown us that GE's problems are not unique, especially when the objective is to seamlessly integrate the offshore partner with the processes and customers of the host organization.

GE's experience in India was, of course, not a search simply for a lower cost structure, but a search for innovative ways to create real efficiencies while improving quality at GECIS, and even as a search for new products and services at JFWTC.

We can sum it up in the most concise terms: Smartsourcing is not a cost journey at all; it is a journey of innovation.

A JOURNEY INTO INNOVATION

Imagine the simplest product possible, something that has only a single ingredient, ideally a pure commodity, abundantly available, utterly bland, and indistinguishable in its appearance, form, and taste. To make this even more interesting, imagine that this product can also be obtained for free.

What latitude could there possibly be to innovate with that sort of a product? It's hard to imagine a bigger challenge. Yet our lack of imagination here is only a testament to our lack of creativity in how well we can innovate innovation itself.

We take innovation for granted as something that naturally happens when we apply ourselves to the task of creatively thinking about a market challenge to deliver a new product or service. That is far from the truth. Most often innovation ends up involving high measures of serendipity and simple brute force. This is an incredibly inefficient way to operate in an area where the stakes are so high.

The ability to innovate has in many industries fallen well below the markets' demand for innovation. As quality initiatives such as six sigma have continued to steadily increase and level the playing field for manufacturers and service providers, the differentiators for any product are ultimately cost and innovation.

The perverse nature of this equation, however, is that while the price we charge for a product may be entirely within our control, the cost of producing that same product may be severely impacted by the R&D dollars spent on its innovation. So while production costs decrease and manufacturing capacities increase, a bottleneck is created in the development of new ideas and products in their journey from concept to market.

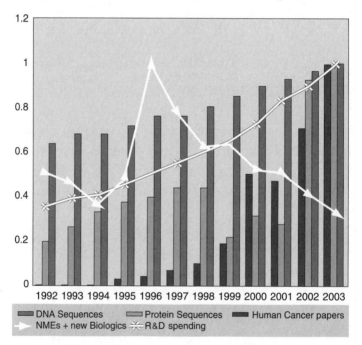

FIGURE 5.2

INNOVATION DEFICIT

Using data from the National Institute for Health, this chart shows that, while Pharmaceutical R&D spending, DNA sequences, Protein Sequences, and publication of papers investigate human cancers, the introduction of novel drugs has actually declined over the past decade. In other words, the increase in knowledge and information does not necessarily correlate to innovation.

George Gaines and Kevin Pang, *The Biopharmaceutical Innovation Plane: A New Industry Structure and Solution for the Drug Development Bottleneck.* J. BIOLAW & BUS., Vol. 8, No. 1, 2005.

Take for example the high-stakes market of pharmacology. In the case of cancer research, and the resulting drugs to treat it, an amazing phenomenon has occurred during the past fifteen years. While the pool of knowledge and R&D have increased at an astounding rate of 300 percent across all categories, the number of new cancer drugs introduced annually has actual declined by 50 percent from its high in 1996!

In our own research of R&D and innovation across many industries we have been struck by the degree to which this is purely a manual task—a numbers game if you will—where many intelligent people are thrown at a problem until discovery occurs. This applies to most every industry regardless of its complexity.

The objective is not simply to apply yourself harder to the task of innovation but to change the very nature of how you and your organization innovate.

While businesses typically focus on only the most obvious form of innovation—new-product innovation—in every organization there are three fundamental types of innovation:

- Creating new products, services, or markets
- Extensions or feature improvements to existing products, services, or markets
- Increased efficiencies in existing products or services

Organizations experience innovation in all three areas but typically have a core competency in only one of these areas. Dell is not known for innovating new products, but it is world-renowned for the efficiencies of its supply chain operation. Apple Computer is known for its innovative product design. Many pharmaceutical companies outsource everything from product development right on through to clinical trials, and innovate solely in marketing and sales. On the other hand, Coca-Cola has made a core competency out of innovating water, with more colors, flavors, and implied lifestyles than anyone could possibly have imagined even a few decades ago. Consider that in most cases a bottle of Dasani (one of Coca-Cola's water brands) will cost as much or more than a similar amount of bottled Coke—and when you put them side by side it is always the Dasani machines that are sold out first—even with a water fountain a few steps away!

This is not an isolated phenomenon. One of the fastest-growing items in the produce section of your local supermarket is not a new genetically altered vegetable but rather mixed greens in a bag, priced at a premium of more than 200 percent over the same ingredients sold separately.

There is also a mathematics to innovation that consistently evades us. Like the unseen forces of uncertainty at play in physics, there are forces at play in highly innovative markets that defy prediction. One of these is the tendency of innovation to act as its own accelerant.

Innovations are like changes to ecosystems; they have unforeseen implications that may impact the market in ways that create even greater opportunity for yet additional innovations. The cascading effect is usually beyond anyone's ability to plan. Cascading innovation is reminiscent of the classic scene from *I Love Lucy*. Lucy is stationed at the end of an assembly line for candies, boxing them as they come. As the assembly line starts to speed up she tries to keep pace, ultimately making a mess of monumental proportions in classic slapstick style.

The automobile industry found itself in a similar situation during the past few decades. With production techniques and computer-aided design and engineering accelerating, new models of automobiles were also running wild. Manufacturers such as Chrysler seemed to be coming out with new models at a rate to rival a five-year-old's Matchbox car collection. But as automobile costs rose, the industry responded by moving quickly to begin pushing leasing as an alternative for noncorporate buyers.

The leasing trend caught on quickly, and for a few years it sparked a boom in buying. But then the aftermath set in. As leased cars reached their term and new models tempted buyers, there was a flood of used cars (albeit barely used in many cases) on the market. In the genius of one innovation the manufacturers had planted the potential seeds of its demise. The solution was yet another rapid move to create certified or preowned car programs that would warranty the *used* cars for periods that were in some cases better than the expectations for most new-car warranties. Interestingly, the genesis of this innovation was with the dealerships that were being buried under mountains of slightly used vehicles that were saddled with a *used* label but were in fact far from the role model of a used car.

The richness of innovation in an industry is often directly related to the transparency of all the pieces of its value chain. This is one of the reasons we will make the case at the end of this book for the role of BSPs (business service platforms) as a means to fully realize the promise and vision of smartsourcing.

While we will freely admit that this sort of accelerated innovation climate can also result in rampant and sometimes irrational behavior on the part of investors and buyers—as is vividly demonstrated in boom periods such as the example of the dot-com bubble in the late 1990s—we should not confuse the increased rate of failure in a fertile innovative climate with the value of those innovations that do survive. A higher rate of experimentation and failure is a natural part of higher rates of innovation. If we are shifting from a service-based economy to an innovation-based economy, we will need to adjust our view of failure and align it within the context of the financial constraints and growth ambitions of our organizations. Certainly nobody would claim that a zero rate of innovation would equal zero rate of failure. The question most businesspeople ask themselves is "At what rate of innovation am I balancing risk and reward?"

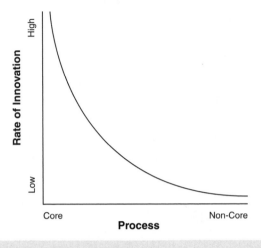

FIGURE 5.3
RATE OF INNOVATION I
As a process becomes core to an organization, the rate of its innovation on those processes must also increase.

The reality is that many organizations often make the mistake of asking that question outside of the sphere of their core competency. As they move outside of those areas that represent their core competency, their ability to innovate dramatically decreases, yet the need to innovate is equally spread across all of these functions.

One of the first mandates for any organization attempting to achieve innovative excellence is to clearly identify which of the three types of innovation described best represents their core competency (i.e., separate the core innovative differentiators of the business from those that are the operational outliers).

An interesting outcome of this analysis for most organizations is that while the areas of core innovative competency may be the source of top-line growth, it is often the noncore areas that consume the largest percentage of an organization's precious resources and management time. In a classic case of the

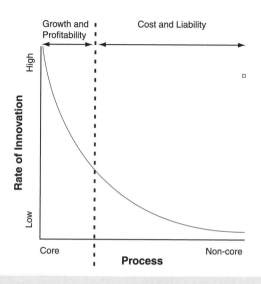

FIGURE 5.4
RATE OF INNOVATION II

The challenge faced by many organizations is that they are so encumbered by processes that are not core that they do not have the resource or cycles to focus on the core. Smartsourcing should focus an organization on its core processes, minimizing its liability and cost while maximizing growth, profit, and innovation.

Pareto principle, the noncore areas consume the majority of your resources and starve your company of its innovative capacity, ultimately being responsible for shrinking or stunting bottom-line growth. These are the factors of risk that often cloud assessments of the rate at which innovation should happen.

Take the classic case of health care. While diagnostics and patient care may be the core competency of most health care providers, it is the support and maintenance of facilities and administrative functions that are often the linchpin for holding down costs and achieving near-term profitability and process excellence. The smartsourcing challenge for a health care provider is how to leverage innovation in their area of core competency (diagnostics and patient care) while also being best-of-class in the support of their patient facilities and processes.

This is apparent even at the level of the individual physician who is encumbered by administrative processes that typically limit his or her ability to deliver quality health care and focus on personal core competencies. The resulting level of triage that is performed results in longer wait times for treatment, shorter face time with patients, and ultimately greater risk for the physician and the patient.

Smartsourcing enables an organization to focus on its core competency while its sourcing partners take responsibility for innovating change and cost control in noncore operations. For example, at Harvard Pilgrim Health Care, Inc., a not-for-profit New England health plan with 800,000 members and 22,000 physicians, smartsourcing was used to create innovations in how claims were processed. In addition, creative IT initiatives were used to develop a secure Web application that allows members to enroll, select physicians, view benefits and eligibility information, update family information, and order ID cards online.

By focusing the service partnership specifically on core strategies and processes, the result was an overhaul of Harvard Pilgrim's claims processing systems as well as its overall IT operations. While traditional outsourcing may emphasize replacing systems and bodies, smartsourcing focuses on the core areas of innovation in which an organization must excel to differentiate itself. Through smartsourcing Harvard Pilgrim achieved excellence across its entire spectrum of innovation. If you take the idea of focusing on the core areas of innovation and apply it broadly to the concept of smartsourcing, some interesting trends emerge.

COLLAPSING THE CAPABILITY CURVE

One of the most basic frameworks to use in understanding how smartsourcing shifts an organization's focus to its core competencies can be applied to any industry. Most vertically integrated organizations can be thought of as having a distribution of capabilities that range from those that are performed with distinction to those that are dangerously inept. We would categorize these capabilities broadly on what we call a *capability curve* (see **FIGURE 5.5**).

THE DANGEROUS DANGLERS

These are the processes that the organization simply should not be involved in. Because of the degree of specialization and resources required in these areas, the organization puts itself at risk by attempting to create capability here. It is not unlike a patient who attempts self-diagnosis without the skills and background to understand his or her medical condition.

THE MARGINAL MINORITY

While the processes categorized as "dangerous danglers" are typically outside of the scope of where an organization

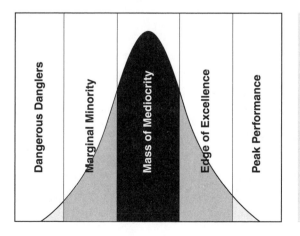

FIGURE 5.5
THE MASS OF MEDIOCRITY

Every organization can separate its processes into five distinct groupings, from those that generate liability (Dangerous Danglers) to those that reflect its core competency (Peak Performance).

should be operating, processes that fall into the "marginal minority" suffer from a different problem. The capabilities needed here are not necessarily out of the scope of the organization but require training time and apprenticeship that creates risk. These processes require a set of skills that take time to develop. The classic case is that of a call center where new hires may be put into a screening role where they determine the nature of the caller's problem before forwarding or escalating the call. Most organizations will argue that the problem here is one of education and mentoring. While these can bridge the gap to some degree, there will always remain a period during which an employee is developing skills and providing less than optimal performance, putting the organization into unnecessary jeopardy. This is especially true in growing organizations.

THE MASS OF MEDIOCRITY

This is the area where many organizations have the greatest difficulty in making a decision to partner. They may sense that they are not fully capable to do the job, but the cost of their inadequacy is typically veiled or even considered an acceptable cost of doing business. These areas of mediocrity are perpetuated until one or more players in the industry decide to change the benchmark. Otherwise there is simply no competitive mandate to invest in change.

THE EDGE OF EXCELLENCE

Any enterprise that has experienced a modicum of success must excel in some way in the processes that support its products or services. While the nature of the excellence may come in a variety of forms, from R&D to sales and marketing, the efficiency of a free market will ultimately eliminate those enterprises that operate only the prior three segments of the bell curve. The irony is that we expect the edge of excellence to remain an edge, that is, to be the thin edge of the blade rather than to define a substantial part of the organization. Our opinion is that this attitude is at the heart of why smartsourcing has been slow to catch on. We would challenge the notion that this must be a thin edge and instead offer (as we will on many occasions in this book) that the majority of an enterprise should and eventually must exist in this and the next segment of the bell curve.

PEAK PERFORMANCE

By definition any enterprise, no matter how efficient, motivated, or exemplary, will have a core group of peak performing processes that occupy this segment of the bell curve. However, it is important to differentiate the notion of peak performers (individuals) from having core capabilities that differentiate the enterprise in the absence of peak performers. Our claim would be that peak performers can create cyclical advantage for an enterprise but that core capabilities and processes, which can be executed with excellence by all performers, are much more vital to long-term success.

While it is arbitrary to expect a normal bell curve distribution among these five segments, it is the case that every enterprise will compete based on its ability to move its capabilities to the right-hand side of the capability curve.

Basic technology infrastructure and the shift to globalization may alleviate some of the drag created by the first three segments and compress these, allowing an enterprise to focus more on its core capabilities, as shown in **FIGURE 5.6.** However, the ultimate ambition and objective of smartsourcing is to move the enterprise almost fully into the two rightmost segments.

At first sight this may seem to be overreaching. However, the premise is not that an entire enterprise can be moved into the two rightmost segments *in whole,* but that it can be moved *in parts.* This is precisely the objective of excellence initiatives such as six sigma, which are already being broadly applied to manufacturing and service organizations.

By moving the enterprise in parts, organizations can first identify the various capabilities and the core competencies of their enterprise, and then profile them individually to see which ones fall into each of the five segments. It is then that organizations can begin to define the areas where they need to improve, re-engineer, and partner. Ultimately, however, the challenge is to envision the impact that this level of scrutiny and discipline will have when applied to every capability involved in how your entire organization is run.

The most basic problem in approaching this challenge is that the processes that comprise the left three segments are almost always the most difficult to describe and the least visible

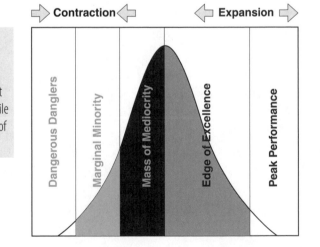

FIGURE 5.6
Outsourcing, globalization, and offshoring should serve to contract the areas of liability while expanding those areas of core competency.

in an organization, while the two rightmost segments are the ones under constant scrutiny and the best understood.

This only furthers the need to move out of these areas as quickly as possible. In a world of increasing uncertainty and complexity, organizations need to focus as much as possible on those things they understand best and are best at. Anything less dilutes their competitive edge and slows their agility.

But to do this you have to begin looking beyond the cost cutting benefits of outsourcing alone and consider the entire scope of the smartsourcing decision. The fundamental questions that need to be answered in order to understand where smartsourcing can be of potential value to an organization are:

- How core is each process of your business to your unique strategic differentiation?
- How competitive and innovative is your organization at each of these business areas?
- How cost-effective are you at the activities in each business area and how much customer value do these processes add?

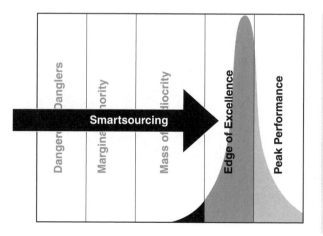

FIGURE 5.7
Ultimately, every organization in an efficient global economy should be doing only that work to which its core competencies are best suited. In this way, smartsourcing leads to not only the lowest costs, but also the highest quality and innovation.

The answers to these questions offer a great deal of insight into those areas that are best suited for sourcing and those that must be the focus of internal innovation. A smartsourcing partner should be able to help in all of these areas.

There is, however, an important caveat to this exercise, which has often been ignored at the peril of organizations pursuing outsourcing; namely, that outsourcing implies absolution. Conventional wisdom favors shedding messy and expensive processes to third-party experts, who will operate in a black box. Nothing is further from the truth. In fact, smartsourcing requires a much more intimate bond of trust, collaboration, and accountability between the organization and its partners. This may result in higher levels of innovation in core as well as noncore processes. In many ways the smartsourcing partner becomes a watchdog for operational excellence and cost reductions, while offloading the organization of this burden allows it to refocus attention on core innovative activities. In addition, this opens the door to new opportunities for partnering on processes in the first three segments of our bell curve that otherwise may not have been considered as candidates.

Savvy smartsourcing partners not only encourage this sort of relationship but also work on an ongoing basis with their clients to identify the areas that are best suited to external innovation. An open collaboration and a high level of transparency in this exercise are critical to establishing the sort of communication, trust, and long-term understanding of the benefits that smartsourcing can bring to the table. In many cases this means complete disclosure on the part of the smartsourcing provider of the costs and business models used to determine the pricing and performance benefits for an engagement, as we will see in Chapter 7.

However, transparency of this sort requires a solid appreciation for the business process being sourced and a methodology by which to adequately describe, monitor, and manage the processes that you are expecting external partners to help with. It also requires a new level of trust and intimacy between organizations and their sourcing partners. Innovation requires intimacy, and it is inherently a trust-based process.

In this respect, smartsourcing is a sea change from the traditional model of outsourcing that has been heavily commodity-based. Smartsourcing must achieve a level of intimacy and integration with the core business processes, philosophy, and culture. While this may seem to obviate the need for partnering, it instead changes the model from a pure commodity relationship to a critical partnership integrated at the highest level of the organization. For many organizations, taking this approach blurs the line of demarcation between partner and enterprise. In the words of one CIO we spoke with, the service provider becomes a "true technology teammate."

To understand this, let's apply the idea to a consumer electronics company, such as Nokia. Long known for its high-stakes investment on in-house innovative product design and research and development, Nokia, along with many consumer electronics companies, has been pulled steadily into the outsourcing of more and more of its functions, including aspects of research and development. In the words of Nokia's chief technology officer, Pertti Korhonen, as featured in the March 21, 2005 edition of *BusinessWeek* magazine, "Nobody can master it all. You have to figure out what is core and what is context."

What happens to a company like Nokia when it starts to pursue a smartsourcing path, especially if that path includes partnering in the cradle of innovation, R&D? In FIGURE 5.8 we show the intuitive effect. At the left-hand extreme of the illustration a company is vertically integrated, performing all of its own manufacturing, finance and accounting, R&D, and customer service. As it partners in each of these areas to cut the costs of each, the total costs to operate should also fall. A purely federated model (which we talk about more in Chapter 10) should be significantly less expensive to operate.

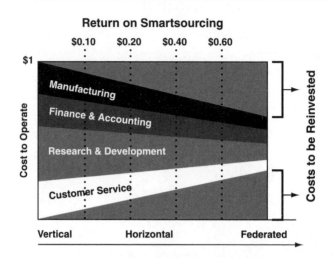

FIGURE 5.8

RETURN ON SMARTSOURCING

The model most of us have in mind when we look at the value of outsourcing today is one that illustrates a steadily decreasing cost to operate each piece of a business. While there are clearly benefits to this, it ignores the greater mandate to reinvest in business.

But on closer inspection you'll notice that while the amount of each dollar spent on each function drops, it creates a vacuum. Nature and capital abhor a vacuum. What happens to the increased margin? This capital does not lie idle; it must be reinvested, but in what?

Current estimates have it that most offshoring examples of this sort of partnership will conservatively yield a return of between 10 to 20 percent on each dollar invested in smartsourcing. In other words, today's smartsourcing return would be reflected somewhere between the first two vertical dashed lines in **FIGURE 5.8,** where a company is saving this much on existing processes. These savings are passed directly to the bottom line of the smartsourcing organization. Although simple in principle, we see the opportunity for much more.

In **FIGURE 5.9** we've taken the next step, which is to plot the reinvestment of an increasing portion of these savings into

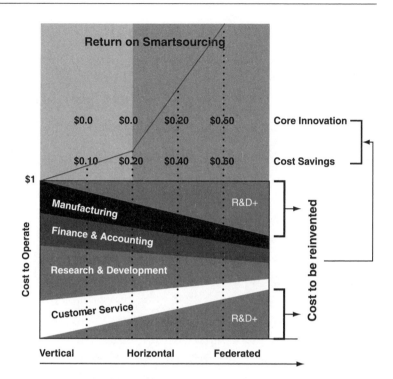

FIGURE 5.9
RETURN ON SMARTSOURCING

Cost savings will continue to drive much of the outsourcing equation; however, we see reinvestment in core capabilities such as R&D driving payback in innovation and growth as well. When you combine the two, the accelerating effect of smartsourcing will easily outpace the benefits of outsourcing alone.

the core R&D function and each partners' innovative capacity. The result, which is already being experienced in industries such as consumer electronics, is a steep increase in the ability to innovate and a correspondingly steep return. This break point from the relatively meager returns of cost savings to the much greater returns of increased innovative investment mark a change in the way organizations view sourcing partnerships and their benefits from simple outsourcing relationships to smartsourcing.

A TURNING POINT

There are, of course, wild cards in all of this. For example: Global labor costs could go up faster than productivity head count reductions; government behaviors, with respect to globalization, could become more protectionist; and counterintuitive economic effects could drive deflation resulting from intense cost-based competition among high-productivity suppliers. Our belief is that this is a natural conservatism that occurs after a boom–bust cycle. But still, none of these should stop an organization from pursuing a smartsourcing strategy.

Your organization is in a competitive arms race to build the fundamental enterprise information technology architecture that will allow you to deliver on the promise of productivity. But at the same time, the intense changes and discontinuity of IT solutions have created a heavy cost, measured not only in profit, but also in opportunity cost and reduced innovative capacity. The burden to develop and maintain this costly and volatile infrastructure is a steep barrier, making it harder to respond to the increasing pressure to do more with less.

Smartsourcing helps you to refocus your business on its core mission and competencies, objectives which may have been long obscured by the fog of technology, but which have always been the essence of what separates the leaders from the laggards in any industry.

You may have built new enterprise systems, optimized your supply chain, and invested in six sigma and ISO operational excellence, but chances are most of your competitors have as well. So any potential advantage from these strategies has been fleeting. Short-term differentiation along the periphery of your business does not create long-term pre-eminence at its core.

You are now at a turning point. It is time to reinvest in those areas that make your organization not just better but in those core competencies that make you great.

CHAPTER 6

A PLATFORM FOR THE GLOBALIZATION OF WORK

"All the world's a stage and most of us are desperately unrehearsed."
—Sean O'Casey

N ow that we have set the stage for the many factors leading to a smartsourcing approach, we need to start looking at the core competencies that you will need to develop—and the central challenges you will need to overcome—in undertaking a smartsourcing initiative. In the next three chapters we will dive deeper into these issues and attempt to create a framework for your smartsourcing decisions.

In many ways this will be a discussion about how to combat the behaviors that have, over time, become accepted ways of assessing your organization's processes, partnerships, and performance. You could say that smartsourcing is like an allergen to these behaviors in that it threatens the existing and accepted way of doing business. The same could probably be said of any change to the status quo. But in the case of smartsourcing there are so many factors that need to be considered that the inertia of the current organization is always far greater than the perceived benefit of change—and this can present a daunting challenge for your organization. So we need to start simply. The best place to start a discussion about where and how to smartsource is by addressing the fundamental issue of where to begin. However, where to begin isn't simply a matter of saying yes or no to a single solution, such as evaluating the use of an accounting system or deciding if you should outsource an isolated business process or a small set of tasks. There is much more at stake that needs to be considered.

Smartsourcing is about looking at the entirety of your organization's processes and asking the following questions: How do we expose and improve the areas where we have core competencies, and how do we shed our risk in those areas? And where do we not have competence, and how can we create excellence in every one of these?

You can well imagine that doing this in an organization of even moderate size can be overwhelming, and perhaps downright frightening. The good news is that smartsourcing is a journey for every organization that embarks on its course. There is no "enterprise" solution for smartsourcing. It is a continual process of evaluation and re-evaluation. In fact, one of the most intriguing aspects of smartsourcing is that processes which you initially shed as noncore may well become core at some future date. Obviously, this raises even more questions for your organization about who has ownership over processes and the knowledge of how they are executed. (This will be addressed in more detail in Chapter 9.)

Keep in mind as you explore where to begin smartsourcing that although many people assume cost to be the driver behind smartsourcing and globalization, there is much more at stake. When asked about concerns over price predictability, stability of service partners, ability to assess competitive bids, and the need for building a cost/benefit business case (all factors of a cost-driven globalization process), firms that have not yet outsourced are still primarily concerned with the risks of outsourcing processes. For the firms not yet engaged in out-sourcing, the message is loud and clear—the decision to outsource will not be made solely on cost but rather on the perception of risk and the level of control that they can exercise over work and performance.

For these firms, that no doubt represent the larger side of the potential market, outsourcing is not simply about replacing expensive labor with cheap labor. In the same light, the adop-tion of a smartsourcing strategy is not simply a handoff, but a partnership of deep assurance and trust. The decision is driven by the ability to ensure control, continuity, and visibility into operations that now reside in a partner's organization.

So how do you start to identify where to develop these partnerships and define where they will have the greatest value? For now let's look at how to simplify the exercise by creating a smartsourcing road map for your organization. The framework used in this chapter will help you better understand how smartsourcing can add value by helping you define a clear understanding of your organization's core competencies and performance. By doing this within a standard framework, you can create a road map for your smartsourcing initiative and identify the areas where smartsourcing will create the greatest impact and support for your organization's ambitions.

CREATING A SMARTSOURCING DASHBOARD

Even if you have not considered a smartsourcing strategy prior to reading this book, like most executives you have probably heard the arguments for re-engineering, continuous optimiza-tion, outsourcing, and offshoring. You may also have consid-ered the merits of each one. But even for those organizations that have pursued a solution in any of these areas, the most chal-lenging and complex issue is the decision on where to begin.

Some of the questions that often come up include:

- Should we re-engineer before outsourcing?
- If something is core should we consider outsourcing it at a substantially lower cost?
- How can we tell if our ability to execute and perform a task is at par with industry best practices?
- What is the relationship between our core competencies and the areas where we perform well?
- What is our confidence level in our performance and competency by task or process?

As we've said, the popular oversimplification of many of these decisions is to just identify the processes that a third party can do for less. While few will argue with the increasing pressure to cut costs, making this the sole driver of a smartsourcing decision introduces two very significant risks:

1. Divesting potential core competencies indiscriminately
2. Oversimplifying the "cost" equation by not properly evaluating the cost of process quality and cycle time

The purpose of this chapter is to present a concise framework and a quantitative methodology to quickly identify the areas of greatest potential for smartsourcing. We will use an approach we call *the smartsourcing dashboard* to illustrate visually, and in simple terms, how to go about this exercise. Let's first begin with some background.

THE PROCESS DRIVERS

In every organization there are two fundamental drivers behind the decision to smartsource: process performance and process importance. Performance defines the degree to which an existing process is being executed at or near benchmark levels of cost, quality, and cycle time. It seeks to measure how well a firm is executing a given process among the ranks of its competitors.

Importance speaks to the degree to which the process creates a differential competitive advantage for the firm. It seeks to measure how much a given process contributes to why customers buy the firm's products or services. The most important processes are by definition its core processes.

For example, while Dell may decide to outsource elements of its call center, there are other aspects of its business, such as information technology (IT) that it would not consider outsourcing. According to Dell CIO Randy Mott, as featured by Andy McCue in a March 31, 2004 report on ZDNet News, "We consider IT a core competency. It is something we look to for sustainable competitive advantage." At the same time it is entirely valid for another PC manufacturer to decide that IT offers no competitive advantage.

If you plot, with relative precision, the importance and performance associated with any process within an organization, you will find that it falls into one of four segments, each dictating a different smartsourcing strategy (see **FIGURE 6.1** on page 124).

SEGMENT 1: PROCESS OPTIMIZATION

Processes that have high *importance* to your firm (i.e., are drivers of competitive advantage and significantly differentiate the company in the eyes of the customers) and also have a high *performance* rating (i.e., have relatively low cost, few errors, and low cycle times) are processes that represent the foundational capabilities of the firm—somehow these processes are tied to your core competency as an organization. These are the processes in which firms create the greatest value, and the ones they need to retain in-house. In the typical manufacturing company, these might include certain product development processes, supply chain processes, and/or manufacturing processes.

SEGMENT 2: PROCESS RE-ENGINEERING

For that same manufacturing firm, poor performance in any of these important processes might be a prescription for processes re-engineering. After all, if customers value the innovations of the firm's products, but those innovations are too slow, too costly, or fraught with poor quality, over time, the firm's existing market position would be at significant risk. Fixing such processes but sending them outside the company's four walls could introduce significant risk, as third parties may not—over the long haul—have the same process improvement priorities that the firm has. It is better to find a reliable process re-engineering partner who can help identify process break-downs, introduce best practices, and improve process performance for these key processes before considering any type of partnering.

SEGMENT 3: PROCESS OUTSOURCING

Not all of your firm's processes will create competitive advantage or differentiate the firm in the eyes of your customer. Does the billing process truly differentiate manufacturing firms in the same way that product development or supply chain processes can? While there are exceptions, in general, back-office processes in the finance, accounting, and HR support functions will not have the same strategic importance. Such processes—in which performance versus industry standards is also weak—provide the classic outsourcing opportunities;

it's the reason ADP, which provides third-party services for processing payrolls, has grown in every single quarter since it went public in 1961!

SEGMENT 4: PROCESS OFFSHORING

But what if your firm's performance in its less-important processes is very good? Is there a smartsourcing strategy for these processes as well? We believe that noncore processes with good performance metrics (for example, cost, quality, and cycle time) make ideal offshoring candidates. An offshore provider will tend to attempt to replicate the current process exactly—but at a lower cost. Offshoring poorly performing processes cements the poor performance into the offshore process; these processes are better outsourced than offshored. However, if the quality and cycle time of well-performing processes can be replicated at significantly lower cost, a very compelling value proposition can be created.

Segmenting your process portfolio by performance and importance is a fundamental step toward gaining insight into your smartsourcing options. By illustrating the relative performance and importance of many processes simultaneously, you can significantly reduce the effort and subjectivity involved in evaluating myriad process candidates for smartsourcing to a much more basic exercise, which provides a simple way to present what is otherwise a fairly complex, and oftentimes convoluted, set of issues.

DEVELOPING A SMARTSOURCING DASHBOARD

Because process importance can be a subjective judgment best vetted from multiple vantage points, the key to developing an

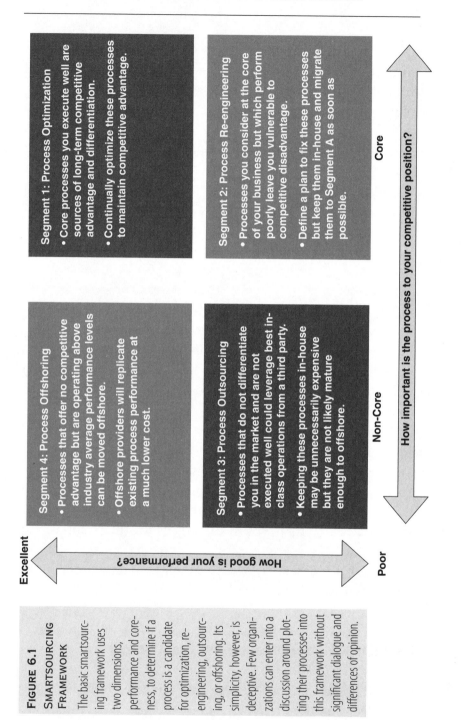

Segment 1: Process Optimization

- Core processes you execute well are sources of long-term competitive advantage and differentiation.
- Continually optimize these processes to maintain competitive advantage.

Segment 2: Process Re-engineering

- Processes you consider at the core of your business but which perform poorly leave you vulnerable to competitive disadvantage.
- Define a plan to fix these processes but keep them in-house and migrate them to Segment A as soon as possible.

Segment 4: Process Offshoring

- Processes that offer no competitive advantage but are operating above industry average performance levels can be moved offshore.
- Offshore providers will replicate existing process performance at a much lower cost.

Segment 3: Process Outsourcing

- Processes that do not differentiate you in the market and are not executed well could leverage best in-class operations from a third party.
- Keeping these processes in-house may be unnecessarily expensive but they are not likely mature enough to offshore.

Core

Non-Core

How important is the process to your competitive position?

Excellent

Poor

How good is your performance?

FIGURE 6.1

SMARTSOURCING FRAMEWORK

The basic smartsourcing framework uses two dimensions, performance and core-ness, to determine if a process is a candidate for optimization, re-engineering, outsourcing, or offshoring. Its simplicity, however, is deceptive. Few organizations can enter into a discussion around plotting their processes into this framework without significant dialogue and differences of opinion.

effective smartsourcing strategy is to validate both the performance and the importance of a business process with a broad audience, and to define specific business cases that quantify the cost/benefit of each element of the process strategy (optimization, re-engineering, outsourcing, and offshoring). In practice, it is best to break this approach into three phases. While these phases are shown sequentially, some processes being assessed may move through all three phases more quickly than others.

PHASE 1: PROCESS ASSESSMENT

In this initial data-gathering phase, it is important to plot each process along the two dimensions in **FIGURE 6.1**. To define the *performance* dimension, you can measure each process's cost, quality, and cycle time. Depending on how deep of an analysis is required, this could include benchmarking of processes relative to industry peers.

To define the *importance* dimension, you need to examine the degree to which a process you are evaluating is core to the business. This often relates to the degree to which the company can differentiate itself in the marketplace through superior performance in this process. While few general and administrative processes (be they finance, HR, or contact center processes) make this list, it is important to evaluate each candidate thoroughly and gain senior management consensus on the degree to which any such processes are core. It may also be worthwhile to involve your customers in this exercise by polling them on what they believe are your organization's core competencies—their insights may provide a stark and compelling contrast to your internal perceptions.

The outcome of this phase of the work is an initial draft, representing a shared consensus of what the smartsourcing dashboard in **FIGURE 6.1** looks like for your firm. In addition, the output of this phase can include a detailed performance assessment using benchmarks of cost, quality, and cycle time of numerous back-office processes. Finally, this phase provides a starting point for defining how to improve process performance—in effect, it lays the foundation for your smartsourcing strategy.

PHASE 2: SOLUTION/SCENARIO ANALYSIS

In the second phase, the initial assessment of process performance and importance is refined. This is accomplished through deeper analysis of processes where Phase 1 might suggest it necessary based on discrepancies in either internal or external perceptions, and by validating assessments of process importance. For example, if executives and customers tend to differ widely on the assessment of core competencies, a closer look is clearly warranted! Often, there is iteration through a set of processes being assessed; on the first pass, certain processes' performance and importance are easily defined and agreed upon, while others require additional iterations, dialogue, and verification. At the end of this second phase, all in-scope processes are evaluated completely and a consensus is reached on what sourcing strategies should be deployed for each group of processes.

PHASE 3: DEVELOPING THE BUSINESS CASE

After defining the sourcing strategies for each subset of processes, a business case can be defined. Here, potential savings opportunities are quantified as are the investments required to attain those savings. Rather than making this an abstract spreadsheet exercise, it is important to rely on empirical data points in the quantification of costs and benefits. In addition to the overall business case developed, this phase should provide a road map that sequences costs and benefits over time, matches this to your company budgets, and identifies "quick hits" that may fund larger downstream transformations.

A Concrete Example:

Let's give these three phases some context. Imagine that you are the newly appointed president of a steel mill in the Midwest. It's a rather small steel mill and, like most of your competitors, you have cut salaried staff to the bone and automated what you could, but you still have not been able to reach acceptable profitability—even after steel prices have climbed. What do you do now? Do you cut your staff again, hoping that those who remain will pick up the workload of those you have let go? Do you make a large investment in technology to further automate certain processes? Or do you step back for a few weeks and ask yourself some fundamental questions: What processes within your mill really are core? How good are you really at performing the work that you do? Do you have a sourcing strategy that has been actively defined, or one that has merely evolved over time?

The steel mill president in this example decided that it was not possible to cut staff again. Both he and his predecessor had reduced salaried staff by 40 percent over the past three years. The result of those previous staff cuts had been to take the workers out of the equation, but not the work. So the remaining staff was running hard, but not gaining any ground; no one had been able to step back and ask themselves how—and where—work should get done.

Stories in the hallways and on the floor spoke about how staff spent time fighting fires rather than preventing them. Senior staff spent their spare time aggregating data from disparate

FIGURE 6.2
PERCEPTION

Processes can be mapped to the smartsourcing dashboard by using a series of interviews with process owners. This first pass can shed insight into the perceived notions of core competencies and smartsourcing candidates. Chances are, it will evoke a fair amount of dialogue and debate around the placement of many processes.

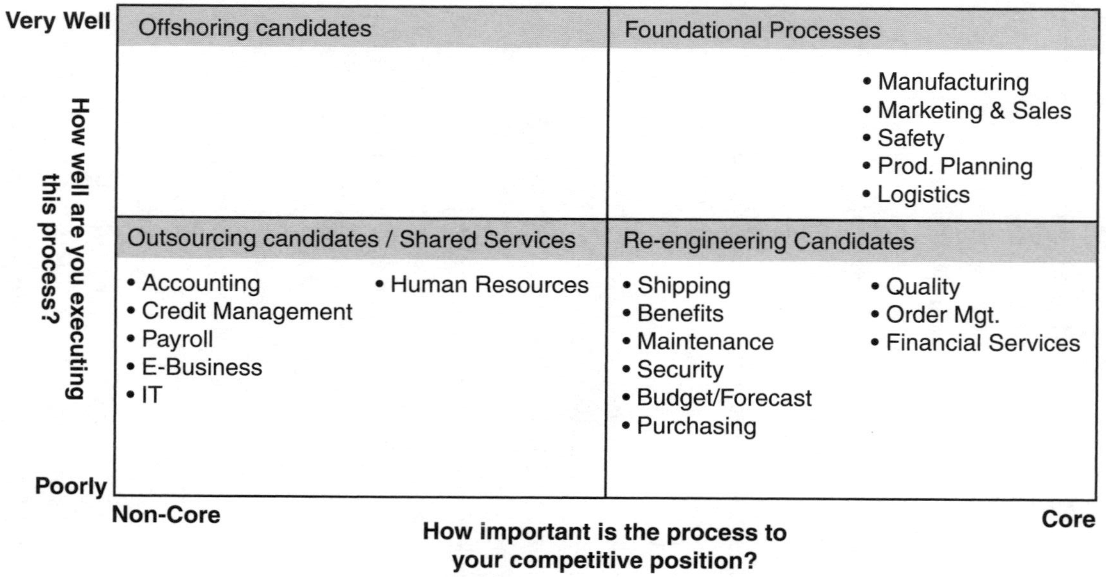

Figure content:

How well are you executing this process? (Very Well → Poorly)

How important is the process to your competitive position? (Non-Core → Core)

Offshoring candidates

Foundational Processes
- Manufacturing
- Marketing & Sales
- Safety
- Prod. Planning
- Logistics

Outsourcing candidates / Shared Services
- Accounting
- Credit Management
- Payroll
- E-Business
- IT
- Human Resources

Re-engineering Candidates
- Shipping
- Benefits
- Maintenance
- Security
- Budget/Forecast
- Purchasing
- Quality
- Order Mgt.
- Financial Services

sources into Excel spreadsheets. Meanwhile, competitors with comparable plants had better cost, quality, and cycle time metrics. This was an organization that was clearly in need of some deep introspection and hard decisions.

We asked the president and his senior staff to think through their core processes. While some of this was done in large meetings with the entire staff, more of this work was done by asking individual executives in the firm to rate all of the firm's processes. What we found was not unusual: a significant amount of consensus on what the mill's core processes were—and reasonable agreement about what the executives thought their process performance was.

On the following page, **FIGURE 6.3** shows what their smartsourcing dashboard looked like based on what they thought.

Aside from the sober assessment of their own performance—they thought only manufacturing and marketing/sales were performing at above average levels—what else was striking about this initial assessment? Take a look at **FIGURE 6.2** and see if you can find anything striking in the smartsourcing dashboard.

To us, it was striking that so many processes and so much work was considered noncore. A full 30 percent of the salaried staff was deployed in these noncore activities, and yet this was the first time the firm had asked itself the question, "What are our core competencies?" In addition, it was revealing to see that the firm's executives ranked the process performance for all but a few processes below average. To dig deeper we objectively verified performance by benchmarking the steel mill's processes with those of comparable mills and comparable firms using available benchmarking information from both public and proprietary sources.

We found—unfortunately—that in many cases the objective data suggested this firm was even worse off than the executives initially thought. Upon additional analysis, we also found that

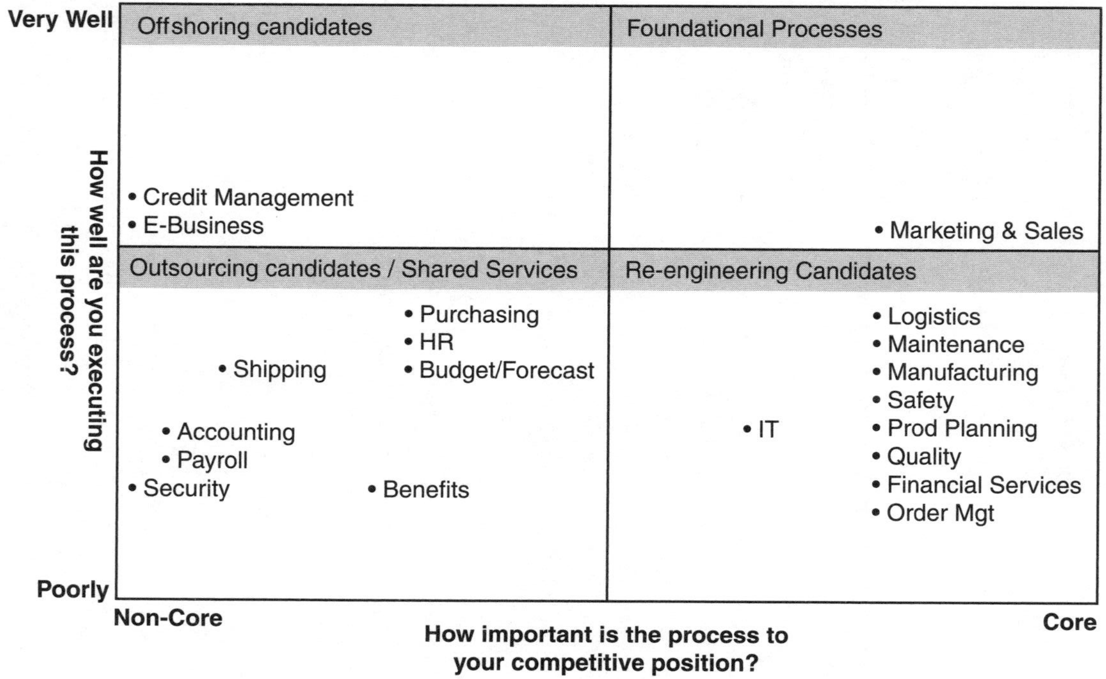

FIGURE 6.3

REALITY

Iterations through the smartsourcing dashboard provide increasingly greater insight into the core versus noncore processes as well as those that are predisposed to outsourcing or offshoring.

	Offshoring candidates	Foundational Processes
Very Well	• Credit Management • E-Business	• Marketing & Sales
	Outsourcing candidates / Shared Services	Re-engineering Candidates
	• Shipping • Purchasing • HR • Budget/Forecast • Accounting • Benefits • Payroll • Security	• IT • Logistics • Maintenance • Manufacturing • Safety • Prod Planning • Quality • Financial Services • Order Mgt
Poorly	**Non-Core**	**Core**

How well are you executing this process?

How important is the process to your competitive position?

some processes, such as information technology, were more core than our steel mill executives had first thought. In the end, we created a revised smartsourcing dashboard, which looked somewhat like the illustration in **FIGURE 6.3**.

The revised smartsourcing dashboard helped the executives to understand that they had some clear opportunities to source certain finance and accounting, HR, and security processes differently.

In addition, our work suggested that many core processes such as manufacturing, production planning, order management, shipping, and forecasting were contributing directly to the steel mill's financial issues. These processes were more expensive, and of significantly poorer quality, than were those of even the average players in the industry.

Of greatest significance is the fact that this smartsourcing assessment was broader than an outsourcing value proposition, or an offshoring value proposition, or a re-engineering value proposition, or a six sigma value proposition, yet it had elements of each.

THE VALUE OF A SMARTSOURCING DASHBOARD

As was the case in our steel mill example, the smartsourcing dashboard is a tool to engender actionable dialogue around the sourcing decision and facilitate comprehensive analysis of an organization's processes within a defined scope of activities, be it finance and accounting, HR, manufacturing, or myriad other areas where an organization needs to achieve process excellence. We have been consistently amazed by the intensity and volume of dialogue that the smartsourcing dashboard exercise and illustration generates. While the questions here are not earthshattering, they are not often enough asked in such a comprehensive framework. It is more often the case that individual processes are considered on their own merits rather than in a larger context along with many other processes.

The dashboard approach also provides a long-term framework for continuous improvement. It highlights the particular opportunities that an organization should consider over a strategic time frame. The value of the dashboard approach becomes more self-evident when you consider that the costs saved by using this approach compound (much like interest on a bank account) as the organization moves certain of its processes through the dashboard's life cycle over time. In other words, it is often the case that an optimized process will lead to areas of process re-engineering, which then lead to outsourcing process elements, and ultimately offshoring well-defined, efficient processes. Like a snowball gathering mass and speed as it rolls downhill, the compounded effect of this progression may create substantial improvements in process performance. Although this is clearly a long-term view of process transformation, it is the essential foundation of any organization's ongoing struggle to improve its performance and reduce its costs, while focusing more of its precious resources on the innovation of core tasks.

However, even though we can imagine a landscape of business processes, with four separate sourcing strategies stratified through analysis of process importance and process performance, how do you know if you are adding value to your organization by sourcing these processes from third parties? In the next chapter we will examine how smartsourcing can create such business value.

CHAPTER 7

MEASURING THE VALUE
OF SMARTSOURCING

"The whole value of a dime is in knowing what to do with it."
—Ralph Waldo Emerson

When we talk about measuring the value of smartsourcing, we need to back up and reflect a bit on how value can be created in the first place. There are four important ways in which smartsourcing can create value:

1. *Keeping the lights on for less*   3. *Transferring risk*
2. *Increasing innovation*   4. *Optimizing risk*

We'll examine each of these value drivers in more detail through an example that is familiar to many organizations that have invested in information technology. Increasingly organizations have been considering information technology (IT) a noncore set of activities. While we realize that there is much debate around the subject of whether IT is in fact core or noncore, our objective here is not to enter the debate but rather to use it as an easily understand example of how you could measure the value of smartsourcing.

If you used the smartsourcing dashboard from Chapter 6, a noncore IT function would mean that your company places the IT function on the left of the dashboard. Whether it is placed in the lower left corner (suggesting an outsourcing strategy) or the upper left-hand corner (suggesting an offshoring strategy) is a function of how well the current IT processes are being performed.

For the sake of this example, imagine that the company considering this noncore IT function also suffers from poor IT performance (as measured in cost, quality, and time to market). So assume that the company—using the smartsourcing dashboard discussed in the previous chapter—is considering smartsourcing its IT function. How would this smartsourcing strategy create value for the firm?

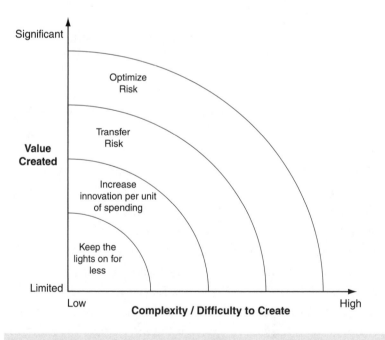

FIGURE 7.1
The four ways in which smartsourcing creates increasingly greater value.

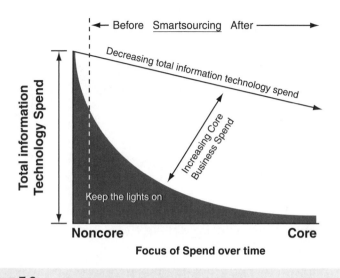

FIGURE 7.2

CORE VS. NONCORE SPEND

The simplest way to look at the direct benefits of outsourcing is to consider how total information spent is decreased over time as the result of outsourcing, and how that decrease allows an organization to spend more on core business activities.

Ideally, an organization should want to spend as much as possible of their allocated budget on activities that enable their core business. However, all too often the "keep the lights on" activities, which are by definition not discretionary, do not leave ample budget or resources to spend on enhancements or development of IT (i.e., innovation). As a result, IT enhancement and development activities are underfunded and the business's core processes are not sufficiently enabled.

If such an IT function were truly noncore to your business—and that will certainly be a decision that will vary from company to company, not from industry to industry—you might look to create value in the smartsourcing partnership by moving as much spending as possible to the "enabling" activities. So let's examine how smartsourcing might create value for this IT function by using the four categories of value creation.

KEEPING THE LIGHTS ON FOR LESS

There are two attributes of value in **FIGURE 7.2**. The first is the reduction, over time, in the funds spent to "keep the lights on." However, decreases in costs must be done without a degradation in service of any kind.

Very often, such improvements will require one of the following:

a. External economies of scale on the part of the smart-sourcing provider allowing them, for example, to buy at lower cost, or,

b. The ability to leverage the assets deployed to keeping the lights on elsewhere (in effect increasing asset utilization), or,

c. Deploying better asset management practices (i.e., process improvements in the management of your IT assets—that requires deep expertise in this IT function).

However, the right smartsourcing provider should be able to offer you scale, increased utilization, and process improvement for your base activities. As a result, the amount of money you will need to devote to keeping the lights on will go down over time—even as the demands on the systems stay consistent or increase.

INCREASED INNOVATION

The second category of value that smartsourcing provides relates to what you do with the dollars you just saved in keeping the lights on. You could, of course, return those dollars to your company's bottom line. If this is the structure of your relationship with your smartsourcing partner, then most likely you are outsourcing, not smartsourcing; you gave up a scope of work to reduce its cost, but have not engaged a strategic partner who will enable your business in new ways. A smartsourcing partnership expands the scope of the relationship to include the activities that go beyond just keeping the lights on to those that include the noncore activities of the same function that are central to enabling your core business.

That sounds a bit roundabout, so let's clarify. Using our IT example, this might be the development and enhancement activities referenced previously. By adding the development and enhancement activities to the scope of the smartsourcing relationship, you allow the smartsourcing partner the opportunity to increase the value it is delivering—effectively, the smartsourcing provider is reinvesting the savings it has identified in your "keep the lights on processes" into the value added, innovation-related processes of development and enhancement. The presumption is that the smartsourcing provider will be able to more efficiently redeploy those savings than you could on your own.

Why should you presume that kind of added value from your smartsourcing provider? For starters, what is noncore to your business must, by definition, be core to the smartsourcing partner's business. This means that your partner should have built its organization around the culture, skills, and tools needed to support what we referred to in Chapter 5 as the peak performance or edge of excellence segments of the capability curve, while the same capabilities in your organization might well be in the marginal minority—or worse.

For instance, in our IT example, a very good applications programmer is ten times more efficient than an average programmer. Not twice as efficient, not five times, but ten times. You should expect your smartsourcing provider to have a greater number of such programmers than your organization currently does. Thus, the value you get from your smartsourcing partner in noncore-enabling activities is increased efficiency, which ultimately translates to more enhancements and development for the same dollar.

How does the smartsourcing partner provide this? Scale is certainly one component of the solution—it helps them attract more of the star programmers. Process discipline is another part of the solution. As the IT services industry of India has taught the world, software development process discipline (embodied in the now famous CMM standards) can reduce software project development costs by over 60 percent and decrease project cycle time by more than 50 percent. It can reduce schedule and cost overruns by over a hundred times and increase programmer productivity by almost three times.

In effect, CMM process disciplines capture some of what makes those "great" programmers great, and allows the average programmer to benefit from the draft. Your smartsourcing provider should be able to demonstrate such value; it is what allows you to squeeze more value from the same amount spent on these activities.

Interestingly enough, in addition to scale (which attracts talent) and process discipline (which creates more and higher-quality output for the same cost), India has also taught us about the value of global sourcing—that is, moving the work to the worker best able to maximize value. This applies not only to IT processes such as software development, but increasingly to transaction processing of all kinds as well, such as claims processing, financial transaction processing, and HR processing.

Simply put, a smartsourcing partner should reduce the cost of an organization's "keep the lights on" activities and increase the efficiency, and therefore the output, of its business-enabling activities. How else should a smartsourcing partner create value for your organization? Let's return to our discussion on risk.

Risk Transference

As the insurance industry has taught us, risk and price are related; the older you are, the more life insurance will cost you. The life insurance contract is really a conversation between you and your life insurance provider about the risk of you dying by some date. Both parties bring different information to that conversation, but, in effect, each party is hoping the other guy is wrong.

The insurance deal is struck at a point where risk and return seem balanced for both parties. In this transaction, you have—in a very pure sense—transferred some of the risk of dying to another party. You pay them premiums for accepting that responsibility because you see value in transferring some of that risk.

That life insurance contract is actually a pretty sophisticated conversation about risk transfer, much more sophisticated than are many sourcing conversations most organizations have today. To build on the earlier IT service provider example a bit more, consider an IT services firm that proposes integrating two applications for you in sixty days, with a team of six people, for $1,000 per person per day. It's a deal worth $360,000 . . . or is it?

What happens if the IT services firm you just wrote the contract with was not thorough in its due diligence and instead needs sixty-five days to integrate the two applications? That's an additional $30,000 on top of the $360,000 you've already budgeted. Do you just pay the $30,000, potentially impacting the financial rationale for doing the project in the first place? Does the IT services firm provide you thirty days of "free" service, potentially eating up the entire profit of the first sixty days?

That depends on a lot of factors, the first being whether or not the risks of not meeting the proposed completion date have been considered. If you have taken that into account, you may have chosen to retain the risk yourself by writing a contract with the IT services provider that pays them a daily rate for their six people until the project is done.

On the other hand, your leverage to ensure that your project provider hasn't overpromised may be the fact that the provider may want to sell you additional services in the future. The firm wants to be good to its word on this deal in order to realize that future opportunity. In any event, if you signed a so-called "time and materials" contract like this (where you pay for the provider's time, not for an outcome), then you have retained the risk of delay yourself.

However, you could have written a contract that shifts the risk of delayed completion to the IT service provider by structuring the contract to have a fixed deliverable for which you will pay $360,000 (in this case, it's the deliverable of integrating the two applications in question). In this model, the IT service provider is obligated to continue to do the work even if it takes more than the sixty days he thought it would take. The IT service provider has taken on the risk of delayed completion. Thus, even in arm's length transactions like a single IT project, risk is a large part of the conversation.

OPTIMIZING RISK

The previous example is what economists refer to as a *zero sum game*. The issue of risk, and who will retain it and for what price, is negotiated with the IT project partner, but not much is done to fundamentally reduce the risk in question. However, it is possible to mitigate, as well as optimize, the transference risk in strategic smartsourcing relationships. And this should ultimately be the objective of every smartsourcing partnership.

Think back to the example from Chapter 2 on the power generation industry at the turn of the twentieth century, that of many distributed power generators slowly being aggregated into fewer, larger power plants. What made that huge shift compelling was not only the increase in the thermal efficiency of the larger facilities, but also the fact that overall capacity utilization could be increased as the service area of the power plant increased.

To explore this point a bit further, imagine a small town with 100 homes or factories and 100 small generators sitting in the basement of those homes or factories in, say, the year 1903. By 1920, those 100 power generators were replaced with a single, larger power plant on the outskirts of town. As the 100 or so users of power turned on their lights or conveyor belts, or (later) washing machines, they used roughly the same total amount of power as they did when they each had their own power supply. However, each home used that power at slightly different times of the day.

In so doing, there was always some base amount of power being used somewhere in the town (see "Typical Capacity" in **FIGURE 7.3**), and power needs would increase at certain times of the day (when the workday began, when it got dark, etc.) in a slightly more predictable manner than if you were to try to predict when each of the 100 homes and factories would turn its generator on each day. This would be represented somewhere in the band labeled "Margin of Risk for Utility" in **FIGURE 7.3**.

In fact, predicting the aggregate power demand (and even its aggregate fluctuation throughout the day) was much easier than trying to predict the power demand of each of the 100 smaller units. This meant that the capacity utilization of the single, larger power plant on the outskirts of town could be predicted quite well. And, in fact, the town needed to buy less power generation capacity in aggregate than it owned when there were 100 separate units in 100 home and factories. This corresponds to the line labeled "Aggregate Peak Capacity" in **FIGURE 7.3**.

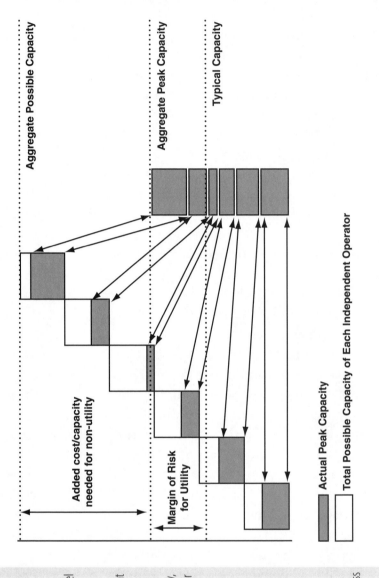

FIGURE 7.3

AGGREGATE CAPACITY AND COST

If you use the analogy of power production as a model for smartsourcing, it is easy to see why a utility based approach provides significant cost savings. If six users of electric power decided to produce their own electricity, each would need a generator that could provide for their peak load usage requirements. This leads to high unused capacity (the white space in each box). However, if you aggregate the power requirements of each customer and deliver these through a utility, there is far less aggregate risk and excess capacity for the utility.

That's because even though there were 100 power plants throughout the town in the early days, they were never all running at full power at the same time—there was a lot of excess power generation capacity in that early model.

The single large power generation facility could be sized with the knowledge that aggregate power consumption would not ever reach more than a certain level. Therefore, less total power production capacity was needed, which increased capacity utilization throughout the day. The increase in capacity utilization was an even more important driver of the move to centralized power than the increase in any one unit's thermal efficiency over smaller power generators.

So how is that relevant to our discussion of smartsourcing value drivers? Well, instead of power consumption, think of a similar dynamic that is created when you aggregate risk. Today, each firm carries its own operational risks. As it learns to partner better, and share risk with its partners, its risk profile will change with respect to those processes it sources from partners. In other words, it will move some risks it currently has in its own operations (like the risk of meeting certain performance standards, or the risk of not meeting an "availability" threshold for instance) to the partner.

The partner an organization contracts with—who will have more than just one customer for the services it provides—will take on risk. However, the smartsourcing partner will be in a better position to absorb that risk as they will be able to leverage their overall scale to reduce risk for each partner, much like the power plant on the outskirts of town was able to increase capacity utilization and reduce power costs for all of its customers.

In the IT example we've been discussing, the service provider—who has many outsourced customers—will likely have used its scale, which will be larger than even the largest single company's IT operation, to invest in redundant power and telecommunications lines, state of the art physical and network security, and leading edge tools to manage an IT environment. The sheer scale of the IT services provider makes it better able to absorb some of the same risks that its individual IT customer could not. Those customers then reduce their risk as part of the smartsourcing transaction.

In this rather simple smartsourcing example, we've demonstrated four important ways that smartsourcing can create value:

1. *Keeping the lights on for less*—using scale and process efficiency to reduce the cost of nondiscretionary process spending.
2. *Creating more innovation for the given dollar*—on discretionary process spending as well as greater access to scarce resources to increase the value of the discretionary spending.
3. *Transferring risk between the partners*—though, in this example, a zero sum game, risk transference is a lever available to partners in a smartsourcing partnership.
4. *Optimizing risk transference*—moving risk to the partner best equipped to absorb it (when scale, or past investment, makes one partner better able to absorb certain risks, shifting risk to that partner can create value for both).

Each of these four value drivers pertain only to the outsourcing example we've discussed so far (i.e., a decision to smartsource a process area that is noncore and where performance is poor). What about value drivers in the other three quadrants?

Let's first discuss value for processes in Segment 4: Process Offshoring. It turns out that though the degree of value created by each of the four value drivers differed in the offshoring scenario from the outsourcing scenario, the drivers themselves are the same.

The smartsourcing provider offers significantly lower cost for keeping the lights on (though wage arbitrage will be a key lever here, perhaps more important than scale).

In addition, the smartsourcing provider must be able to create more value for the given discretionary spending than the in-house provider. The presumption is that you are choosing the offshore provider (as opposed to an onshore provider) because your current process is already performing well. You may not get as much value from this part of the equation, but, over time, the offshore smartsourcing provider should be able to deploy new processes and systems at least as fast as you could in-house. (But as we will see in Chapter 9, the issue of process orchestration will be an important part of meeting this objective.)

The risk transfer equation is again similar between the outsourcing and the offshoring provider—with the additional consideration that you may be moving your process across national borders. This may introduce some additional risks (consider political instability in your partner's country, for example). But the ability to transfer risk—often with great efficiency, should not be underestimated.

What if you decide the process in question is core—meaning you are not going to transfer its operation to a third party? Do the value drivers still apply? Let's consider Segment 2, Re-engineering, first. Your smartsourcing provider in the re-engineering partnership will help you improve the performance of your noncore processes. That means it will look to improve cost, quality, or cycle time for each process in question. The provider will again seek to reduce cost in the "keep the lights on" portion of the operation. It will also seek to increase the efficiency of your "business enabling" processes. However, it will be more difficult to transfer significant portions of your operating risk.

How can you transfer this risk to your partner if that company will not be performing the process after it is re-engineered? You can do a bit of this by structuring the contract governing the re-engineering so that risks (of timely completion, budget, quality, etc.) are specifically addressed. But there just isn't as much risk on the table in a process that stays in-house—presumably that's a good thing.

Finally, value in the optimization relationship—Segment 1—has a bit less on the table than does the re-engineering relationship; the good news is, those processes are already working. In these processes it may be less about shedding risk or cost, and more about gaining access to innovation in a timely manner.

So, no matter what smartsourcing strategy you choose for a given business process, there are four drivers of value for the smartsourcing relationship. Measuring that value is an exercise in quantifying the expected value and in tracking whether you and your smartsourcing partner are meeting those expectations consistently. While that is a bit easier to do for the more quantifiable value drivers linked to cost reduction and increased innovation, we've tried to make the case that it is possible and important to measure risk as well, and to track the partnership's ability to reduce the overall risk associated with any given process.

CHAPTER 8

WHY IS IT SO DIFFICULT TO SMARTSOURCE?

"Because a thing seems difficult for you, do not think it impossible for anyone to accomplish."

—Marcus Aurelius

The basic premise of smartsourcing is that it simplifies an organization by allowing it to focus on what's most critical for the business. Attaining that simplicity, however, even after deciding what elements of your organization are right for the various forms of smartsourcing, requires that you navigate significant challenges. This chapter discusses the primary impediments to smartsourcing. We will look at the subtle and not so subtle errors that organizations make when they try to smartsource, and offer advice on how to spot and correct these before they undermine your smartsourcing initiative.

Let's start by reviewing the key attributes of a smartsourcing decision; it is one that:

- Is based on a firm understanding of your company's core versus noncore activities.

- Opens the door to sourcing complete business processes to third parties for your noncore operations.
- Looks to embed process improvement into the fiber of your core activities—this often requires a third party to help you assess the performance of your current operations and/or assist you in improving them (which is, in effect, another sourcing decision).
- Looks for a partner whose core activities correspond to your noncore tasks, that has economies of scale that can be leveraged, and that has a capacity to bear (or mitigate) risk that you do not.
- Creates a tight partnership between you and your smartsource provider, which makes the strategies and operations of both partners transparent to each other (only through this tight partnership can your smartsourcing partner provide a way to increase the return on the investments you need to make in your processes).

The attributes of a smartsourcing decision can be represented as five steps along the decision tree in **FIGURE 8.1**. Only if the sourcing decision process incorporates all five attributes can you really expect the benefits of a smartsourcing decision (versus the pitfalls of an outsourcing decision, for example).

However, most firms tend not to think about their sourcing strategies in this context, so they outsource rather than smartsource. They select "vendors" based on cost and write contracts to protect them from outages. They write in specs for "server up time," but they do not think about the value of spreading their operational risk to a party that can invest in technologies or processes that can significantly reduce risk. To avoid those pitfalls, let's explore each of the five elements of the decision tree—and the most critical smartsourcing impediments to each.

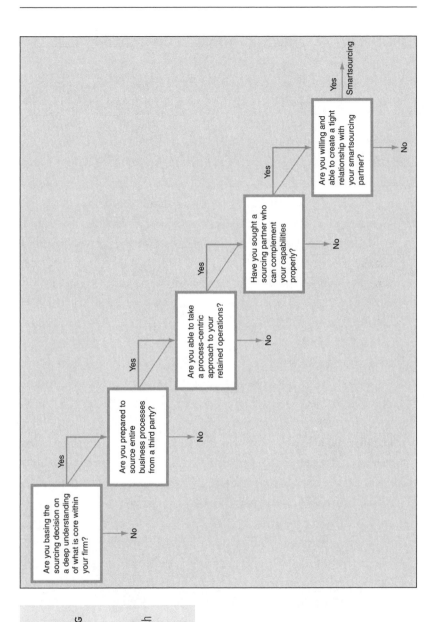

FIGURE 8.1

ARE YOU STRUCTURING A SMARTSOURCING PARTNERSHIP?

The basic steps in determining if you are ready to establish a smartsourcing partnership.

Impediment 1: Understanding Your Core Processes

Have your ever led your company through an evaluation of its core competencies? Have you ever reached consensus in the conversation? The bottom line is that no company wants its processes to be considered noncore. Typically, you have two options in an analysis of this kind: Perform it from the top down without much input from the management team of your operations, and run the risk that the senior team is wrong; or do it from the bottom up, including a large number of executives, and struggle through the implications of arriving at a consensus.

We have helped many firms through the core competency conversation using both the top-down and the bottom-up approaches. And we will admit that at times, the top-down approach can work; but more often it fails and the implications of failure are relatively severe because they often include decisions to shed some core competencies. In addition, the irony of the top-down approach is that it works only when the viewpoint from the top is dictatorially singular. This means that while definitive it can also risk being myopic. In a moment of severe crisis this may be the only option, as consensus of any other sort will just take too long. But in the absence of a severe crisis, we see high risk in this sort of an approach.

Our preference—with all the "messiness" it implies—is the bottom-up approach. The way this tends to work in practice is to corral a group of senior executives responsible for a process, product, or function and ask them to rank not only the coreness of their own operations, but also their peer's operations. In effect, every executive is rating not only how "core" their own processes are, but also how "core" the processes of all the other executives are. This is actually done using a standardized survey tool that ranks the importance of each process for each executive. The resulting assessment is illustrated using the same smartsourcing dashboard approach we used earlier in Chapter 6.

Armed with this data, there is often a clustering around both activities that are clearly noncore, and some that clearly are. It is rare that all activities end up clustered in between the two extremes of core and noncore, but if they do you would have good case to wonder why you are still in business!

The ones that do end up in the middle of the road will require further analysis, but the problem with these processes is often that senior leadership has not adequately articulated the vision and ambitions of the organization. If they had, it would be much easier to assess how critical the processes are to achieving that vision. In these cases senior executives have to step in and express a future strategic perspective in order to shift over the remaining middle-of-the-road operations. In some cases this alone is worth the trouble of going through a smartsourcing dashboard exercise. We recall one instance where the CEO of a large manufacturing operation looked at the dashboard and after some anxious moments said to us, with more than a tinge of self-critique, "If my execs can't tell what's core, then it's my fault for doing a poor job of telling them where we want to go."

We have found that executives using this approach often find noncore activities within their own operations even when the total operation is very core. This can lead to some interesting small-scale sourcing discussions that might otherwise have been missed (such as moving some transcription service to a third-party provider, or sourcing imaging and mailing solution from a partner, and so on). That said, the core/noncore decision is never a simple one and, in the end, an inability to make these decisions creates some of the greatest impediments to smartsourcing.

IMPEDIMENT 2: CREATING INSUFFICIENT PROCESS SCOPE

Think back to your last process-sourcing decision. Perhaps it was a noncore area such as performing background checks on candidates for hire. Perhaps it was as complex as sourcing your HR processes (payroll, benefits administration, recruiting, performance management, etc.). Which decision was easier to make? If your company is like most, it's easier to outsource the subprocess (performing background checks) rather than the broader business process (recruiting), never mind the entire suite of processes (the human resources operation).

But, as we discussed in Chapter 7, the benefits of a smart-sourcing decision go well beyond saving on your "keep the lights on" processes (for example, performing background checks). Part of the reason to smartsource is to gain access to rare skills and innovations available through the smartsourcing provider that could make the discretionary spending you have available for your noncore function go further.

In order to create a way for your smartsourcing partner to create those benefits, the scope of the process being smart-sourced must be sufficiently large. Often, this means considering the smartsourcing of an entire business process like "order to cash processing," or "procure to pay processing," or IT infrastructure management from a third party.

To get at the third, and perhaps most important, benefit of smartsourcing—that is, risk transference—the scope of the relationship must be broad enough to materially influence the risk equation. While it is certainly true that having a third party perform your hiring candidates' background check moves the risk of timeliness and accuracy of those checks to the third-party provider, you may be leaving risk transference gains on the table by keeping the scope of this too narrow. For example, if you were able to expand the scope beyond background checks for new hires to include the entire candidate sourcing process, there might be new risks, such as the risk of not identifying a sufficient number of qualified candidates for an open position, that you would also be able to transfer to your partner—where they would be significantly reduced by the partner's investments in those same processes (be they maintaining networks of executives, like those of Korn/Ferry International, or technology investments, like those of Monster.com).

If your company went all the way to deciding that human resources processes as a whole are noncore, you are better off expanding the scope to the entire suite of HR processes (including payroll, benefits, compensation management, recruiting, training, performance management, and perhaps even HR strategy), and finding a single partner that can service all these needs. By bundling this all into a single relationship, your company would be able to cut through the myriad complexities of the HR processes to the business outcomes they want the process partner to provide.

In this model, you have in fact left the "details" to your partner, who should be in a better position to define how they will reduce cost, give you the newest innovations, and manage your risk—because these processes are core to what makes your partner's firm great.

IMPEDIMENT 3: TAKING A PROCESS-CENTRIC APPROACH TO YOUR RETAINED OPERATIONS

Smartsourcing is not only about the processes that you source from third parties; it is also about how to manage and improve processes that are core and that you will keep in-house. How do you smartsource these processes?

Begin by thinking of the processes involved, rather than the functions. Think in terms of the "order to cash process" rather than the finance function. That is often hard to do; it seems that we have all been conditioned to think about organizations as consisting of functional silos and perhaps geographic or product specific business units, rather than process that cut across these boundaries. By moving your organization to a process-oriented mindset, the foundation is in place to create objective measures for process improvement. This is a key point and an easy one to miss. We don't know how anyone can objectively measure the performance of a finance function, or for that matter a customer support function, or any other broad-based function in a way that is meaningful from a process improvement standpoint. While you could claim that a good finance function is one in which errors are minimized and a good customer support function is one with few complaints, neither measure tells you how to improve the function, only that it is not working as it should. There are no consistent standards of what define most "functions," and so there are no metrics to identify how we can improve performance—only that we should improve it. But an "order to cash process" or "time to close a call" can be measured in terms of cost, quality, cycle time, or perhaps more specifically, in terms of number of remittances processed per day or calls closed per employee. By taking a process-oriented mindset to its core processes, a firm can establish objective measures of performance, can track its performance against those measures, can compare its performance to those of its peers and to best practices in other industries, and can then identify ways to improve its performance.

This sort of process mindset is simply missing in many organizations. High-level metrics are defined in order to track performance, but these same metrics tell you little about how to improve performance within a function and even less about the details of the activities and tasks that span multiple functions.

Smartsourcing is based on a deep understanding of underlying processes. And only when you take such a process view can you then think about truly improving your operations, and identify a smartsourcing partner who might be able to assist you in improving your performance. Too few firms have a process view, and it makes thinking about smartsourcing very difficult—if even possible.

IMPEDIMENT 4: THE INABILITY TO FIND THE "RIGHT" SMARTSOURCING PARTNER

Finding the "right partner" for your smartsourcing decision is the impediment we hear about most frequently: "I'd smart-source this if only I could find someone who knew how to handle my processes" is a refrain we've heard many times. And finding the right partner is not an easy task. But there are some best practices that you can employ in managing the process.

1. *Document your current processes and evaluate the cost, your performance quality, and cycle time before you begin your candidate sourcing process.* As we noted in Impediment 3, this is easier said than done, but if you've followed us this far, then you're probably already well on your way to adopting the process-oriented approach we are advocating. You've probably segmented your operations into business processes, scoped those processes around well-defined boundaries, documented the processes, and perhaps benchmarked the processes to some industry standards. If not, then start now!

2. *Use a knowledgeable intermediary to help you run the smartsourcing process.* These firms will help ensure that you:
   - Have built a solid foundation, including a proper process scope and a solid business case.
   - Have identified a comprehensive list of potential smartsourcing partners—both ones that you or the

intermediary have worked with before and ones you have not.

- Designed an objective Request for Information to your potential partners.
- Manage a Request for Proposal (RFP) process for your short-listed vendors (We would encourage you to use an RFP process, though in the end the process should not be the master of the decision).
- Have, in the end, an apples-to-apples comparison of the various candidates.

3. *Make sure that—in addition to the more quantifiable information the RFP process may have provided—you are choosing a partner who shares your culture, and with whom you can work well over the duration of the relationship.* These are long relationships and, though a contract will likely exist to specify responsibilities, compatible cultures are a better way to solve sticky problems over the life of this relationship than are legal contracts.

4. *Make sure that the risks in the deal are articulated and fully understood and that you choose a partner who can manage and absorb those risks for you.*

How can a company looking to share risk through smartsourcing go about doing that in a partnering selection strategy? Well, for starters, find partners who understand your company's business and understand the risks inherent in it. If you are a health care insurer considering partnering with someone who cannot spell HIPAA, you are unlikely to have a partner who will be able to mitigate your risk substantially—regardless of the cost savings they propose or the scale they might have in other processes.

If you really have documented your current processes and quantified your performance, used a knowledgeable intermediary to help you set up and manage the smartsourcing process, and allowed an appreciation of culture and risk to factor into your smartsourcing decision, then you are well on your way to a smartsourcing relationship.

IMPEDIMENT 5: INABILITY TO CREATE MUTUAL TRUST AND TRANSPARENCY

We've left this attribute of smartsourcing relationships for last—certainly not because it is the least important, but rather because it is, in our opinion, the hardest part of smartsourcing. It may also be smartsourcing's greatest impediment.

You have determined what processes are core to your firm, insured as broad a scope for the smartsourcing decision as possible, documented operations at the process level and engaged a third party to assist in managing the candidate sourcing process. And you think you've found a partner who shares your values and who can complement your firm's strategy and operations. But can you work with this partner? And what does it take to work with them in a smartsourcing capacity?

If we had to put one label on what it takes to make the smartsourcing relationship work, we'd choose *transparency*—transparency in many differing respects. Smartsourcing a noncore, but still important, business process from this partner will force your firm to be open with your partner about many sensitive business issues.

Consider a health care insurer who is looking to source claims processing (a transaction intensive business process increasingly noncore for many health insurers). The health care insurer must now provide the claims processor all of the billing information, employer program pricing, adjudication processes, and rules on how to handle billing exceptions. And the insurer would turn that information over to a claims processor who may provide similar services to the insurance company's competitors. It's tough to be transparent here—and legal contracts can't be the only element of the solution.

Now think about not just the information that must be shared to begin the smartsourcing relationship, but think about how that information changes over time as well. For instance, the health insurer knows it is about to win a new, large employer contract. How will that affect billing volumes, and how will the claims processor prepare to handle that new volume if the two companies are not able to discuss those issues frequently and openly—we'd say "transparently"? There must be a governance model in place to allow for such ongoing, open information flow.

That governance model is likely to require communications at three levels: the operating level, the management level, and the executive level. At the level of the claims processor, it's possible that the insurer's employees and those of the claims processor are sitting in the same building, on the same floor, in cubes that are adjacent, and, we'd suggest, intermingled. Communication at this level must be seamless. To achieve that, there must be transparency in business processes—the handoffs from the insurer must harmonize with the processes from the claims processor, and vice versa. Deep process integration is a part of this governance model. Often, that means that not just the smartsourced business processes must change, but also the adjacent business processes as well. If the claims processor wants to leverage its facility in Tulsa, Oklahoma, for the evening batch job of a certain type of claim, this may affect the accounts receivable report that the in-house finance function sees in the morning.

Above the working level, governance requires the synchronization of the operations of two companies to achieve a single set of goals. This means that the firm looking to source its processes from a partner (the health care insurer in our current example) can clearly articulate its goals. What metrics matter, what levels are acceptable, how should certain anticipated situations be handled? Presumably, this has been spelled out in the smartsourcing arrangement (and the legal language that accompanies this). But the two parties still need to be able to track how they are executing and must have a structure in place to adjust their course when needed.

Usually this requires a shared sense of purpose and a set of incentives for both parties that ensures—as best as possible—that they equally share in the benefits of meeting the stated goals. But it also requires the creation of relationships and mutual trust to bridge any gaps that might appear.

Finally, there must be a corporate governance process that is able to transparently communicate relevant longer range or strategic issues that the other partner must know about in order to manage its end of the partnership. These might include such positive events as signing a new, large customer or an expansion into a new service line. They might also include news about potential retrenchments, or product/service specific profitability issues. In short, the two companies must be able to communicate about such issues, even though the parties carry different business cards. And the relationship must be transparent and flexible enough to change as the business of one or both parties changes as well.

We believe that all three levels of governance—the operating level, the management level, and the executive level—must be transparent. At each of these levels, such transparency requires a harmonization of the two businesses and their respective operations, it requires measurable outcomes that define success for both parties, and it requires relationships and trust that both parties have the good of the partnership at heart. Those are not easy challenges and we've seen many a potential smartsourcing relationship fail to meet this test.

Smartsourcing is more than just defining core processes and being willing to partner to source them from third parties. It requires a deep understanding of current and future process performance, a well-defined set of objectives for the smart-sourcing partnership, a choice of a partner that is both a proper complement and a cultural fit, and a governance structure that creates transparency, relationships, and trust at many levels.

It's a tall order, but it can be done. And as we will see in the next chapter, it can now be done in ways we could barely imagine even five years ago as the reorchestration of disaggregated business processes is becoming more possible than ever before through the formation of digital value chains.

CHAPTER 9

DIGITAL VALUE CHAINS

"Coming together is a beginning. Keeping together is process. Working together is success."

—Henry Ford

The concept of a value chain, that being the coordinated series of activities that go into creating products and services from the procurement of raw materials to product delivery, is deeply embedded into the collective wisdom of business leaders. In many ways, a generation of businesses has been shaped by the concept of value chains. Enormous efficiencies have already been gained from how we organize and manage them. However, the next round of efficiencies will come from how we organize and manage the production, delivery, and use of the information, on which value chains are built.

The modern value chain is far more complex than the value chains of even a decade ago. New levels of connectivity, relentless focus on cost cutting and core competency, and market demand for innovation have created monstrously complex interactions between enterprises. Even Michael Porter, the person who first coined the term *value chain,* has said, in his book *Competitive Advantage,* "Organizational structure in most firms works against achieving interrelationships." We would go further to say that the very structure of value chains and the inability to integrate the many repositories of information they rely upon work against achieving interrelationships both within and among enterprises—and this is especially true of the sorts of alliances and partnership we are describing in a smartsourcing relationship.

And it is not letting up. The trend for nearly all businesses over the past several decades has been toward increasing value chain complexity. The challenge, however, has been that the information and the technology applications that house it have increasingly become more fragmented over time. The result is often to limit the free flow of value chain activity between employees, partners, suppliers, and customers.

The problem is often that the systems and infrastructure needed to support this partnering are either homegrown, proprietary, fragile, extremely difficult and costly to support, or simply unable to keep pace with the shifting demands of employees, suppliers, partners, and customers—especially in a global context where transactions often lack high levels of standardization and predictability.

Businesses today need a new notion of the value chain, one that considers the impact and the payback of a tighter integration of information and applications into Porter's original concept—what we are calling a *digital value chain.*

The easiest way to understand the digital value chain is by imagining all of the information sources and information creation involved in the journey of a product throughout its creation, delivery, and use. This includes not only traditional information systems such as purchasing, manufacturing, inventory, marketing, sales, and support, but also connection to the information systems of suppliers, customers, and partners. Synchronizing these vast networks of interconnections presents a daunting challenge for any organization but especially so for organizations that undertake a smartsourcing initiative that will distribute the value chain among even more partners.

WHY A DIGITAL VALUE CHAIN

The most visible consequence of a smartsourcing initiative is the distribution of work among a larger number of partners, which are often located across the globe. In this sort of an organization it is easy to envision how the flow of information and work will need to be more tightly managed and controlled. However, using a traditional notion of control may create far too rigid a set of processes to deliver the sort of agility and responsiveness an organization needs to move with its market.

The objective of a digital value chain is to facilitate interactions among partners in a global setting while balancing the dual requirements of process integrity and flexibility.

In many ways, however, this has become a third rail for political and social discussions. In a fully deployed digital value chain, work will go to wherever it is most advantageous for the work to be done. That is most often interpreted as meaning the movement of jobs en masse.

While our view on the topic may be fairly transparent in the ideas and concepts we are proposing in this book, we strongly feel that much of the discourse around globalization is purely an academic discussion. It has merit in that it helps us to think through the issues we as individuals and organizations will have to contend with, but it will not stem the tide toward global enterprise. The reason is tied directly to the notion of digital value chains.

We have already made the case that commerce today is fundamentally about the transfer of work. But if you consider how the content of work has changed most dramatically over the past century, it is clearly in the shift from labor on physical objects to work as an intellectual exercise conducted with information objects. This shift makes any debate about the merits of globalization moot. In those nations that operate under a free-market model, the economic efficiencies and fiscal policies of enterprise and the buying power of these same free markets will ultimately make the decision about globalization. The fundamental reality is that digital value chains can't be confined by geography and national borders any more than the Internet can.

But what is even more important to understand in appreciating how the changes in the flow of information and work are spurring globalization is the nature of the sort of information that can now be transported through digital value chains.

Although business has already seen how capital and currency markets were facilitated by the move to online transactions, these systems were almost exclusively comprised of structured data and rigid processes. The digital value chains we are describing are rich in unstructured information, such as documents, video and audio, and real-time access. In addition, they are not governed by rigid processes but rather are based on roles, rules, and business objectives. These are not subtle shifts. They offer foundational changes in the ways knowledge work can be distributed and performed.

What impact does the idea of a digital value chain have on your business? To appreciate the answer, let's start with a simple case. Consider for a moment the notion of any business not as a vertically integrated organization, but instead as a collection of digital, information-based activities that occur within a specific context. For example, a customer service representative in a remote call center may need to access a range of structured and unstructured information about a customer to resolve a problem. This may include information about the firm's products and services, supporting third-party documentation, customer history, component supplier information, regulatory and safety concerns, and much more.

While it is not possible to anticipate all of the combinations and sources of information the call might require, the speed and clarity with which this information is accessible to the representative will determine its ability to build a solution and provide an answer—in short, to meet customer expectations. Now imagine having the ability to address each such problem or opportunity by assembling the right combination of information sources and instantly being able to communicate, coordinate, and respond appropriately to the situation at hand.

This sort of access provides the information needed "in context" and "on demand" based on the users' immediate needs; it is a far cry from the sorts of hardwired flow charts many call centers follow when dealing with customers today.

The value in this sort of on-demand digital value chain is created not just in the processes that generate the information, but also in the ability to access that information regardless of its location and repository, and then deliver it to the right individuals at the right place and time. Indeed, when looking for opportunities to optimize the value chain, the latter is often the greatest source of inefficiency.

In the case of even simple outsourcing, the obstacle many organizations face is that as their businesses change in response to market stimulus, their outsourced back-office operations move at a torturously slow rate. In these cases, outsourcing may cost much less from an operational standpoint; however, these costs could be easily eclipsed by opportunities lost in the inability to synchronize the many pieces of the organization. Now multiply these problems by the more complex and involved components of a value chain and it becomes clear that responsiveness can be limited far more by mechanics than it can by innovative capacity.

In a digital value chain, efficiency results from the free flow of information across what are otherwise natural barriers to its

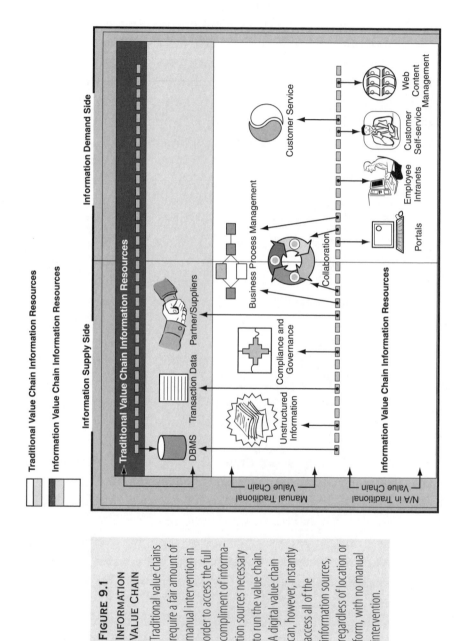

FIGURE 9.1

INFORMATION VALUE CHAIN

Traditional value chains require a fair amount of manual intervention in order to access the full compliment of information sources necessary to run the value chain. A digital value chain can, however, instantly access all of the information sources, regardless of location or form, with no manual intervention.

flow. This sounds incredibly obvious, yet think of the number of times that you have called a support line and have had to repeat the information about your account, problems, and history to several people in sequence as your problem is handed off.

Nowhere is this more apparent than in the realm of health care, where the patients end up being the point of coordination and linkage between the many elements of the process (do we dare call it a value chain?), which involves various health care providers, specialists, insurance companies, and pharmacies.

The degree to which businesses are able to seamlessly share, exchange, modify, and enhance this information across employees, partners, suppliers, and customers determines virtually every aspect of an organization's efficiency by reducing transaction times and increasing responsiveness. It is easy to recognize factors in today's enterprise practices that are destructive to achieving higher velocity of digital value chains: information overload, lack of integration of business information, difficulty of finding online information, lack of process context in information work.

A poorly structured digital value chain may result in delays during the transfer of information from one task to another, extending the time to react to a situation beyond the window of opportunity. For example, the rep in our previous call center example has at most a few minutes to achieve customer satisfaction. More importantly, however, the ability to integrate otherwise unrelated stores of information, structured and unstructured, is essential to creating a unique value for a service or product. The innovative capacity of an enterprise will ultimately depend on how well and how fast it is able to do this.

The best way to understand the way information velocity and the digital value chain operate is by using a simple four-quadrant depiction (FIGURE 9.2), which illustrates the relationship between the internal and external components of a digital value chain and its awareness and responsiveness. In each of the four quadrants we can point to specific technologies and behaviors that help to increase the sharing and flow of information. Equally important, ways in which information is transported across and among the four quadrants needs to be identified.

Many factors have contributed to the higher rate at which information must flow through these four quadrants, but perhaps the most pronounced has been the increase in uncertainty and risk that was referenced earlier in the book. Planning horizons have become increasingly tactical and visibility has decreased from years to quarters.

	Internal	External
	KNOWLEDGE PRACTICE	
Awareness	Always collectively aware of strengths, weaknesses, skills, and resources across functions and business units.	Creating high intimacy between the organization, its customers, partners, and communities to form trusted relationships.
Responsiveness	Able to instantly organize global skills and resources through the enterprise and its partner networks.	The persistent ability to meet the market on its own terms: anywhere, anytime, even when the market cannot articulate or anticipate its needs.
	INNOVATION PRACTICE	

FIGURE 9.2
THE INNOVATION CHAIN

The Innovation Chain is a series of interactions that constitute an organization's cycle of innovation. Good innovation management creates permeability among the four cells of the chain and accelerates the speed of innovation. The four stages of the innovation chain define the flow of knowledge through an enterprise and the speed of innovation.

Most organizations have hardwired their value chains to deal with anticipated problems and opportunities, rather than deliver on-demand services, products, and solutions that are best suited for the precise requirements of the moment.

One of the greatest impediments to achieving this level of agility in "home grown" solutions is the ability to deal with unstructured information from all possible internal and external sources in the value chain. A properly constructed digital value chain must have this capability. Otherwise it will always be limited to dealing only with anticipated and structured situations.

So how does an enterprise achieve this level of digital value chain agility? The first thing that becomes clear as you examine any complex business model is that becoming exceptional at your business means becoming extraordinarily efficient at handling exceptions—breaking out of the anticipated and structured. This is the very foundation of innovation and, we would claim, it is impossible to do this without the latitude to focus exclusively on your organization's core competency.

You need to approach the market with the expectation that exceptions are the norm and then prepare your organization to deal regularly with the unanticipated. With that lens toward the market, you will see that few really important transactions are routine or unexceptional.

One way to think about this is to ask what the level of expectation is on the part of your customers when it comes to your ability to handle exceptions. There are probably few cases where the expectation set is low. If it is low, then the market represented by that expectation set is ripe for competitive innovation or a government-sanctioned bureaucracy. Chances are far better that your customers have high expectations for how well you should be able to handle exceptions.

The framework we have used to explain this plots an organization's response into two categories, predetermined and

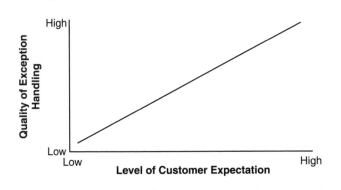

FIGURE 9.3

LEVEL OF CUSTOMER EXPECTATION

Simply put, as customer expectations rise, so too must the ability to deal with a greater number of exceptions in a manner that allows each exception to be treated as though it has already been anticipated.

innovative, against a market's two categories of stimuli, anticipated and unanticipated. Most old economy value chain models rely on predetermined organizational responses to anticipated market stimuli.

Addressing opportunities and problems other than anticipated business stimuli using routine processes requires agile and spontaneous interactions with information that was often not developed or even contemplated prior to the appearance of the opportunity—what's needed is something far more dynamic than the relatively narrow value chain solutions available to date.

In addition, most structured information management systems do well at dealing with anticipated external stimuli by using planned responses. The classic example is a transaction processing system, or enterprise resource planning (ERP). However, today's digital value chains are rich in unstructured information and unanticipated market, regulatory, and economic stimuli.

Organizations that are able to deploy technologies to address the upper right-hand quadrant of the innovation model must have a digital value chain that provides distinct competitive advantage and customer value. They will have the ability to access unstructured information regardless of its form or location; apply that information in current context, not just as it was anticipated; react with greater velocity to opportunities and problems; and ultimately differentiate themselves based on higher levels of innovation.

The question that remains for us to answer, however, is how these digital value chains can be created in a way that does not hardwire them to old or outdated processes. The answer is process orchestration. In a smartsourcing environment we have to move beyond rigid and overly structured process models to a level of orchestration that allows far greater agility in the way we respond to change in both the market and in our partnerships.

BUSINESS PROCESS ORCHESTRATION

In their classic 1983 *Harvard Business Review* article, "The Information Archipelago," McFarlan, McKenney, and Pyburn laid out a thesis that has defined information technology for the last three decades. In many ways, we are still living among islands of information. But these islands are now best characterized as continents. Enormous investment has gone into their creation and enormous value lies not only in each of these collections of process knowledge but, more importantly, in the many manual connections between them. One only has to look as far as the failings of U.S. homeland security in bridging the challenging disconnects between agency repositories to see this.

Organizations have built these islands of automation with packaged software solutions intended to solve specific operational problems such as customer relationship management, financial systems, human resources, and other defined process problems. But the legacy left by these systems is an integration problem that today consumes the lion's share of most technology budgets and increasingly more than its fair share of profits.

While the challenge of integration remains largely unsolved, it has nonetheless moved closer to the forefront after years of custom application development, a rising tide of regulatory pressure (now presenting criminal liability thanks to the Sarbanes-Oxley Act), and for many firms a morass of system complexity after waves of M & A (mergers and acquisitions) activity. Forced to contend with these new challenges in the face of profits that are being increasingly consumed by integration and maintenance costs, it is no surprise that business process management (BPM) has seen such a rapid rise in interest during the last decade.

Amazingly, however, 27 percent of organizations that we have surveyed told us that the primary obstacle to partnering on their processes is the lack of an adequate understanding of the candidate process. While there may be some appeal to taking a process that is costly, nonperforming, and poorly understood and simply outsourcing it, such is a recipe for failure.

How can so many organizations be at a loss to describe their processes if business process automation has been around for so long? The solutions that have been available to date work well when a process is already understood and simply needs to be translated into an online process. But when the process involves even moderate levels of spontaneity and agility, the tools available quickly become inept at handling exception processing. Then introduce multiple roles, tacit knowledge of the tasks required, and rules driven by business objectives rather than predefined procedures into the mix, and business process automation comes to a grinding halt.

Where process automation has been successful is in the transaction-based functions of an organization. These are often, although not always, areas where the process is already well scripted and rarely expected to change. However, we believe that even in these areas organizations are finding it increasingly more difficult to stem exception handling. As markets demand an ever-faster rate of innovation, even the most stable processes start to succumb to the necessity for change. What we are experiencing is an innovation cascading effect that trickles down to the lowest levels of an organization, causing every process to change more rapidly than in the past.

One way to look at this is to plot the stimulus for change against the way in which our processes respond to change (**FIGURE 9.4**). The lower left-hand quadrant of this framework represents the processes least likely to change, where the market stimulus is anticipated and the response is routine. However, we would claim that an organization that lives solely in this quadrant will slip in its ability to meet its market as the market matures.

One way that the market matures is through innovation in the products and services it is using. However, the creation of these new products requires that the processes used change periodically. When this happens as the result of an organization's

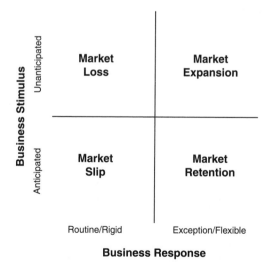

FIGURE 9.4
STIMULUS/RESPONSE MATRIX

If you plot business stimulus (how the market triggers you to react) against process response (how you actually react), you can quickly get a sense for how innovative or not innovative an organization is. Ultimately, any organization must spend a significant portion of its time in the upper right hand quadrant of this matrix.

own initiatives, the organization moves to the lower right-hand quadrant of this model where it is able to retain its market with some minimal innovation and process change. Still, even in this case, the market will mature and ultimately present an organization with unanticipated stimuli. These may take the form of a decline in interest for existing products, competitive innovations, or simply new demands from a new set of interests. For example, when Apple introduced its first iPod, 5 gigabytes of storage for 1,000 songs was plenty for most users. But as the ability to download music became easier and the selection of music to download became broader, Apple quickly had to deliver greater storage capacity. This was hardly a monumental innovation.

If an organization is able to address these new requirements with substantially unchanged processes, it has moved into the upper left quadrant of our framework. But you will notice that staying in this quadrant is perhaps the riskiest place to be in our framework. We would best describe this quadrant as the place where you want to spend the least amount of time. The reason is that when a market moves on you may be able to address it for a short time with the repackaging of existing offerings (old wine in new bottles), but while you are expending effort to repackage products the forces of a competitive market will soon snatch the market from you with new innovation.

This is where the upper right-hand quadrant reflects the greatest, and we would claim the only, avenue for growth and long-term pre-eminence. Creating new processes to deliver new services and products is the place where organizations need to spend the most time. In fact, if the four quadrants were drawn to scale, based on time and effort that should be expended on each, they would look more like **FIGURE 9.5.**

In order to respond to external stimulus that require rapid process change, we need to shift our view from that of process automation to process orchestration.

Process orchestration is on the cusp of what may very well be the final boom of the software industry. Born from the need to keep pace with continuously changing business environments, this phase will be led by a new mandate for the componentization of software applications as a collection of business objects that can be stitched together when and as needed. But to lay this entire opportunity at the feet of technology would miss the point entirely.

The true linchpin for the realization of this opportunity is the ability to connect the basic capabilities and competencies of an enterprise, the true components of its success, through a framework of orchestrated business processes—and by doing so transform automation infrastructure into reusable business assets and to share that architecture across a global network of business partners in a smartsourcing solution. This is a new charter for the partnership of business and information technology.

After spending thirty years building "islands of automation" with packaged software, organizations today are looking to bridge the gaps these have left across operational processes.

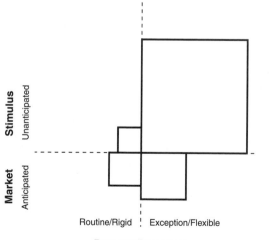

FIGURE 9.5
STIMULUS/RESPONSE MATRIX II

The relative amount of time and effort that should be spent in each quadrant of the stimulus/response matrix.

The growing trend to address this has been greatly influenced by changes in software development that have led to easier separation of business processes from applications, fueled in no small part by the Internet and newer technologies such as Web services. In their simplest form, Web services provide a mechanism by which to standardize the way in which technology components can work together and be spontaneously delivered over the Internet, as they are needed. This provides the bedrock for delivering technology as a utility; think back to our discussion early in the book about how the electric industry moved from proprietary and expensive localized solutions to a utility model.

An even simpler, and more familiar, example is that of the cycle of product development that took place in the consumer electronics stereo market. Stereos were originally marketed as self-contained systems. Early stereos came complete with the entire fundamental infrastructure necessary to enjoy music, namely a turntable, speakers, and amplifier in one package.

This configuration had remained consistent from the days of the Victrola (the record player of choice in the 1920s) up until the consumer electronics boom of the 1970s. Yet by the 1970s, the role of the audiophile came into its own (music's power user), and the market for stereos became "componentized." Component stereos took each piece of the system out of the container, made it modular, and then optimized it.

Soon there was a proliferation of specialty components such as amplifiers, speakers, tuners, preamplifiers, and tape decks. Rival vendors in each new category led to fierce competition, and innovation drove down prices and shortened product life cycles.

Without industry-wide standards in place, many competing component manufacturers pursued their own paths and soon re-created the same problems as before. The lack of interoperability between competitors' products forced consumers into purchasing a single packaged application. The result was a market on the verge of implosion due to consumers bewildered by mismatched components and competing approaches.

The component manufacturers answered that need by developing packaged component systems. These were all the components necessary to produce music, packaged as a complete system. The problem of integration was solved with specially developed cabinetry that housed all the components.

Standards arose so that components could be interconnected via cables, with consistency across product lines extending to such granular details as the color and size of cable connectors. This for the first time allowed components from different vendors to be assembled into a "best-of-breed" system. Since this development the market for consumer electronics and stereo equipment has flourished with virtually every home having at least one system, and the ability to interchange components between all of them is now taken for granted.

A very similar cycle is now emerging for information architecture. The first-generation applications, delivered as packaged applications, were analogous to the portable record player or consoles. They were ready-to-run applications with minimal capability of customization. Long gone, however, are the days when an organization could deploy a single application with the expectation that it would meet the need for the enterprise for years to come. Today's reality is that of a rapidly evolving business computing environment where the platform is required to support the overlapping life cycles of new applications.

The greatest threat to the agility of any organization is locking up mission-critical processes within the inflexible structure of yesterday's packaged applications. If the information architecture is to be responsible for a business architecture that includes outside partners and customers, it then must be delivered on a secure, scalable, high-availability platform, with support for wide-scale access across business and sourcing partners.

By separating business process management as an independent function, and effectively componentizing it, applications can be designed around existing processes, and thus take advantage of shared business logic rather than reinventing and recoding a process for each application and each partner. This is essential to maximizing the economic value of smartsourcing.

ORCHESTRATION VS. AUTOMATION

Although we would like to sidestep the tour of the boiler room here and avoid the nuts and bolts discussion about how orchestration actually works, what we have described so far would be little more than dogma if we did not at least make an effort to pull back the covers. We will take a much higher-level look at these issues in Chapter 13 when we talk about the xEnterprise.

First, a caveat: Don't confuse business process orchestration with what is commonly known as business process outsourcing (BPO).

While BPO is typically used to refer to the outsourcing of back-office processes such as accounting, HR, sales and marketing, research, compliance, and even legal, it can include nearly any aspect of a business for which a substantial volume of rules are needed in order to follow correct procedure.

Whatever your acronym, the problem faced by all of these business process efforts is that the rules by which processes are executed are far too rigid to allow for good judgment and often prolong what should otherwise be an expeditious process.

Take, for example, a call center where technical support is being provided for complex technical equipment. One of the frequent problems with this sort of an environment is that the diagnostics required to solve a problem remotely include various processes to help walk the technician in the call center through the situation. If these processes are highly regimented they may work well for a novice technician, but they may also prevent the most expeditious route to a solution for a more experienced technician.

In an automated approach the rules are defined in what we would term a highly procedural fashion—meaning they are tightly scripted. Orchestration, however, provides greater latitude in how the rules are interpreted and applied, what we would call a declarative manner, allowing the solution to form on demand. The analogy is similar to how a real-time GPS would work to reroute traffic based on current rather than historic conditions. Most automation is the equivalent of a published paper road map. Orchestration is the equivalent of a real-time, always up-to-date GPS.

The basic notion of orchestration involves the development of processes as a set of loosely coupled activities, rather than explicitly coded steps. This is rooted in the fundamental shift of application design toward the delivery of software as a service, something that has shaped both the philosophy and fundamental technologies behind nearly all software development today but especially business process management.

Think of an application as simply a set of activities strung together for a specific purpose or function. The philosophy that governed application development until only recently was that of building an amalgamation of activities through which business and application logic are inseparable. As is vivid in virtually every enterprise today, the inevitable result is a rigid and nearly unmanageable morass of code.

SOA AND PROCESS ORCHESTRATION

Componentization and its inherent benefits for software reuse has been long understood within the world of programming. Connecting two software applications is not by itself revolutionary. What is, however, is building libraries of components into a vast network of distributed services. In this sort of context process takes on new meaning, not as a set of discrete tasks to be coordinated but rather as a common foundation from which a set of business goals can be achieved. This is the concept of software on demand, or what is increasingly referred to as a service-oriented architecture (SOA).

While most of the early attention focused on SOA or on demand has largely been dominated by Web services, it is important to realize that these standards are merely a means to an end and not the endgame itself. The true value of SOA comes from the ability to orchestrate these components across executable business processes. An on-demand model provides a foundation for smartsourcing that radically broadens the options available to a partner while also increasing the integrity and reliability of the processes being partnered.

By definition, the use of SOA presumes that automation is already in place (i.e., SOA enables connectivity between automated activities), yet very often this exists as our proverbial islands with no visibility between them. One system might handle the technical support documents, while another coordinates call center schedules, and another tracks problem resolution status. Thus each system is responsible for a discrete function, yet lacks the ability to determine if or where a process may have broken down within any of the related but otherwise disconnected systems.

Whether or not your business involves a call center or support desk, this is nonetheless likely to be a familiar scenario for any firm that has invested in automation without orchestration. One approach to this problem would be to manually integrate these otherwise disparate systems with hardwired points of integration. Such a construction would allow specific data to be passed from one application to another, but only that data. This sort of an approach would work for those situations that you can anticipate in the lower left-hand quadrant of FIGURE 9.5. For example, most accounting systems are built around a set number of operations that can easily be predicted and anticipated, such as posting entries to a general ledger, preparing purchase orders and invoices, and so on.

Yet this would not address the need for process coordination, it would not help with handling exceptions in the other three quadrants of FIGURE 9.5, and it would come at a very high deployment cost given the manpower required for all of the manual integration. Exposing these application capabilities as Web services would offer visibility without the rigidity of manual integration, and over the long-term would be much more cost-effective to maintain. What we mean by "exposing" is that larger, rigid applications are broken down into small, standardized component applications and made available over the Web where they can be recombined in almost limitless combinations. But Web services alone would do little to help coordinate processes across these systems. There is also no inherent capability, without a process-based add-on solution, for the Web services to be "discovered."

This represents a significant first stage of moving from automation to orchestration and the vision of SOA, by combining process management with Web services. It allows for the sorts of external applications present in a smartsourcing environment, and data, to be integrated into executable business processes with minimal programming effort compared to what would otherwise be required. It also leverages the inherent flexibility of SOA over other integration approaches.

Because it is expressed as a Web service, the service component is self-describing and self-contained. In simple terms this means that you do not have to have any prior knowledge of how a Web service works in order to use it. The Web service will actually tell you (or more precisely the application) how to work with it. That's a pretty radical notion. Until now changes in application needed to be anticipated and coordinated well ahead of time. In the Web services model changes within the application (such as adding a new data table or moving up to a new system version) will be resolved through the Web services definition and will not require a redesign of the process. Anyone who has dealt with other forms of integration knows full well the problems involved with application changes breaking integration connections. In the context of live processes, these changes will bring work to a screeching halt.

However, the combination of Web services and process management provides the ability to design processes based on specific goals and outcomes, without having to explicitly define every possible permutation or flow path. To do this within a traditionally automated process would require volumes of coding, making the BPO model much more costly and prone to inconsistency.

PROCESS ORCHESTRATION MYTHS AND REALITIES

The role of orchestration in smartsourcing offers a vivid illustration of evolutionary advances in current business process software over earlier approaches to process automation. It should be noted, however, that orchestration is not a "quick fix" for managing processes without proper analysis of business logic.

What an orchestration-based approach does offer is the ability to manage global processes of greater complexity with far more efficiency than is otherwise possible without components. The key to this is a modular approach to managing business rules, relationships, and activities.

Given the inherent complexity and constant changes within any real-world business environment, effectively managing processes requires the agility to shift with changes in context, rather than always being bound to the same scripted flow. In a smartsourcing relationship this is a critical element of keeping partners synchronized through business changes.

BUSINESS PROCESSES FOR A BUSINESS AUDIENCE

One key thing to keep in mind is that process deployments are predominantly led by line-of-business managers and business process owners—not technologists. This is not to suggest that process efforts do not require the involvement of technical resources. Some degree of expertise will be required for process orchestration just as with any other major software deployment.

The reason for the increased involvement of line-of-business owners is that the two most significant components of a process orchestration effort are defining business logic and integration points. This requires the ability to express requirements in nontechnical terms, including process flows, as well as complex business rules and relationships.

If processes are not properly articulated and validated in the design phase, they will fail upon deployment. Treating end users as the test bed for processes not properly validated through a business lens will result in significant cultural resistance and reluctance to cooperate with further iterations. Being able to adequately translate business rules into a technical architecture may indeed be the linchpin for a successful smartsourcing effort.

Process orchestration also involves cross-functional process teams. The lingua franca for these teams may initially be flow-charting tools, but at some point (ideally earlier than later) this needs to switch to the actual process design environment used to create process definitions. The later in the deployment process this segue occurs, the greater the probability for the misinterpretation of business requirements as they are translated into process definitions.

It is unequivocally the case that the first step in defining any process is to understand it. While the objective of any process-modeling exercise is ultimately to create a more efficient process, process modeling requires that you first be able to model a process that has some resemblance to the process at hand, and that is far more challenging than you would ever expect.

UNDERSTANDING THE INVISIBLE: MAPPING BUSINESS PROCESS ORCHESTRATION

Although we may have made the case for the importance of orchestration in smartsourcing a process, we still need to address how you create the orchestrated processes to begin with.

The most pronounced challenge in business process orchestration is transferring the knowledge of what needs to be outsourced to the party doing the outsourcing.

This needs to be considered first within the smartsourcing framework we presented in Chapter 6. Those aspects of what an organization does that are truly competitive and core should be kept in-house. We often mistake our inability to articulate deep understanding of complex processes with some inherent but invisible core competency. Far too many organizations perpetuate the perception that if a process is impossibly complex it is also immensely competitive. This is a holdover from the old notion of a value chain as being something that should be invisible and impossible to replicate. Taken to the extreme this belief often mutates into the illusion that the most competitive processes you have are those that even your own organizations cannot understand. Of course, this sounds absurd when you read it here in black and white, but ask any well-paid knowledge worker to describe what they do and their initial response will be incredulity at the thought that what they do can easily be described—after all, isn't that why they get paid the big bucks?

If the offshoring of manufacturing demonstrates anything, it should be that a factory can be almost completely transparent in its manufacturing processes and yet still gain significant competitive advantage in how it innovates and markets. This does not take away from the value of the knowledge worker; instead, it makes what they do even more valuable as the true, and perhaps only, differentiator in any process.

A striking example is the Volkswagen Phaeton, a high-end luxury automobile built in Dresden, Germany. While the Phaeton did not meet the high expectations of Volkswagen in its market performance, the automobile and its history are anything but unimpressive. The Volkswagen Phaeton plant is a great example of how a philosophy of transparency does not undermine competitive stature.

VW built its Phaeton factory almost entirely out of glass. It is an amazing architectural structure, but its link to our story lies far deeper than the magnificence of its façade. The Phaeton is one of the most advanced automobiles on the road, rivaling cars well above its price tag, which at nearly $80,000 is hardly inexpensive to begin with. The manufacturing techniques and assembly methods used to build the Phaeton are indeed unique in many cases. For example, the chassis of the Phaeton is transported in a suspended rotating gimbal throughout the manufacturing process in a way that revolutionizes most manufacturing techniques. So why would VW build a factory out of glass to put on display all of this highly competitive technology?

When one looks at the glass factory the first thing that comes to mind is arrogance. Not in the negative sense of the word but in the most positive sense. Arrogance in understanding that the greatest competitive assets of most organizations are not found in the visible processes but rather in the invisible; that is, those things that cannot be seen by the naked eye, no matter how closely the process is scrutinized—no matter how transparent the physical factory.

And this is precisely the problem with process orchestration.

Many first-time implementers of process orchestration quickly realize how little they actually know about some of the processes they most need to smartsource.

The result? Many organizations are in irons when it comes to defining the processes they need partners to help them with. To further the problem, these same organizations are experiencing the cultural backlash involved in trying to define many of these processes. Simply put, cooperation on processes definition can be as much of a challenge as any other aspect of the exercise. But without an organizational mandate to change, what's the solution? Many organizations have figured out a way to do just that, without the risk of disruption and resistance that often accompanies business processes re-engineering.

As with most process solutions, the first step in designing a process orchestration solution begins with an understanding of the work environment, the work processes, and the users.

The foundation of a well-designed orchestration effort starts with a baseline depiction or schematic of business processes. In its simplest form this is a graphic illustration that will be used throughout the entire analysis and design process to assist in understanding how information and resources flow through the process, both internally and externally, and how the proposed process orchestration environment will (or will not) be supported by existing or planned IT, business, and governance.

The primary objective of the business process schematic is the development of a common understanding of the organization's existing process and technology infrastructure among the organization and its partners. The secondary objective is the development of a framework that identifies the major areas of concern and potential difficulty in the process orchestration implementation.

One of the most interesting aspects of the business process schematic is how few organizations already have one in place. Imagine if someone were to ask you the question, "Do you have a complete and up-to-date graphical depiction and description of your organization's hardware, software, technology infrastructure, and process rules readily available for a candidate smartsourcing process?" Could you produce it within less than one hour if that person were to walk into your office and request one right now? Amazing as it may seem, less than 2 percent of the people we have surveyed said "yes." The remainder simply do not have such a road map of their organization.

Without this road map you start with two distinct disadvantages. First, your assumptions about the existing process will be based on hearsay and fragmented perspectives, rather than an objective view of the actual infrastructure in place for facilitating the process orchestration. Second, because process orchestration can have an enormous impact on access to existing applications and will be limited in its process scope by the availability of existing systems and platforms, you will need up-to-date detail of your IT infrastructure in order to assess the availability of process orchestration technology alternatives or required modification to the infrastructure.

As we said, however, it is not unusual to encounter resistance to the process of documenting existing "as is" infrastructure. The incorrect perception is that by doing this you will be paving the cow paths. In other words, why bother trying to figure out what you are currently doing if what you are currently doing is not optimal? The answer is simply that without a business process schematic in place assumptions will be made about the infrastructure and the business process that fail to manifest existing inefficiencies. In addition, there is no denying that much of the legacy in applications and data that you have in your organization resides in the existing infrastructure. Ignoring this will undermine any attempt at process redesign.

That's precisely the point of the business process schematic. Making an assumption that there is a *right* answer, simply because you know where you want to go, before evaluating the existing infrastructure and process is paramount to skydiving without first checking wind conditions, altitude, and equipment. You'll go in the right direction and arrive at your destination one way or the other, but not in the same condition.

Building a process schematic can be done in many ways with a variety of tools that are available on the market to diagram and flow processes. Although the explanation of how to create a system schematic is not something we will describe in this book, here is an outline of some of the key steps in and outcomes of the system schematic.

DEFINE A SOLID BASELINE PROCESS DIAGRAM

The baseline will be the hardest part of your system schematic. In this phase you are likely to encounter much of the cultural resistance to process design that challenges any effort of this sort. Our recommendation is to establish a fast-track agenda during which you spend time interviewing a core group of participants in the process. Take an equal-opportunity approach to these interviews; that is, spend the exact same time with each interviewee—no more, no less. This will establish some sense of fairness in the perception of the process. Second, keep the interviews to the point and expeditious. This is not a process that should take hours; a forty-five-minute interview with each participant is enough.

ACCEPT INCOMPLETENESS

Accept that you will never create a complete baseline from just the interviews. No matter how astute you are, the baseline that results from the interviews will always be flawed. You will need to augment this and contrast it with process data gathered from other sources as well. These may include diagnostic tools that are already in place to measure process times, customer or partner surveys that measure process times, and data about the overall process times that allow you to cross-check the individual process times you gathered in the interviews.

ILLUSTRATE THE GAPS

Once you have a set of baseline data from all of these sources, create an illustration that can then be shared again with the interview group. It is at this point that your most valuable fact-finding will occur. When the process participants review the baseline process, they will start to see the delta and the gaps between the various perceptions and perspectives cast by different sources. Use caution here as to avoid creating an engine for the persecution of the participants. The point is not to be soft-handed in the approach but rather to acknowledge that much of the inefficiency in any process does not result from malice or ineptitude on the part of any one participant; rather, it is the outcome of the lack of understanding on the part of many participants as to the true nature of the process and the overwhelming role that nontask time plays in the process.

For example, in our experience, we have found that for any given process it is likely that 90 percent of the time it takes to perform it is attributable to either queue time (wait time) or transfer time. Even in pure online systems these time delays play a critical role in moving work from one task to another. This may seem somewhat absurd, especially in an online system. After all, the time to transfer even extraordinarily large quantities of data from one point on the globe to another is insignificant given the network bandwidth available today. But remember that what is being discussed here is not the transfer of information; it is instead the transfer of work. Work involves nuances in its transfer and execution that is often not explicit in the process or embedded as part of the information. I could send you a packet of forms and data, with instructions on what to do with them, and yet you may still be unable to perform the task needed due to a variety of factors—from your own workload, to your perceived priority of the work, to basic skills and cultural gaps.

The point of the system schematic exercise, whatever tool you choose to use, is to vividly illustrate these gaps and to then gain some concurrence as to their existence. Once this has been achieved the most critical aspect of the analysis phase is behind you, and you can move on to re-engineering the process to moderate or eliminate the transfer and queue times and to optimize the specific tasks. But to optimize 100 percent of the 10 percent of the time it takes to perform a series of tasks before re-engineering the other 90 percent of the time it takes to transfer work to and from each task is clearly a waste of time.

MOVE ON TO THE TASKS

However once you have tackled the queue and transfer time issue you can now begin to ask the question, "What is the potential for each of the tasks and resources in the process?" By "potential," we are referring to the opportunity to do a smartsourcing analysis on each of the tasks or groups of tasks from the standpoint of where it falls on our capability curve (Chapter 5). As we go through that exercise, natural candidates for smartsourcing will begin to emerge.

The result of the system schematic will typically be a series of "to be" scenarios that an organization can now assess based on the costs, merits, and capabilities of each. But even if you were to disregard these new scenarios as a route to re-engineering or optimization (the right-hand quadrants of the smartsourcing dashboard), they will at the least provide a higher level of confidence in partnering on the process and allow your partner to source them in the way most appropriate to their model of work, making the system schematic necessary for any sort of smartsourcing effort.

However, we have admittedly left out a critical component of process analysis in all of this that is far too easy to ignore in our zeal to digitize all aspects of an organization's value chain, and that is the physical dimension of the process.

Until recently this was a separate and distinct set of problems and solutions that were most likely to be relegated to a logistics function. We see that changing. As the physical resources and assets of an organization are integrated much more tightly with value chains through new technologies such as Global Positioning Systems (GPS) and Radio Frequency Identification (RFID), we will need to extend the concepts of sourcing, governance, and on demand to our physical assets as well.

THE PHYSICAL DIMENSION OF THE VALUE CHAIN

While most discussions about any type of sourcing involve only consideration for the way digital work and information is transferred from person to person and location to location, the reality is that many businesses are still very concerned with the location and the status of physical assets. For example, Wal-Mart's supply chain is predicated upon having immediate knowledge of where a shipment of goods is and when it will arrive in a store. These sorts of discussions about the physical dimension of an organization often get sidelined in the enthusiasm over digital environments. The reality is that digital value chains are not pure online structures. Increasingly, sourcing has to take into consideration the way we manage risk and leverage an organization's physical assets.

Part of the shift has to do with the fact that as a society we are becoming increasingly less tolerant of an inability to account for physical assets. We are unforgiving of the errors that result from the delta between what we think we know about the physical world and what we should know; in the post-9/11 world we have good reason to be less tolerant.

The other side of this is that new technologies for tracking physical assets are now available. GPS, RFID, and a growing network of global sensors and satellites are all creating an incredible greenfield of opportunities to track, manage, and control in real-time almost any level of physical asset with amazing precision. The implications are far reaching and difficult to project. However, a somewhat analogous shift occurred about 100 years ago.

As incredible as it seems to those of us who live our lives by the dictates of computer-based schedules, conference calls, and travel itineraries, as early as the turn of the twentieth century, a mere 100 years ago, there was no way to agree upon standard time in anything but a local geography! In 1905, standardized time zones were just beginning to catch on in commerce. Greenwich Mean Time (GMT) was not even established in England until 1880. Still, it took the better part of the next two decades for the idea to catch on in the industrialized world.

As modern-day businesspeople we look back on that period and are confounded by how it was possible to conduct commerce without the benefit of standardized global time. How could one establish a time for a telephone call, coordinate a meeting of people from several geographies, estimate the local time one would arrive at a particular destination? The absurdity is readily apparent. Of course, none of these was a problem as all business that occurred in a time frame spanning less than twenty-four hours was simply local business. It was the mobility that fueled commercial expansion and the industrial revolution that ultimately required us to marry time so intimately with business.

Today we are undergoing a similar revolution as the acceleration and the continuing global mobilization of commerce brings about an entirely new set of challenges in how we manage global networks of work resources, people, and materials. In the same way that our ability and sophistication with respect to managing time accelerated rapidly at the turn of the last century, we are now finding that our need to integrate the concepts of location and proximity is becoming increasingly more important to managing risk and opportunity.

While smartsourcing may seem to diminish the need for the concept of proximity and geography in terms of how these relate to where work is performed, the importance of coordinating work, and its attendant physical assets and resources, cannot be ignored.

In some ways globalization makes the problem even more pronounced because neither the logistics nor the people and information being dealt with have inherent borders. Battlefield strategy, military assets, and soldiers are being orchestrated in control rooms that are hemispheres removed from ground zero. Support for supply chains requires instant location and status of materials that might be in transit anywhere among a dozen time zones. Global disruptions in on-demand business processes may not only involve identifying and rerouting materials instantly, but also anticipating problems, obstacles, and threats. It is a subtle aspect of globalization that impacts nearly all smartsourcing cases where physical goods and services are involved.

The mythology we find ourselves buying into is propagated by a decades-long increase in the speed of information transfer. We have been lulled, like a child immersed in a video game, into believing that the world really does consist of just bits and bytes.

The real world has not been obsolesced by digital value chains and high bandwidth communication. If anything it has only become harder to keep track of. As individuals, businesses, and nations we have become acutely aware of the role of location and spatial information in our lives. If a crisis occurs locally or halfway around the globe, what is the first thing that you will reach for as a reference? Most likely it will be a map. To talk about globalization as though it consists only of information, without considering the integration of the physical world, is akin to architecting buildings with no consideration for the flow of materials and machinery needed to construct the buildings.

What has not kept pace with this virtual revolution, however, is our real-time ability to track and manage the movement of the physical assets and materials related to work. The lag between what we know about the way a process should perform and its actual status has exceeded the window of opportunity to manage and deploy resources. Put another way, we must make the link between data, resources, and decisions instantly responsive.

The disconnect between these two realms—information and physical assets—creates a significant element of risk for global organizations.

Not surprisingly most crisis and risk management systems and methods revolve around this same fundamental concept of geographic proximity and interrelatedness of physical resources. Whether it is planning evacuation routes for a region threatened by a hurricane, rerouting supply chain routes around a dock strike so that demand chains don't dry up, or simply taking advantage of greater efficiencies in real-time coordination of mobile resources, the notion of where our assets are and what can be done with them is increasingly taking center stage as part of good organizational governance.

Increased velocity, globalization, mobility, uncertainty, and risk have all created intense pressure to track and coordinate our physical assets as well as we track and coordinate our information assets. But the challenges of dealing with the physical or spatial world are far greater than those involved in managing data and information. Ignoring a strategy that accounts for both can be catastrophic in a global smartsourcing solution.

THE RESPONSE GAP

Until very recently physical assets were merely tagged and represented as pieces of data in the many specialized applications of an enterprise. But the schism between what we thought we knew about our assets and what we needed to know was vast and growing. While databases reflect a neat and tidy inventory of resources, they do not reflect the real world and the real-time location and situation of these resources; and they certainly do not reflect the potential and possibilities for using these resources based on their objectives. The delta between these two extremes, what we know and what is, is called the *response gap.*

The response gap is one of the most basic challenges in marshalling our physical resources in response to an unforeseen opportunity or crisis. With 85 percent of the typical organization's assets being spatially related in some way, this gap has enormous and often untold consequences for an organization.

In the days after 9/11 this became especially apparent in many areas of government and emergency services. In one not so well publicized case, a military transport truck run by a civilian operator was delivering "daisy cutters," one of the most powerful conventional armaments, to a military facility that was under a lockdown order. When the driver was turned back, he parked his vehicle in the nearby lot of a local retail establishment where it stayed for the next three days until it was finally tracked down.

It is difficult to imagine a three-day gap of knowledge in an age when so much of what we need to know is at our fingertips. But physical assets do not live in databases. They live in a real world that is often out of sync and out of reach of search engines, databases, and business process rules.

Imagine instead a world without a response gap, a world in which every physical asset is intimately and immediately linked to the data about its characteristics, capabilities, locations, context, and proximity to other assets. Imagine that this physical world is not only reflected in our business applications but that it is nearly indistinguishable from it and can constantly be synchronized with it. Imagine that this world is predictive, in that it can respond instantly to threats and opportunities presented by on-demand orchestration of physical assets to address the threat or respond to the opportunity at hand. Lastly, imagine that all of this information about our physical assets is available to the global network of smartsourcing providers that you partner with.

Is all of this possible? Just barely. But it is quickly becoming an expected behavior and capability. And for competitive organizations it will be a central element of success.

Businesses have learned that accountability must be much more than a slogan or line in a mission statement. Accountability means command of our organization's assets and the ability to marshal them to meet the needs of the market. It also means transparency and visibility in every aspect of our value chains, from the flow of materials, to the flow of the assets, and the people that manage those materials. In short, long gone are the days when the response "I'll get back to you on that" had any standing. Nowhere is this more apparent than in situations where the physical assets and the people who are responsible for them are so increasingly separated by time and place.

While information technology has attempted to bridge the response gap, it has been limited by its lack of an ability to geographically pinpoint mobile resources. In a smartsourcing scenario this information needs to be instantly available without regard for the challenge of geography.

Geographic information systems, popularly known as GIS, have offered powerful first-generation technology tools to help many organizations track assets for engineering, scientific, and research purposes. However, GIS has been relegated to the nonbusiness aspects of most organizations. GIS attempts to create a Copernican view of the world in which every other application in the business revolves around a GIS epicenter. The result of this has been a GIS-centric model of the organization that is rarely embraced by the business community and rarely incorporated into a smartsourcing solution due to the difficulty of integrating it easily with other applications.

While GIS is a powerful and necessary technology it is no more at the center of most organizations than any other application. To truly create agility and responsiveness in how information and physical assets are managed, organizations must use technologies that can establish a peer-to-peer level of integration with any other application in their enterprise portfolio. And this is where spatial information solutions differ dramatically from their predecessors.

Spatial information systems represent a second generation of technologies that integrate readily to support any business application by linking it to the spatial data that describes the location, status, and potential of an organization's physical resources and resource events. Notice the key phrase, *resource events*.

FROM OBJECTS TO EVENTS

First-generation GIS technologies were and still are very adept at dealing with resources as items of inventory. However, if you consider the greatest value of any business system it is the ability to deal with the role of an object within an event or a series of events. This is especially true when considering how these events will be managed as part of an unintended or unanticipated set of consequences.

However, this sort of agility is not limited to high-risk environments. One of the fallacies that has been perpetuated by the complexity of first-generation GIS technology is that real-time spatial data is only needed for exceptional applications well outside of the mainstream of most businesses. The fact is that the increasing availability of location-based technologies, remote sensors, and wireless communications have brought this capability directly into the mainstream of business applications, allowing organizations to achieve entirely new areas of competitive advantage.

For example, in many states, commuters are now able to access a real-time view of the drive ahead. Web sites provide a map-based graphical overview of traffic conditions, including lane closure and accident alerts and live video feeds, showing conditions on the roadway, including weather, traffic volume, and speed.

Traffic engineers located in the same state or halfway across the globe at remote monitoring centers can monitor and respond to traffic problems in real time. Using the monitoring cameras, they can see when the state highway patrol shows up, as well as ambulance units and wreckers. Typically, they see an accident—or its immediate aftereffects—before it is reported, and notify the appropriate emergency agencies. When cargo trucks are involved in an accident, the cameras allow operators to read the warning placards on the truck about what kind of substance or chemical might have spilled. In that case, the engineer can contact the department of environmental quality and alert them as to what they will have to deal with on the scene, so they know what equipment to bring and how to approach managing the spill.

Another capability made possible by the online technology is the ability to actively manage traffic flow through remote control of traffic signals. While monitoring traffic near a construction zone or accident scene via a remote camera, for instance, traffic engineers can see when things are backing up, and then remotely control the traffic light over a fiber-optic network to resolve the problem.

In fact, one offshore business we spoke with, which was in its formative stage, had developed a business model based on 24/7 staffing of video feeds located in strategic locations such as bank and store parking lots, airports, and other sensitive or secure locations. Trained personnel would monitor these cameras and notify local authorities of anything unusual.

None of this is futuristic. It is here today and it is only a short step from this to the integration of remote sensing devices in roadways, vehicles, machinery, and other assets that can provide even greater precision of information that not only describes the current conditions of a roadway, for example, but projects and predicts future conditions, alternatives, and options.

Spatial awareness is slowly creeping into every aspect of our lives and our businesses. It is increasingly becoming a critical aspect of how we manage the processes of a global organization. It is creating a new class of event-based assets that have location and potential intimately entwined with their other business attributes.

The result is the formation of incredibly agile and complex digital value chains that are not limited to just digital information but can also include physical assets and can respond to their markets at the very instant an opportunity or challenge presents itself—or better yet, just before.

In many ways these value chains can now be managed at a lower cost and with less overhead because they provide a level of self-service that could otherwise only be achieved through layers of management and manual effort. The classic example is that of a battlefield where assets (people, equipment, and armaments) are scattered across a large geography and constantly in flux. Access to spatial information about the location and status of each asset, its capabilities, and its value relative to the location of other assets means a battlefield commander can make an immediate decision in support of an objective rather than having to delay action or involve a larger manual effort to gather and then validate this information. In addition, that commander's actions are instantly part of the spatial information available to other commanders in the same geographic area.

Because of the uncertainty in these situations, this is where the interactions among the constituents of a value chain or a battlefield become least predictable and most risky. By orchestrating these interactions and providing immediate visibility into the many factors to be considered, next-generation spatial solutions promise to alter the value chain in a manner as radical as interchangeable parts altered manufacturing.

WHAT'S DRIVING THE SPATIAL ENTERPRISE?

There are six fundamental dynamics at the core of the spatial enterprise and the shift from object-based businesses to event-driven businesses. Each of these has had a dramatic impact on how we perceive opportunity and the time available to respond to it:

■ Increased mobility of work leading to increased mobility of physical assets
■ Increased uncertainty and volatility in the behavior of markets and economies, fueled by geopolitical unrest
■ Increased enablement of wireless technology with which to communicate and orchestrate the actions of mobile assets

- GPS technology to track and monitor the real-time location and trajectory of assets
- Sensors and RFID tags embedded to identify the current status of an asset's environment
- Web services that allow applications to access spatial information about objects via the World Wide Web and that integrate this information with other local applications

When combined these factors have led to the equivalent of a competitive arms race as businesses raise the bar for responsiveness with alarming acceleration. The effect is similar to what we experienced with just-in-time (JIT) inventory systems, which revolutionized supply chains and the notion of inventory management for behemoths such as Wal-Mart and Dell during the last two decades. But JIT was still a fairly regimented and predictable transfer of objects in support of predictable events. While frequency and volumes changed, subject to sophisticated projections, the process remained relatively stable. The ability to go the next step and actually enable each object to be an event on its own propels supply chains into yet another quantum orbit, yielding what will be benefits as unimaginable today as the economies and efficiencies of Dell's model were a decade ago.

LOOKING FORWARD

If the idea of a spatial enterprise is tough to buy into because of its complexity, you need only consider how far organizations have come in using information systems to manage the enormous complexity of their businesses in nearly every other area. This capability now needs to be applied to the physical world.

The practical reality is hard to ignore. We have entered a period of immense volatility and uncertainty that makes planning a daunting challenge. Our physical assets and resources need to be coordinated and mobilized on a global scale in order for us to be competitive. For organizations and economies to survive, the fundamental architecture of our information technologies and our spatial awareness must evolve to keep pace.

In the same way that the foundations of a building remain intact and immutable while the structure may be remodeled many times, the foundations laid for information systems must support an ever-malleable organizational structure, which can take the shape most appropriate to its environment.

The spatial enterprise may still involve a large dose of vision, but it is fast making its presence known throughout government and enterprise as a mandate and a clear prescription for global organizations that expect to remain viable, agile, and responsive in the decades to come.

PART III

THE FUTURE OF THE SMARTSOURCING ENTERPRISE

"Tomorrow belongs to the people who prepare for it today."

—*African proverb*

CHAPTER 10

DEORGANIZATION

"Don't try to build structures that will anticipate the future. Build structures that will withstand it."

—Thomas M. Koulopoulos

To set the stage, think of the way the notion of organization has changed in your lifetime. What are the precepts that you began with at the start of your career and what are they now? How do you think your ideas may change in the course of the next five years?

No matter your age, if you are just entering the work force or just exiting, you have been part of a profound change in the way the notion of an organization is understood. And this change is not purely the result of the business factors that are at play. Look around the globe at the last several decades and you will see a reconstitution of borders and political alliances, the formation of new organizational structures such as terrorist cells, the emergence of social networks across national borders. We are witnessing a mutation of the very genetics of community. Trying to build an organization within this volatile new firmament may at times simply seem impossible.

The attempt to build organizational agility and responsiveness is hardly a new one. Organizations have always struggled with the balance between governance and decentralization. The Egyptians recognized this as early as 2600 B.C. in their attempts to create decentralized organizations, while 2000 years later Sun Tzu spoke of the importance of adapting to change in his now cultish treatise, *The Art of War*. However, it took the rise of limited liability corporations in the sixteenth century; the movement toward individualism and industrialism, inspired by the rewriting of the social contract and the works of John Locke in the seventeenth century; and the evolution of capitalistic thought as portrayed in Adam Smith's *The Wealth of Nations* 100 years after that for the issue of agility to start taking a prominent role in how organizations were conceived and structured.

Those developments were only a beginning. It has taken the better part of the last 200 years to work through the hierarchical organization. In an allegorical twist we could say that the classic pyramid structure organization that the Egyptians conceived of nearly 7,000 years ago has remained intact; it has simply become more mobile. Technology enables us to virtualize and globalize the pyramid, but it is a pyramid nonetheless. What may surprise you, however, is that the problem is not in the structure of the pyramid or the hierarchy but, rather, in the inability to quickly decompose and reconstruct the pieces of the pyramid.

THE EXTENDED ENTERPRISE

Let's start by drawing several threads together.

First, there is the simple premise that we have stressed throughout this book, which is that the only way to create enterprise excellence is to focus on core competency. If you go back to the discussion in Chapter 5 about the capability curve of a typical enterprise, you will recall that an organization needs to stay within the two rightmost segments of the bell curve in order to achieve core competency excellence and at the same time, develop a set of skills in partnering on the three leftmost segments of the bell curve. Doing this removes risk, liability, and cost.

Second, we talked about the importance of process orchestration across the digital value chain in order to increase the velocity of information flow and the agility of processes and partnerships.

Third, we began the book with a discussion of the important role that uncertainty would play in how we organized ourselves and approached the processes of decision-making and partnering.

If these three precepts are used as the cornerstones of how the ideal organization should be structured, we then start to form an image of the type of organization that is best suited for the new global environment. Organizations based on these precepts have an uncanny ability to govern themselves in a way that defies predictability and is nearly impossible to plot on an organization chart. In fact, we would go so far as to claim that the organization chart has little meaning or utility once you drop down below the board and executive level necessary for corporate governance.

The reason is that every organization's structure we are familiar with shares one common feature—all are, by definition, structurally focused or *spatial*. We recall one senior executive at a large manufacturing company who demonstrated his organization's virtuality to employees and customers by using a child's toy that could be pulled apart or compressed to take on a variety of forms, from a pyramid, to a diamond, to a flattened circle, or just about any other shape the user wanted. His point was that his organization could look like any of these to the customer. What he failed to recognize was that both his employees and customers did not care for the flexibility that his organization could apply in dealing with others; they only cared about what the organization looked like to them. The employees saw themselves being bounced here and there or alternatively squashed and stretched in these virtual organizational gymnastics. Partners saw an organization that was impossible to work with because there was no clear way to navigate it. Customers saw an impossible organization to navigate through.

Employees, partners, and customers want their touch points, responsibility, and accountability to be clear. This does not mean that the organization must be rigid. Therein lies the challenge and the power of building an extended enterprise based on a federated organization structure.

Federation is based on the premise that structure is necessary but in smaller autonomous working units, what we have come to know of as cells. Cells consist of clear lines of accountability internally but can be recombined with other cells quickly to form a structure of required permanence.

Given the pace and substance of technological change, the abundance of organizational options made available by technology, and the need to ensure that organizational structure serves strategy not ownership, we see federation as the optimal organizational structure for the twenty-first century. Because of its lack of a permanent structure, the federated enterprise is less of an alternative structure and more a way in which to best enable any organizational form yet still retain the trust, leadership, and autonomy needed for a strong organization.

In fact, cells have the added value of providing an inherent ability to partner and a much higher ability to innovate. From a partnering standpoint their modularity allows you to define in consumable and manageable chunks the processes of an organization. Cells also provide an inherent standardization of inputs and outputs. In other words, it is far easier to ask a cell to define what it needs to get a task done, and what the results of the task will be, than to address the same question to an amorphous organization. These natural groupings of capabilities can then be easily transported to partners. Note that we are not suggesting that this can be done as easily as interchangeable parts, nor that it should, but we are suggesting that in the course of constant self-examination an organization be able to ask these questions and make decisions about what capabilities it wants to retain versus those on which it should partner. The other benefit of these cells is that they form long-term bonds of trust and intimacy that allow them to be incredibly innovative within an organization. These bonds of trust form the sort of open-systems dynamic referenced in Chapter 4. They also have greater license to experiment and take microrisks that may offer quantum innovations over time.

A federated organizational structure:

- Can adapt itself to its dynamic macroeconomic environment
- Is organized for continuous flexibility
- Is chameleon-like and can change radically from one project or function to the next
- Can simultaneously utilize hierarchical or vertical forms, and virtual relationships when necessary
- Relies on a federation of tightly knit cells rather than the more common departmental division of labor

Keep in mind that the federated enterprise is not a lack of structure. Instead, it has the ability to incorporate all aspects of structure. Its strength is not merely the ability to connect workers outside of the traditional organization in the form of partnerships and sourcing relationships, but also to reform itself around new market needs, innovations, and core competencies.

Cells are the lowest divisible form of organizational structure in an organization, not unlike the quantum objects discussed at the beginning of the book. So why isn't the individual the lowest divisible form of the organization? Because an individual cannot in and of him- or herself provide trust, creative dialogue, truthful inquisition of his or her own ideas, and the redundancy of resource necessary for persistence (persistence meaning the constant availability of the resource). Think of the simple analogy of doctors or lawyers who most often work in a practice setting in order to leverage the benefit of shared services, shared expertise, and backup. A cell not only offers this but it is also self-sufficient in its ability to generate, validate, and nurture new ideas.

This is where the federated enterprise presents a significant advantage over any other form of organization. Any cell can quickly become the center of gravity for a new innovation. When this happens the organization rallies other cells around the new idea to form a new product or even a new competency in this space.

If you consider other forms of organization that you may have experienced, from hierarchical and matrix to virtual, it becomes apparent that each one is trying desperately to fight against the entropy that slowly dismantles organizations when uncertainty mounts. But what if this entropy and the accompanying uncertainty were necessary phenomenon that could be channeled into an organization's evolution? In other words, it is only by dismantling the organization that we can continuously build it back up again in a form appropriate for the uncertainty of tomorrow's market, economic, and cultural challenges. But dismantling typically comes with a high price. People are shuffled into and out of positions. Core knowledge is lost. Customer and partner relationships suffer in miscommunication, or noncommunication. The use of cells allows the dismantling and reconstructing to happen while preserving the core integrity and trust that exists in an organization. Authority in these autonomous groups is still evident, although not through traditional command and control. Instead, a small central company exists with senior people who exercise their judgment over investment and marketing decisions. But groups also try wild-eyed ideas, some of which turn out to be very successful—and financially rewarding—for their participants. This structure is suited to dynamically changing markets.

EXTENDING TRUST

Two of the essential and basic challenges faced by federated organizations are going to be their ability to create levels of trust that can keep pace with the ongoing reconstitution of teams and the ability to maintain some degree of open-systems thinking in the organization.

We see both of these being facilitated by the development of social networks that cut orthogonally across an organization, no matter what its current structure. These social networks will join the people in global organizations in a way that allows them to leverage local relationships and bonds of trust across large, loosely coupled extended enterprises.

For the uninitiated, social networking often looks very much like knowledge management, which has often been derided as an obtuse technology with far more hype than application. Some of the larger, more expensive, and convoluted knowledge management systems have certainly proved the point! They had escalated a complex concept (getting knowledge trapped in brains out to the free world), into a hideously complex system as they attempted to codify every bit of implicit and explicit knowledge that might poke its head out of office cubicles. Other than providing plenty of fodder for the *Dilbert* cartoon, knowledge management amounted to little more than hyperbole. It wasn't long before many declared knowledge management dead, and good riddance.

With social networking, however, at least one guise of knowledge management has resurfaced with a vengeance: the ability to form communities of interest and to identify expertise. Knowledge management was about separating knowledge from people. Social networking is about connecting people to each other, and this is where its application to smartsourcing plays a potentially significant role. Knowledge of and about people, expertise, location, strong and weak personal relationships—all of this information becomes incredibly difficult to capture in any sort of a systematized manner. And as our network of partners expands, the irony is that we need this sort of localized knowledge even faster and with greater frequency. But the question, of course, is how do you create a local look and feel to a vast global network? *New York Times* journalist Thomas Friedman has termed this the problem of "glocalization"—the ideal blend of global and local, but also the ultimate challenge.

Everyone has some sort of personal network, and between these networks there is at least some overlap. If I know you (in any capacity) and you know Bob, then Bob is 2 degrees away from me. There is a fairly good chance that you would introduce me to Bob and that Bob would accept the introduction. There are many SN (social network) advocates that would say that the networks that are formed help create bridges that begin to automatically connect people of like minds, or with at least some similarity of experience, skill set, or other shared interest. This creates a connection between parties that would otherwise have no concept of one another's existence.

We can use a variation of a well-known metaphor to illustrate these relationships (see **FIGURE 10.1**).

In "traditional" knowledge management, this grid represents that holy entity "Knowledge," but in this instance, we're speaking of knowledge about people. To illustrate SN for you, assume that you "Know Who You Know" (KWYW)—that is, your immediate, directly connected network of relationships

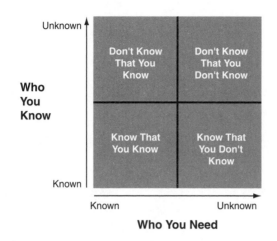

FIGURE 10.1

DKDK

Your social network includes not only the people you know, but those who others know as well. While your immediate network of a few dozen—or even a few hundred—people may be known to you, there is probably a network of several million people only three or four degrees removed from you that includes many resources you would never have known of or considered in your network. Tapping into this broader global network is the promise of social networking.

within your immediate local organization—in the vernacular we introduced earlier in Chapter 9, this may be your cell or adjacent cells. This is no doubt not a very large number, and easily mapable and trackable. There are likely to exist well-formed bonds of trust in this near-hand social network.

However, in large organizations there are plenty of named people that you "Know (by name but) That You Don't Know" in a way that allows you to meaningfully connect with them (KTYDK). There are also people that you "Don't Know That You Know," perhaps a coworker's close friend from a previous project. These folks are several degrees removed from you, but not so removed you couldn't find them if only you knew to ask a close friend to make the introduction. And there is the rest of the known universe (unknown to *you*), those in the "Don't Know That You Don't Know" (DKTYDK) camp who may have skills and experience that you need to perform a task but you would never know to reach out to and even if you did would not have a connection to.

From a smartsourcing point of view, establishing a mechanism by which to develop some transference of trust and integrity to these three other quadrants is going to have a direct and substantive impact on how well an extended enterprise of the sort we have been describing will operate.

The purpose of social networks is to do just that by allowing you to map the people you know across all of these quadrants and then provide you with access to this network based on degrees of separation. In other words, the social network figures out how and through how many people you are connected to someone else and then offers a path for you to extend your relationships and those of others to reach a particular person that may be many degrees removed from you.

While the most familiar versions of this are in public social networks that have recently started to emerge for job finding, dating, and hobby enthusiasts, it is the private versions of these social networks that we believe are going to be most important to keep track of and deploy within an extended enterprise.

In some cases that will involve populating the social network with information about the skills and capabilities that people throughout the extended enterprise have. A strong word of caution here, however: *Do not* expect or mandate that people define themselves to a social network. It will simply not get done. This basic premise was also the fundamental flaw in knowledge management. People who are busy will not take the time to do it. People who are not busy will dominate it. You can guess which ones have the knowledge and skills you are most in need of networking!

The solution is to establish ways that allow you to capture the ties that bind the social network as part of the normal course of events. For example:

- E-mail content is often one of the greatest sources of detail about a person's actual experiences. In a private social network there are many ways to filter content to include relevant e-mail content (while maintaining the content's privacy). For example, part of the postmortem that has been conducted on Enron, in the wake of its financial and governance difficulties, involved reviewing the flow of e-mail traffic to identify high-level indicators of irregularities. What regulators found was that the e-mail traffic itself (sans content) was a very good indicator of potential trouble. Tracking word usage and phraseology in the e-mail (even when any single e-mail may have appeared completely benign) provided another level of insight as to when and where problems at Enron started. From a security and policy standpoint, this certainly raises questions about who has the right to look at e-mail and under what circumstances e-mail can be mined. However, in the context of an ethical approach, the point is that an organization can still protect individual privacy while offering some mechanism for connecting people in networks that individuals would not otherwise be able to easily create on their own.
- Document content can also be similarly mined and protected while still offering ways to connect people with like interests.
- Customer experiences and contacts can be captured in the form of customer deliverables, proposals, and diaries.

Keep in mind that with each of these approaches it is still the person-to-person linkages and the inherent trust between people that is ultimately being extended by a social network. It's not just a matter of finding the person with the right skills, but also in connecting to them via a chain of links that have already established bonds of trust.

So what might this federation look like from the standpoint of a global partnership? Our belief is that we will see at least three distinct forms of federation: corporate federation, value chain federation, and business services federation. The first two are fairly easy to envision. The corporate federation is a tightly bound collection of cells that are held together through ownership or some sort of equity participation (think of our description of keiretsu in Chapter 3). The value chain federations are held together by strategy. They have joint financial and performance metrics that are used to assess the strategy's merits, but ultimately they can succeed from the federation if these metrics do not justify their participation. For example, most sourcing arrangements have service level agreements that spell out clearly the expectations and requirements on the part of both parties. The third form, however, is one that we are just beginning to understand more fully, the evolution of business service platforms.

CHAPTER 11

THE INVISIBLE HAND
OF COMMERCE

As we move toward the external economies of scale that we began this book with, a new platform for commerce is starting to take shape. This new platform will incorporate many of the benefits of a utility such as shared services and external economies of scale, but it will also provide a dependable and reliable foundation for the creation of new businesses that would otherwise not be able to scale on their own if they had to rely on their resources to deliver these same services.

We call this a business service platform, or a BSP. BSPs are already emerging as hubs of enormous networked communities. They are a critical component of the smartsourcing movement because they provide much of the glue that will hold together the vast networks of partnerships and technologies needed to make smartsourcing a viable and reliable approach. Driven by some of the largest global companies today, BSPs hold the potential to revolutionize the way we trade, alter the role of software providers, and transform the very nature of trust among business partners.

The first generation of BSPs is being driven by companies such as Dell and Wal-Mart, which are building hubs that will emerge as vast electronically enabled networks of traders that include both suppliers and customers. Within these networks, suites of business processes will begin to standardize how commerce works within an industry. While smartsourcing provides a compelling vision, it is ultimately the BSP that provides the security within a particular industry needed for a critical mass of suppliers and partners to invest and make the leap of faith to smartsourcing.

This company-driven, first generation of hubs will be followed by a second generation that will be more open—that is, they will be places where multiple, competing product and service providers do business. Imagine, for instance, a BSP that both Wal-Mart and Target might use. That wave of BSPs will be managed by third-party facilitators—possibly IT service or software providers—supported by one or more major industry players. For example, we expect that in each major industry, such as automotive, aerospace, retail, medical supplies, health care, insurance, pharmaceuticals, etc., a single BSP will evolve to deliver the basic technology and standards needed to make smartsourcing a secure investment.

These specialized smartsourcing service providers will have deep business process skills in their respective industries. These facilitators are "process aggregators," and we strongly believe that they will ultimately become the industry platforms for the delivery, investment, and innovation in smartsourcing.

However, you need to stop yourself right here if you think hubs of commerce are radical and new. Hubs of commerce are not an entirely new concept. ADP in payroll, First Data in credit card processing, and Sabre in airline reservations have already demonstrated the value of process aggregation in their industries. It also wasn't that long ago that a similar concept swept through e-commerce circles. It was called B2B (or business to business), and it was the last vestige of prosperity and vision before the dot-com demise. Despite some busts, some great ideas came out of it; and the lessons of B2B players have much to teach us about the way commerce works and the fundamental behaviors we need to adopt before the new generation of smartsourcing hubs will start to pay off on the promises made years ago.

A FISH STORY

Let's take the example of Neal Workman. In November 2000, his B2B marketplace, Gofish.com, was on a roll. Workman had raised $42 million in venture funding and the site was poised to be the online exchange for buying and selling fish around the world. No overnight success, Workman was a sharp guy who had grown up in the fish business; Gofish.com was his moment in the sun.

Workman, of course, wasn't alone. Dozens of online exchanges had sprung up on every electronic street corner, from energy exchange AltraEnergy.com, to metal exchange e-Steel.com, to janitorial-supplies portal janCentral.com. And, like these, most failed.

If you listen to Workman tell his story, the failure was due to the reluctance of buyers and sellers to move to an entirely online mode of commerce; they only wanted to *dabble* in online commerce. That reluctance belied a much deeper set of issues having to do with trust and reliability that undermined the Internet-based B2B commerce hubs, which were once thought to be the cornerstones of a new economy.

These B2B hubs promised to deliver new levels of liquidity for markets by reconfiguring supply chains to meet changing market requirements. Like economist Adam Smith's invisible hand, online markets would swoop in to shape commerce. The idea was elegant and simple. An online hub had unique visibility into both the supply side and demand sides. This would enable the hub to identify opportunities for products and services, and then orchestrate and recombine components of the supply chain on demand to deliver these new products. In other words, the hubs would become market makers, taking positions in each market—and transaction fees to boot.

But things never materialized quite that way. Something important was missing from the B2B recipe that technology alone couldn't make up for. Although the message at the time was that B2B exchanges would become vast communities of commerce in every industry, they never succeeded as business platforms. It was as though the market was trying to make bread rise without the yeast.

What happened to the promise of B2B hubs is a lesson that anyone considering smartsourcing needs to learn. After the hoopla subsided, the true hubs of commerce that emerged weren't the third-party facilitators or online marketplaces, but the industry gorillas themselves. The rise to power of the Dells, Home Depots, and Wal-Marts is perhaps the most valuable lesson in how commerce works—online or offline.

While Workman's assessment of the market's reluctance to move to new ways of doing business is accurate, it doesn't explain *how* to move markets.

Smartsourcing is fundamentally about complex processes and relationships, and both are built over long periods with substantial investment. While the promise of liquidity and growth may have conceptual appeal, it's ultimately cost that prevents change. The barriers to entry for any new technology are often steep. If these aren't removed by a moment of severe crisis and a pronounced external mandate for change, technology alone won't succeed in causing any substantive change in the way markets behave.

In addition, there was a clear and present danger for any business moving to a hub model if the particular hub they chose didn't end up as the only, or at least the dominant, hub for its industry. The catch here was obvious: No one wanted to place a big enough bet until the winner had emerged and the winner would not emerge until someone placed a sufficient bet. In this winner-take-all scenario, competition was fierce. The prize went to those who could build the community the fastest. In this way, the initial stages of the B2B rollout more resembled a nineteenth-century homestead land grab than a twenty-first-century sale of e-commerce technology—each contender was seeking to out-partner the other.

But the ultimate winners were not the technology players. This wasn't a technology issue; it was an issue of market leadership and trust. The promises that online markets made about liquidity and growth were well founded, but merely shadows on the wall compared to the power and credibility that a Ford or a General Electric can wield with suppliers.

Today's smartsourcing service providers need to heed this call to leadership and integrity. If Black & Decker, the Gillette Company, Newell Rubbermaid, Procter & Gamble, and myriad other large brands are going to bet double-digit percentages of their businesses on these new hubs, there will have to be more to bet on than the promise of technology. A complete range of services, a clear perception of integrity, and a level of trust and accountability will need to form around these new hubs of commerce. The call to these mandates and the responsibility to look beyond technology is clear if smartsourcing is going to genuinely reshape the way business is done.

EVOLUTION OF A BSP

How will BSPs evolve? Primarily, they'll occupy leadership roles in industries in which they take large-scale risks and then distribute these risks across very large populations. They will also circumvent the risk of having to pick and choose the technology winners, because part of the BSP's role is to establish the technology platform. In these cases the risk is taken off the partner and put onto the hub—think back to our earlier discussion of risk transference in Chapter 7.

For example, consider the confused and costly state of affairs in health care. Repeated efforts to "fix" the system have only created mounting costs and pressure on all sides of the health care equation, from patients and providers to insurers and payers. It may well be (and it is our opinion) that the only way to "fix" health care is to take transformational risks through investments that no single provider, insurer, or payer would ever be willing to undertake on its own.

But let's not be overly naive; there's a downside to the BSP model, too. The outcome of these efforts is often an industry-specific and proprietary software environment, with specific industry-oriented domain knowledge, collaborative capabilities, and embedded business processes. This can easily lock partners into a hub, make transfer costs high, and in many cases require participation in multiple BSPs. But the price is one that most BSP hub members have already demonstrated they are willing to accept on cost alone. Imagine now how that payback increases when the benefit is not only measured in reduced costs but also in increased quality, reliability, opportunity, and growth.

The BSP model may be as significant a step forward for the evolution of smartsourcing as operating systems once were for computing, and even more significant for business than the advent of factory automation. It may be a radical thought for many who have developed an IT supplier's view of the world, but the BSP is quickly becoming the driving force in determining the software and technologies that companies need.

Herein lies the most elusive problem for software vendors to address: process management. The efficiency of commerce, its speed, and ultimately, its liquidity, are based mostly on how well the complexity of tasks and activities are orchestrated. All businesses have access to the same fundamental technology components; it's the way in which they use these technologies to coordinate activities across myriad inter- and intraorganizational boundaries that determines how well they execute. Simply put, process capability is 99 percent of competitive success in any industry. Rather than merely hosting horizontal applications for individual companies, BSPs provide the process platform for an entire industry.

Why is this so radical? It represents a previously unknown level of process integration. Think of the simplicity and process transparency of an online service such as ADP's payroll outsourcing, and then apply this notion to all the touch points across your digital value chain. That's the promise of BSPs. Instead of just presenting an Internet hub offering specific applications and technologies, with no explicit continuity among process participants, this new breed of BSP exists as the business process itself. It's provider, producer, and conductor of the fundamental process activities.

BSPs offer another benefit that is key to the transparency needed in smartsourcing: that of letting companies share centralized information from process to process. BSPs will assume the role of process aggregators, leveraging the information to provide additional value–added services. It's not farfetched to imagine a BSP with deep visibility into supply chain capabilities identifying entirely new ways to reconfigure partners' competencies and resources to develop new products and services in a way that would otherwise be invisible to hub participants.

Will BSPs succeed where the software industry in general has failed? We believe they will. Since the BSP model is industry-centric, rather than technology-centric, it benefits from the dynamic of increasing returns: The more organizations within the industry that use it, the more valuable it becomes to participants.

For those who look back and say, "Hey, it's not a new idea," take heart. It was and is a good idea. But good ideas abound;

it's the trust and the power needed to shape a community that we often underestimate, as well as the time and effort required to build new ways of doing business. In the end, though, something else has been going on as well. While BSPs have been taking shape a quiet technology revolution has also been taking place. It's called *on demand,* and it is a revolution that is already shaking the bedrock of the way technology is sold, delivered, and integrated into business. ("The Invisible Hand of Commerce," by Thomas Koulopoulos and James Champy, originally appeared in *Optimize* Magazine's July 2004 issue. Excerpted for this chapter with permission.)

CHAPTER 12

ON DEMAND

"On demand" is also known as utility computing, real-time enterprise, virtual infrastructure, agile enterprise, and other synonyms generated by the technology industry hype mill. The promise of on demand is simple and appealing: less expensive, more transparent, and more effective deployment of technology resources and services to meet business goals. By whatever name you call it, on demand has already moved to the forefront of technology suppliers' commercial messaging.

While the topic of on demand may seem to be related more to technology issues than to the business issues surrounding smartsourcing, it is a core aspect of how technology is shifting to better address the needs of business and away from the overly restrictive era of one-size-fits-all enterprise applications. It is also an essential ingredient of coordinated and integrated business processes that are increasingly crossing organizational and global boundaries.

That said, it is difficult to find a provider of technology or technology services that has what we would consider an on-demand or utility computing agenda. Despite the advanced marketing programs under way, most of this welter of current activity only amounts to minor modifications to the acquisition and financing schemes under which customers are purchasing technology resources and services from various providers. The on-demand acquisition model calls for paying on a throughput, usage, or transactional basis, not on the conventional basis of outright purchase of hardware and "perpetual" enterprise licensing of software. It is amazingly similar to the era of telecommunications, now long gone, when consumers had to use the telephone company's equipment on their premises but were able to pay for it over time—effectively buying the equipment many times over.

This approach certainly removes the onus on the customer to tie up working capital in technology "inventory" that may or may not be needed for current business operations, and also provides a smooth ramp to bring on new capacity on an as-needed basis. But simply acquiring compute cycles by the dose is not only not new, but at the moment it is also not really "real time." Arguably, any large business transition has to start somewhere, and these incremental business practice adjustments at least represent a change from the status quo.

In their simplest form, on-demand services provide a mechanism by which to standardize the way in which technology components can work together and be spontaneously delivered over the Internet, as they are needed. This provides the bedrock for delivering technology as a utility. Think back to our discussion early in the book about how the electric industry moved from proprietary and expensive localized solutions to a utility model.

WHICH ROAD TO FOLLOW?

On demand is at a fork in the road. Two distinct paths are emerging. The first is the path that leads to the evolution of on demand purely as a development environment for technologists, hidden from all but the applications providers; this is clearly the path that is most obscure and least meaningful to a businessperson. The other path leads to on demand as an open environment of business objects that can be developed, shared, and owned by end users. The two paths lead to two very different futures for on demand and the role of information systems in business. What is clear is that for on demand to come at all close to its promise of transforming the way we build and buy business solutions it must somehow end up in the hands of business users.

Our focus is on the second of these scenarios—where on demand represents a new set of business tools that can be used to not only orchestrate our own organizations but also to easily partner with other organizations and build the sorts of digital value chains we described earlier, in Chapter 9.

Not surprisingly the immediate appeal of on demand is its lower cost of buy-in. The pay-by-the-dose cost structure and

End of the Enterprise Application Software Era

Function-centered Enterprise Applications

First Wave:	Second Wave:	Third Wave:	Next Wave:
• Financial Acc't	• ERP/CRM	• Verticalization	Smartsourcing
• Payroll	• Human Resources	• BPM	Web Services
• Inventory Mgmt.	• Supply Chain	• Outsourcing	Orchestration
	• Collaboration		

1970 - 1980	1980 - 1990	1990 - 2000	
IBM	SAP	EDS	????
			Service
McCormick &	Oracle		Oriented
Dodge			Architectures
Host-based	Client-server	Early Web	
Architectures	Architectures	Access Models	

FIGURE 12.1

SOA

There are at least four distinct waves of innovation in the way software is packaged and sold. The latest wave, Service Oriented Architecture, has no clear leaders yet. However, the components of its technical architecture are already firmly in place.

the promised degree of standardization in the integration of internal and external processes has been heralded by many as the next era of enterprise software.

The mandate in this new era is simple: Invest incrementally, integrate what you have, and phase out old solutions. But that last point does not bode well for many of the software technology vendors such as IBM, SAP, Oracle, and EDS that profess to be so clearly behind this new trend. The problem that traditional technology vendors (first, middle, and last wave) will find with this great new charter is that it signals the death of single-vendor dominance and opens the door to a level of software commoditization, componentization, and interchangeability unimaginable just a few years ago. It is the reason on demand is so hot and yet still so invisible.

On the one hand, the old guard of software providers cannot simply roll over. And the plain truth is that there is too much at stake in these already entrenched legacy solutions for most end users to want them to roll over. On the other hand, the cost benefit, flexibility, and payback is impossible to ignore from the buyer's standpoint and clearly represents a new business model that, over the long term, will obsolesce current enterprise applications.

While on demand will make the cost of entry lower and the cost to scale a technology solution incremental, we have no doubt that the overall cost of each individual solution will also drop dramatically. That spells two things for vendors of technology: Innovate or die.

DOING MORE WITH LESS

The group that is arguably best poised to take advantage of on demand are the IT service providers that are able to deliver not only a platform, but also a set of services that address the critical issues of specific industries. In our estimation these companies will play a pivotal role in the implementation and realization of the on-demand vision and ultimately form the basis of an entirely new industry.

Critics, however, have pointed out that an on-demand change in service provider practice will limit customers' range of choice in technology deployments and perhaps exclude the benefits of either leveraging previous disparate investments or taking advantage of potential new investment in best-of-breed components that don't happen to be featured in providers' standard offers. While customers may expect an IBM or an HP to offer in-house brands for the new on-demand projects, there clearly has been an expectation that the independent services firms would be just that—independent, free to treat each customer's configuration as a special case. But as the industry moves into an environment in which hardware and software for all kinds of applications is much more closely integrated, standardized, and componentized, much higher standards of performance and quality will be applied to solutions of much lower cost.

The sort of relentless precision we are describing reminds us of a remark made by a Boeing Company executive responsible for the 777 commercial airliner program. He succinctly described the 777 as "one million parts flying in close formation." On-demand business will require a similar level of engineering discipline, quality management, reliable uptime performance, life cycle maintenance, and efficiency. It is no wonder that the kind of supply chain and quality issues that have faced all the advanced practitioners in the discrete manufacturing industries and elsewhere are now entering the discussion of on demand.

In effect, by bringing together a closed supplier consortium to rationalize the supply chain for on-demand offerings, service providers are choosing to pursue an economy of scope for services—one based on a controlled supply chain environment designed to lower access and implementation costs enough to be competitive with single-source suppliers. This is precisely the shift we described at the very outset of the book! And it will lead to some major upheaval and pressure on the services industry to lower costs and deliver more.

The Advent of the Global Grid

One way that these costs will be substantially reduced is through the advent of a new computing model called *grid computing,* which provides the ability to access a worldwide network of computing power by tapping into the unused capacity of other peoples' and organizations' computers. The largest public grid of computing networks already includes several million CPUs linked together to provide power in excess of the largest supercomputers. In the simplest terms, these grids aggregate the unused power of existing computers and then redeploy that otherwise idle capacity on demand. Today, organizations such as grid.org are doing this with 3 million volunteer PC users on projects ranging from the search for cures to cancer, treatments for advanced-stage anthrax, drugs to combat smallpox virus postinfection, and the search for extraterrestrial intelligence. Private grid computing is already in use by nearly every large service provider as a means by which to deliver utility computing in the model of the electric power grids already in place across the globe.

The great promise of this sort of ubiquitous computing has previously conformed to the much-lauded "Moore's law"—that the processing power of computing devices would double every eighteen months. The problem, however, is that the applications' requirements have grown at a faster rate than the devices that support them. Just the operating system alone requires a hundred times more computing resources today than it did a decade ago. The processing demands of an extended enterprise will outpace even Moore's law—assuming we can continue to accelerate the power of individual computers at this sustained rate.

Think instead of a multiplier for Moore's law that factors the ability to combine the power of existing computers. Let's call it Moore's second law; namely, that when the power of individual computers can no longer double every eighteen months the ability to recombine computers will continue to increase available computing at least at this same rate.

The price of entry to the global grid for most users will not be an access fee, but rather raw computing power. As a new twist on the time-sharing model of years' past, the global grid will present a worldwide bank of capacity where resources are utilized by the collective network of participants, in exchange for access to others' computing power during times of peak demand.

What is interesting to consider is who will own these banks. In the idealists' view we will each link up our desktops and servers to the global grid and share and share alike. This is no more likely than everyone having a generator in his or her basement. At the end of the day, simplicity and economics will lead the way.

The opportunity for the "big money" here is through dramatic reductions in the cost of computing power as utilities form and in the commercial delivery of microtransactions. These include access to virtually vast libraries of minisoftware components delivered on demand where and when they are needed. By lowering the threshold for participating in these services (by leveraging the set of standards emerging around Web services and the global grid), a vast new market will emerge to support the many business processes now necessary to run most organizations, yet which represent the core competency of just a few.

THE NEW ECONOMY OF MICROTRANSACTIONS

Both manufacturers and service providers will transform what were previously laborious tasks into a mix of fee-based Web Services, thereby greatly increasing the efficiency of how they are delivered. Many cost centers will become new profit centers as the economy of microtransactions offers the ability to charge for what was previously a nuisance, too insignificant to monetize.

This new vision of computing would present an integration nightmare within today's mode of enterprise computing. Building the numerous connections between systems and data structures required to complete the various tasks would present a Sisyphean struggle—completing one connection only to find that ten others are now out of date.

What's worse, an integration project of this scope would involve costly technical staff and resources, who would have a harder time keeping pace with the changes in context of content and applications. It would be nearly impossible to keep on top of all possible changes, creating a significant bottleneck in the process of using and delivering these services.

The only manageable approach is for applications themselves to be self-aware. This requires the content they provide to be self-describing. For example, content from the parts database must be able to identify itself after it has left its host system, and to find its way back again. Each application component—the mini-"chunks" of software—must be aware of its own role and responsibilities.

While this may sound like a bit of hocus-pocus to anyone who is not a technologist, it is actually very straightforward and increasingly accepted in the software community as a standard approach to developing what are being referred to as component-based open systems. The open systems can work with each other due to this ability to actually describe to one another what they do.

To simplify it, think of the analogy of people presenting a resume with capabilities and skills. The resume helps provide a way to select the individual best suited to a job. In the same, but far more detailed manner, software components can now be selected based on their capabilities and stitched together in elaborate collaborative applications when and where they are needed.

JIT SMARTSOURCING?

But haven't we heard all this somewhere before? It sounds remarkably similar to discussions in the auto industry that led to just-in-time manufacturing—or JIT. Consider the issues auto manufacturers faced twenty-five years ago (or thirty-five years ago in Japan) in beginning to try to rationalize a supply chain with thousands of suppliers (most of which were small firms) providing increasingly sophisticated parts and assemblies through several tiers of component and assembly subcontractors.

What automakers sought was a permanent reduction in cost and capital requirements, and a new set of product development and manufacturing practices that would allow them to be much more responsive to their markets. What they could gain with a simplified, rationalized, and higher-quality supply chain was dramatic: permanent decreases in working capital required to support large inventories, better prices from fewer suppliers handling more volume, the ability to shift risk to the supply chain, reduced costs associated with handling rejected parts and rework in the production cycle, reduced time-to-market for new vehicle models, and improved performance in order-to-delivery times for customers with specific requirements.

In many ways, large services and outsourcing firms play a similar role in final production and delivery as that played by the major auto brands. In the auto context, the just-in-time environment and the rationalization of the supply chain involved a new set of what are called *service level agreements*. These had to do primarily with "integration work," like specifications for metrics on part dimension tolerances, allowable defects per thousands of parts shipped, delivery window constraints, and new kinds of business volume commitments. While the subject matter of on-demand business is different, the requirements for compatibility—zero-defect software, uptime reliability, time-to-value, and new kinds of business commitments—trace many of the same paths to a similar territory.

While the analogy is thought provoking, it is still important to bear in mind that auto manufacturers do not deliver (or attempt) custom cars in a mass-customized model. Currently, however, the vision of on demand extends to that level of personalized business solution. The reality is that in advanced manufacturing the inevitable tradeoff is between standardization of processes and interfaces, and limitations on the range of possible product configurations. In other words, you still can't order a Ford pickup with a convertible top and Cadillac-like fins, no matter how much we would like one.

On demand promises to fit the business, like a custom car for each organization, but so far organizations clearly lack the capability to put into place a rationalized software/hardware supply chain. All service providers will face challenges of technical integration and licensing inconsistencies within a "standardized" configuration approach. Clearly, no one today has a just-in-time set of on-demand solutions that could operate at anything like the level of the Boeing 777 and its million parts.

While it's a great idea to get started on a standard description of the parts, this is a very long way from standardized processes in the industry that might support on-demand provisioning of business processes. Don't expect a personalized provisioning environment for your firm to arrive "off the shelf" for some time. In other words, consider on-demand business to be a verb rather than a noun for the time being. But what you should do in the meantime is make sure your firm's technology and business executives understand the issues of on demand, and track the progress of product and service offerings as they unfold.

To get a head start, begin to look at the business processes across your organization within the framework of the smartsourcing dashboard and the capabilities curve, and add a layer of analysis that asks which of these processes is best suited for an on-demand environment by considering the following questions.

For processes in the leftmost quadrants of the smartsourcing dashboard and the three leftmost segments of the capability curve:

- How easily can the process be separated from the technology legacy it is built on?
- Is the process well defined? If not, what effort would be required to define it?
- How standardized or commoditized is the process in your industry?
- Can service level metrics be defined for the process?
- Will an on-demand solution provide process controls to monitor and track the process in real time?

For processes in the rightmost quadrants of the smartsourcing dashboard and the two rightmost segments of the capability curve:

- Is an on-demand solution capable of providing the customization necessary to address your unique value proposition for these competencies?
- Will on demand allow you to control the modifications necessary to innovate in these process areas?
- Will an on-demand solution deliver the process controls needed to link these critical tasks with other in-house systems and processes?

The first category is where you are likely to see the most dramatic shift in the way on demand will couple with smart-sourcing to change the nature of the way in which business is conducted and enterprises are run in the near-term. This is an easy decision to make if the answers to the previous questions are mostly affirmative. Costs are lowered, control is maintained, and metrics can be assessed to determine if service levels for performance and quality are being met.

But on demand is just the beginning of what we expect will be a test case for the long-term potential of smartsourcing and the creation of a new industry of services—an industry that will ultimately become the catalytic factor in shifting to an innovation economy.

CHAPTER 13

EVOLUTION OF THE
xENTERPRISE

O n demand and grid computing are only setting the stage
for what we believe will be the final transformation to
our vision of smartsourcing. Although, bringing all of this to
a conclusion by projecting where smartsourcing will take us
may be far too presumptuous, given how much still needs to
happen. However, we feel compelled to at least paint a vision of
one possible scenario of the future, and the types of organizations that will fuel it.

Predicting what these enterprises will look like and what
will drive their agility in partnering may be pure speculation
if we attempt to delve into the details, but at a higher altitude
the view is not so difficult to describe. It is the evolution of
an extended or xEnterprise where smartsourcing is architected
into the most basic aspects of its business systems, governance,
and financial model.

The xEnterprise is the result of a radical leap in how businesses are built—a loosely coupled confluence of increasingly
granular pieces of technology, business rules, process and infrastructure, delivered on demand and held together only by the
gravity of strategy.

The xEnterprise brings the discussion on smartsourcing
full circle. It requires management, technology, and business

systems that keep pace with the velocity of uncertainty. It focuses obsessively on core competency and develops antibodies to anything out of its core. It has deep skills in partnership and alliances in order to govern myriad sourcing arrangements. It seizes opportunities to innovate by using a cell-based, federated organization structure. But most importantly, it exists because of the evolution of a new industry of services that will support unprecedented levels of innovation. BSPs are the genesis of that industry, but it is as difficult to use them as metaphor for the true potential that is being envisioned as it would be to see an oak tree in an acorn.

We believe that this new industry will become the defining institution of the next age in globalization. In the same way that manufacturing was driven by the advent of interchangeable parts and moving assembly lines, telecommunications was driven by universal dial tone, and the Internet by a set of standardized protocols, such as HTML, HTTP, and JAVA for universal compatibility of Web-based applications, xEnterprise will be driven by the ability to deliver reusable plug-and-play business components when and where they are needed through a network of vertical-focused business service providers.

This ultimate evolution of the BSPs discussed earlier will form an industry that we believe will dwarf the technology industry of the last fifty years. Software applications, proprietary hardware platforms, and siloed technology solutions will give way to universal platforms for global xEnterprise that are served by these vast BSPs.

By using vast libraries of components to create on-demand applications for any business, these organizations will add a third dimension to the marketplace that increase the liquidity, velocity, and reliability of any business while dramatically reducing its costs. To most of us, from where we stand today, it will appear to be a far more complex solution with a far greater propensity for failure.

If it is tough for you to buy into because of its complexity or the somewhat circuitous route the service takes to get to the user's point of access, consider the analogy of telecommunications, which did not take off until it evolved similarly through the use of vast ubiquitous networks. If you had suggested to someone fifty years ago that they would take a route that may involve several thousand miles of network traversal to call someone only a few miles away, they would have clearly laughed you out of the room. Yet that is precisely the way telecommunications and the Internet have evolved. Both mask enormous complexity and an intricately brokered model where even the most basic peer-to-peer communications are routed through very complex gateways and channels.

We'll admit it's an exceedingly difficult scenario to envision. But such is the nature of any great revolution. Organizations have been hardwired to deal with anticipated problems and opportunities, rather than deliver on-demand services, products, and solutions that are best suited for the precise requirements of the moment. They spend their precious bandwidth on areas that have little payback and detract from the core competencies and mission at hand. And it is only recently that the platforms, network interoperability, and standardization have evolved to a point where they can support the vision of a distributed, object-based organization. But, as we've already said, and perhaps more to the point, the current economic climate has forced a crisis upon every organization. In this economic context there is a tremendous desire to somehow change the rules of the game.

TILTING THE FIELD

At the risk of sounding like technology bigots, we think the answer to this crisis and the foundation of xEnterprise will come in the form of a breakthrough that dramatically tilts the field, causing dominant players and products to lose traction as they seemingly fall off the edge of the market while new players and products rise to prominence. It's happened before. Unfortunately, however, our memories are short and we quickly forget that the way software platforms can change business so dramatically does not serve us well in anticipating the future and seeing the next shift.

Consider this: Who was the leading software-only vendor in 1980? It wasn't Lotus, Oracle, IBM, or Wang, as most people would guess. It is a name long forgotten by most people and unknown to anyone under the age of thirty: Cullinane, which later changed its name to Cullinet and revolutionized the software industry with packaged enterprise (then known as departmental) applications.

These applications allowed enterprises to achieve greater levels of agility by not only automating many of the mundane transaction-oriented processes of accounting and administration but also allowing for standardization in back-office systems for more reliable, faster, and portable solutions. In many ways they were the early precursors to the sort of federated approach we have been talking about. A caveat is due here, however. These same systems are credited with creating the islands of automation we have so often mentioned. But our view on this is that the silos created around these technologies were due as much to the proprietary and closed nature of the technology as they were to the overhang of the vertically integrated organization and its internal economies of scale that we discussed at the outset of the book.

During this same time, however, applications underwent the equivalent of an enterprise land grab as each enterprise software vendor attempted to occupy as much enterprise real estate as possible. No wonder then, given this winner-take-all market mentality, that in the current economic and organizational context, the most frequent topic of discussion is that of lowering the cost of ownership of these monolithic business platforms.

However, these seemingly adequate solutions, when insulated from one another within the stovepipes of an organization, are now horribly inadequate for use within an integrated framework. Even closely related enterprise applications for accounting, sales, and customer relationship management have been extraordinarily difficult to integrate with a partner's equivalent application. The scenario is not unlike taking best-of-class automobile parts from several automobile manufacturers and then trying to build a working car—which must then be rebuilt each time it crosses state lines in order to conform to local transportation codes.

With this fragmentation across enterprises, digital value chains have been anything but integrated. The vast majority of the glue that holds today's digital value chains together is made of elbow grease and manual intervention in the form of splintered processes that have come to define the lion's share of costs and effort in building partnerships.

EVOLUTION OF COMPONENTIZATION

Onto this stage has stepped the World Wide Web and with it an alternative and a possible antidote for the Stockholm syndrome that enterprises have developed for their enterprise technology providers.

During the last two decades enterprise applications have increased in numbers, complexity, size, and cost. Despite the enormous reliance on enterprise applications, fragmentation has created fiefdoms and poor integration with little practical architecture for future integration. Instead, the enterprise application landscape was an architecture built for competition and dominance.

However, while applications were evolving, so was infrastructure. Suddenly the availability of the World Wide Web as a platform with which to deliver on demand the basic services shared by all of the piecemeal parts of an enterprise solution became a reasonable option.

As the Web grew in its importance and became a platform for business transactions, aided in large part by various standards for services and components, it began to subsume applications. Generic applications such as ERP (enterprise resource planning), CRM (customer relationship management), and sales force management can already be consumed through pure Web-based applications. But these first-generation Web applications are primitive in comparison to the sort of fully virtualized model that we are envisioning taking shape over the next five years.

The final enabling aspect of this architecture is easy to miss but critical to its evolution—a "virtual channel" through which to broker the services. In the virtualized model services do not now flow directly from application or infrastructure externalities to the user, but rather through a virtual channel. These composite applications will lead the way to virtualized enterprise applications where infrastructure and applications blur into virtualized services within the next decade.

CHAPTER 14

A NEW SOCIAL CONTRACT

"We are living in an interdependent and interconnected world."
—Mikhail Gorbachev, 1986, in his address
to the first Communist Party Conference
as president of the former Soviet Union

I f you are still with us at this point, congratulations, you've
completed the first part of the journey. You understand the
forces that are shaping globalization and sourcing, and hopefully you are better equipped to make the decisions that you
will need to make for you and your organization to succeed in
the uncertain and opportune times ahead.

However, we're not quite ready to let you go into this new
era without some final observations of the landscape ahead.

At the end of the day, all of the efforts and investments we
are making in globalization, smartsourcing, extended enterprise, core competency, innovation, and productivity have to
culminate in a way that betters the human condition on the
broadest possible scale.

So how will the ideas we have espoused in this book do
that? Well, we would like to say that they will *only* do that. But
the truth is that, as with all revolutions, the sword will cut with

both sides of the blade, for better and for worse. To look at just one side of that equation would be naive at best. So in these final pages we'll briefly examine both sides of the equation by looking at what we believe are, and will continue to be, the defining trends by which globalization will change our world, our organizations, and our lives.

THE SHIFT TO A PROCESS-CENTRIC ORGANIZATION

If you think back to our interview with General Croker, one of the concepts he vigorously reinforced was the critical importance of *process* in building agility in organizations. For many this is counterintuitive. Processes, after all, are supposed to be rigid—the antithesis of ad hoc. For those who are closest to the process management space, these sorts of discussion become religious wars. In a blog we ran not too long ago, this sort of a debate raged on for several months between a number of bloggers. They went back and forth trying to defend their stance on what processes were and why process management was an oxymoron.

It is amazing how limited we can be in our ability to find new solutions once we have ascribed a label to old solutions. Process management is something that has been done throughout the evolution of industrialism. We have put in place disciplines for how we define and manage the flow of materials, their assembly into final goods, and their distribution to the market. All of these are processes. And all of it is necessary.

But if you stop to look at most organizations, you realize that they are anything but process-centric. Instead, they are organized functionally, by departments, disciplines, professions, markets, and geography—by anything but processes. Yet when we succeed in breaking through to the next level of performance and innovation, it is typically because we are able to sidestep or step out of the functional boundaries.

Our challenge, as we see it, will be to understand how organizations will shift from these still-pronounced functional silos to process-centric collections of cells that are self-orchestrating across functions. This is not a matrix organization—it is not about spatial structure at all. Instead it is about being able to create a collective awareness across an enterprise of the capabilities, skills, resources, and availability that exist to seize a specific opportunity.

So how will this happen? Well, that is the next book that needs to be written. For now, a few things are clear. First, we need tools to orchestrate processes that are as accessible to workers as spreadsheets are today. We know that some of the largest technology organizations in existence are already developing these tools with an eye toward making them a standard part of the desktop environment of every computer user.

Second, we need to figure out a way to inventory the capabilities of our organizations in real time. Look at this as a means by which to turn the potential energy of an organization into kinetic energy. Every organization has far more depth of experience in how it recombines its resources that it can ever leverage, but all too often the opportunity to connect these resources is confined by the functions, geography, and structure of the organization.

Third, we have to adopt an outside-in view of our organizations. Every organization should have sanctioned horizontal business units that cut across the organization in an orthogonal manner so that otherwise disconnected resources can be connected in ways that create the open-system dynamic we talked about at the beginning of the book in our discussion of uncertainty. Processes must sometimes be scripted, but in as many cases processes evolve organically; they mutate and evolve—and if an organization does not capture this it slowly dies, imploding under the weight of its own corporate memory. This is where the importance of value-centered leadership becomes critical. Without an incredibly strong set of well-articulated values, an organization in an environment of high uncertainty will flounder due to the absence of guiding principles in those moments when there is no policy or procedure—or where the existing policies are outdated. Do not underestimate this simple fact. Leadership is the single greatest counterbalance to a volatile marketplace, or economic or political threat. This is not because a good leader is a seer, but rather because a good leader will put in place those values by which a skilled group of individuals can make the right decisions in an unpredictable context. We should caution that all the values in the world will do little if people are not trained well in the skills needed to perform the job at hand, but equipped with the right skills these firm values become an indispensable part of an agile and responsive enterprise.

Lastly, we need to stop thinking of a process as a prescription for how to do work, and instead concentrate on what work should be done. The question must turn from how do I best execute the processes, to what are the right processes to execute?

It is likely that in the next twenty years this shift will obviate the need to think of functions as collections of people and skills and instead focus us on the concept of processes as shifting magnetic poles within an organization, around which the right skills and people can instantly align.

THE EVOLUTION OF FREE-MARKET ECOSYSTEMS

As we develop our skills in deploying a processes-centric model, the natural outcome will be that organizations will also be able to partner with greater ease. Processes can be extended across partners and sourcing relationships in a way that more closely resembles the federated extended enterprise described in

Chapter 10. But this is only one degree of complexity beyond where we are today. The real question to ask is what this ease of partnering will look like when it is three or four degrees removed from its source. In other words, as the partnerships develop into more intricate webs (or as we termed it earlier, "a mesh") of networks, how will supply chains and markets change?

Our vision is of the formation of vast ecosystems of alliances that self-select their participants over time. This is not unlike the BSP model, but with the added twist that the increased competency in partnering now creates more of a confederated approach than that of a federation. Simply put, in a confederation you can decide to succeed from the union of alliances, whereas in a federation you are tightly bound to the alliance by the high entry costs of joining a new alliance. In the same way that standardized skills provide a level of emancipation for workers, this creates emancipation for organizations.

In these free-market ecosystems participants are closely measured by their ability to maintain high stability and reliability in the two rightmost segments of our capability curve. Any leaning toward the left of the curve is immediately recognizable and cause for quick modification or replacement.

While this sounds unyielding, it's no more so than measuring tolerances in a factory automation environment would be today. If a parts supplier does not meet a certain level of defects (think six sigma) or a defined set of tolerances, their participation in the supply chain is in immediate jeopardy. These free-market ecosystems become the future analog for the keiretsu we discussed earlier.

This spells a massive diss-aggregation of capabilities as organizations sift out the core from noncore competencies, and a re-aggregation of these core competency providers as an outcome. Again, this is not something that will happen in the next few years; it is a phenomenon that will take the better part of the next decade to evolve.

THE NEW EMPLOYMENT

This re-aggregation is going to create turmoil in the way organizations determine which resources are necessary in order to execute their core competency. Even with the current relatively low level of outsourcing going on, we often hear the quip "I work for you but I am not your employee" from employees of outsourcers who feel a fundamental allegiance to their clients. Understanding how this shift will change the ethics, loyalties, and responsibilities between employee and employer is one of smartsourcing's most daunting questions.

Smartsourcing creates a new culture in an organization. The traditional bonds between employee and employer are altered in peculiar ways, thus raising questions about even some of the most basic aspects of corporate governance—such as, whose policy do I really follow, the organization that pays me or the one I work for? Understanding these issues is essential if organizations are to build values and reinforce behaviors that support quality and teamwork, or the sorts of cell-based organizations described earlier. The nuances and practices of this new culture are probably far more complex than can be predicted. But there are some indications of what this might look like in the near-term.

First, it is likely that the global aspect of this issue will continue to gain more than its fair share of the headlines. It is one undeniable side of any shift in globalization that jobs will be moved away from some sectors and organizations. If the quest for improvements ends at cutting costs, then this is indeed a sad moment in the history of both our organizations and many countries. But it should not and will not end there.

For every dollar of work offshored, estimates tell us that a $1.20 to $1.40 is created in additional returns for the organization moving the work. So the question then becomes, Where will that money be reinvested? In the same way that a tax cut spurs spending, which in turn spurs economic prosperity, we believe that these returns will be the venture capital of the innovation economy we have so often alluded to. Our take is simple: Those nations with the greatest capacity for innovation are now being subsidized by those nations with the greatest capacity for work. And this effect cascades as new nations build out their own innovative capacity.

Second, employment is not only about whose name is on your paycheck. It involves the more complex emotional issues of camaraderie, self-fulfillment, praise, and intangible rewards for a job well done, a sense of principled leadership at the helm, and the foundation of certainty and stability. Optimizing these is much more a function of *how well* the individual's contribution is realized and valued rather than *how much*, in pure financial terms. Though the rate of remuneration must have some bearing on fairness and equity, these factors are almost always moderated and kept in balance, at least on a domestic basis, by an increasingly open and mobile employment market. Ultimately, these nonmonetary forms of recognition will decide the primary allegiance of employees.

So what does that mean? Something quite radical in the context of the vertical or functional organization. Our vision is of vast holding companies that will slowly purchase the noncore capabilities of organizations and consolidate these into pools of workers who are paid by the holding company but devote their primary allegiance to the client for whom they actually work. And over time these clients will be more easily identified as the final buyer or consumer of the services they support. This sort of an employment relationship is largely undefined as such today, despite the fact that it is being done in many sourcing relationships and even in some of the world's largest organizations. For example, the call center representative in India who helps you install your new desktop computer systems is paid by an Indian offshore firm and is identified as a PC manufacturer's employee, but ultimately works for you. The degree to which his or her satisfaction and performance comes from the relationship with you, the end user, is far greater than the degree to which it comes from PC manufacturer or the outsourcer.

THE ENDLESS NATURE OF GLOBALIZATION

So where does the cascading effect of globalization end? It is certainly a question that is being asked more frequently. Will we tap out the available resources for globalization of work in five years, ten years, twenty years? And when we do will we reach equilibrium of pay scales, this time on a global scale?

It seems as though the global land grab of the twenty-first century is to get into the offshoring game fast and cheap. If the production offshore industry is any indication, getting in fast allows you to build out the necessary infrastructure to dominate, as did relatively small nations such as Japan and Taiwan. But the infrastructure required here is vastly different and in many ways already available through the Internet. While basic technology and facilities will be needed to house work, the cost of these in comparison to building factories and massive shipping and warehousing operations is slight. Thus the implication would be that we will see a fast ramp up and a quick equilibrium established. We don't think so.

Let's add some perspective here. The total ranks of the unemployed hovers at about 200 million worldwide. This figure represents employees who are able to work but are not employed. The number of underemployed (defined as those whose pay scale is less than $1 (U.S.) per day) is nearly 600 million. And as the world population grows, both numbers are increasing steadily. In the decade from 1993 to 2003, both of these numbers increased not only in total but also as a percentage of total population. Thus we are experiencing not only a growing unemployed work force but an accelerated growth. We would also claim that both of these numbers are very conservative. But even if they are rounded to a still-conservative 1 billion unemployed or underemployed worldwide, the increase by 2030 could well approach 2 billion.

It does not take much to realize that the gap between the prosperity of what we have labeled as the innovation economies of the world and the underdeveloped economies of the world is immense and growing. Bridging this gap will not come by simply exporting personal computers and high-speed Internet connections across the globe. The numbers and impact of educational institutions from the basic elementary education through post-secondary levels will need to be multiplied. We will also need to create an economic and political climate that supports the development of economies at every point along the chain, from manual labor to knowledge work.

The sheer enormity of this leads us to believe that we are looking at a trend that will likely last the better part of this century. In other words, get used to smartsourcing and the idea of a global extended enterprise, because the challenges will certainly outlive all of us.

THE DEATH OF THE SOFTWARE INDUSTRY (AS WE KNOW IT)

If all of this is starting to get too far out there, then let's descend back to Earth for a few minutes. While we can speculate on the impact extended enterprise and smartsourcing will have on the world at large, there is one consequence that will be felt directly in our own backyards, and that is the slow but predictable demise of packaged software. The departure of the one-size-fits-all solution, unless you spend buckets of money to customize it, in which case it only fits you and none of your partners, is long overdue. The near monopoly that some of these vendors have had for the last few decades was a necessary part of laying the foundation for information-enabled enterprise. But enterprise has outgrown the model. As we detailed in our discussion of componentization, the evolution of BSPs, and the creation of xEnterprise, the future lies in the ability to orchestrate standardized pieces through vertical channels, not through software packages.

So what happens to your favorite provider of ERP, DBMS, CRM, or SFM? The same thing that happened to your favorite provider of word processing, spreadsheets, and e-mail (no, they don't get acquired by Microsoft); they become fodder for part of a larger food chain. The battle between these behemoths is that of trying to grow and be the first to occupy that next rung of the food chain before another species evolves. But with perhaps one or two exceptions, we just don't see that happening.

CIO TO CSO

Within organizations the move away from packaged software toward components will have a different but equally radical effect. Although today organizations rely on their CIO (chief information officer) to plan and deploy their technology investments, the need for coordination of partners above and beyond the coordination of technologies is inevitable. As we described in the beginning of the book, for the early electric power industry the progression from an internal coordinator of technology to that of a coordinator of providers is typical of the move from in-house technology to outside providers.

The role of the CIO is following the same trajectory. CIOs are a relatively recent development. In the 1970s and 1980s, directors of MIS (management information systems) would work with homegrown technologies in order to coordinate their highly proprietary interactions with business systems. In the late '80s we saw the maturing of packaged applications and the appearance of the CIO, whose task it increasingly was to work with external providers of packaged applications in order to integrate these with internal systems and other external solutions. Throughout this period the majority of the costs that made up an information technology budget were controlled internally.

Today however, the role of CIO is in transition. The CIO is tasked with the responsibility to work with an increasing number of external suppliers of complete business solutions that often fall well outside the realm of a specific technology. This is where we see the need for a new role with core competencies in the area of coordination of sourcing partners rather than the coordination of technologies. We don't expect that one will eliminate the other in a direct effect, but we do expect that the need for the latter will increase as the need for the former decreases. We've termed this role *chief sourcing officer*.

The CSO will be responsible for understanding the most detailed nuance of selecting and managing a sourcing partner, from the governance of the extended enterprise to the use of dashboards that provide a fly-by-wire metaphor for driving the organization's extended partnerships and their performance.

THE ECONOMICS OF TRUST

As our description of free-market ecosystems, componentization, and coordination takes shape, another question begins to emerge. If we are successful in creating these very efficient confederations of partners who can easily plug and unplug from alliances, and if the technology platforms make this even easier to do because of their standardization and component interoperability, what holds these alliances together?

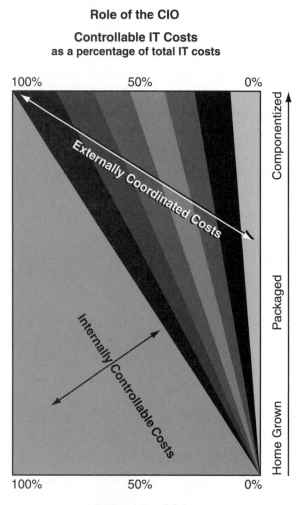

Role of the CIO

Controllable IT Costs
as a percentage of total IT costs

Role of the CSO

Coordinated IT Costs
as a percentage of total IT costs

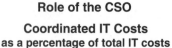

FIGURE 14.1

THE CHIEF SERVICES OFFICER

As we saw in Chapter 3, eternally coordinated costs are becoming a far greater part of every organization's value chain. Managing these costs in the case of information technology will increasingly become the role of the CSO versus the internal cost focused CIOs of today.

Think back to our discussion of the move toward strategically aligned organizations. Our premise was that ownership would no longer be able to hold these organizations together as a single coordinated entity. But what we had not yet introduced was the notion of a purely efficient market where much of the proprietary technologies that hold together today's alliances was no longer a salient factor in these decisions. As we said a few pages back, the transfer costs—that is, cost of unplugging and plugging back into another ecosystem—is no longer a measurable impediment.

It does not sound as though we have much left to bind these loosely coupled partnerships. But what if it was never the technology that should have held together the partnership in the first place? What if technology, like a messy application of superglue, was often at fault for joining partners because of all the wrong reasons, and once attached created little opportunity to reconsider the relationship without significant and costly surgery?

We believe there is and has always been more to the best-performing partnerships. And for lack of a better term, we would simply call it the element of trust. Trust is based not just on a warm feeling but on a proven track record of performance, delivery capability, and reliability. In a smartsourcing context it is also a critical part of how you evaluate the ability to entrust a partner with your intellectual property and innovation initiatives.

This is not trivial. In a 2005 intellectual property infringement case between Lexar Media and Toshiba it had a direct, severe financial implication. Lexar had entered into an intimate partnership with Toshiba whereby Toshiba had invested in Lexar and was working jointly with them to develop new storage technologies. At the same time, however, unknown to Lexar, Toshiba was working with another partner and, according to a court decision, sharing Lexar's secrets with this third party. The breach of trust and ethics cost Toshiba over $400,000,000 (U.S.).

While this is an isolated incident, imagine the sort of complex flow of intellectual property in the sorts of free-flowing ecosystems we have described. How is IP protected? How can you verify and preserve your investments in the innovations you share with a sourcing partner? And what about those innovations that result from the ability to aggregate the processes of multiple competitors by a sourcing partner? To whom do those belong?

Again our views here are not overly complex. We believe that trust will evolve as more than a feeling about a partner. It will be part of the reputation and brand of this new generation of BSPs. And if partnership denies the degree of innovative capacity an organization can express, then the lack of a brand of trust will only undermine the competitive stature of any member of this new free-market ecosystem.

Our advice is to focus on building the primary role of trust in your brand and pick partners who have done the same. Measure the elements of trust in discrete and quantifiable terms, and put them front and center when you partner. Mutual verifiability is the basis of any partnership.

THE EMERGENCE OF THE INNOVATION ECONOMY

As the saying goes, "It is always the sacred cows that make the best burgers." While we beg the pardon of our vegetarian readers, the point here is aptly illustrated: The greatest advances come from crossing into the areas that we most often avoid without question. So what might that mean to smartsourcing? During the past few hundred years we have crossed the line many times as industrialized nations moved from economies based on agriculture, to textiles, to manufacturing, to services, and now finally to innovation. Earlier in the book we talked about the prevalence of the "Made in China" label that had become such a common moniker of the late-twentieth-century shift to offshore manufacturing. The question we feel that is most relevant as we enter the twenty-first century is not where will goods be manufactured, or even where will services be developed, but rather where will they be invented? This is not a biased question being asked by two U.S. authors. Any country would be similarly threatened if it were to consider the "Invented in" label followed by anything other than its own name. This may be an oversimplification of a much more complex set of issues, but we believe it cuts to the essence of the challenge that we all face as we enter the innovation economy. Innovation has no inherent boundaries, and placing a national label on it will be an extraordinary challenge.

But why stop there? Is innovation the last frontier? We don't believe so. It is just one more sacred cow. It is our next safety net. But we want to look beyond the next wave and talk about what might come in its wake.

The notion of an innovation economy often evokes images of overcaffeinated conclaves of engineers inventing one new product after another. The notion being that today we do not innovate quickly enough or often enough. But what if that is a misconception? What if we do in fact innovate rapidly but our innovations die rapid, premature deaths? In our own research we have found that organizations that are considered to be the most innovative are still very much at the mercy of brute force and serendipity in how often they come across new innovations. As was touched on in our dialogue with General Croker, these companies have adopted a mass firepower model that puts large numbers of uncoordinated resources to the task of innovation. They encounter redundancy, missed opportunities, and high liability in the exposure of their intellectual property by doing this. It is here, in the ability to change the mechanics of innovation and our ability to manage it, that we do see the opportunity for some degree of competitive differentiation among organizations and nations.

Our impression is that what we lack is not the capacity to innovate but the mechanisms, tools, and disciplines to manage innovation throughout its life cycle, from conception to consumption. Creating an innovation economy is not about accelerating the pace of good ideas or invention. In an educated and motivated society, which one would hope increasingly describes the world we and our children will inhabit, ideas occur freely. The question is what happens to them after they occur. Do they languish or thrive?

Innovation management will fast need to evolve as a formal discipline by which to develop the untapped innovative capacity of our organizations. There are many elements to this, but two are of special importance in a global setting.

On one hand, smartsourcing a digital value chain of activities that were once housed in a single vertically integrated organization means being able to track and manage innovation across a much more complex set of partnerships. Eliminating the redundancy of efforts and aligning innovation with a global marketplace will require the ability to manage highly decentralized innovative capacity.

On the other hand, however, the increased transparency and partnership required to smartsource will also increase the risk of infringement and exposure of intellectual capital. To counter this, organizations will need to better track all of their ideas from inception and measure their contribution and developments of existing ideas with high precision.

In many cases the objective is not to increase the number of innovations but rather to adequately and quickly filter and move the best innovations through the life cycle, from inspiration, to development, to implementation, to protection—and to do this across all of the smartsourcing partnerships an organization may have established.

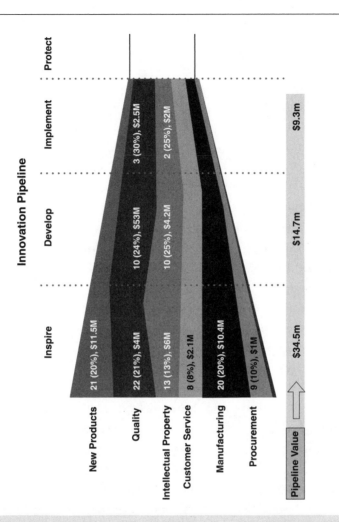

Innovation Pipeline

	Inspire	Develop	Implement	Protect
New Products	21 (20%), $11.5M			
Quality	22 (21%), $4M	10 (24%), $53M	3 (30%), $2.5M	
Intellectual Property	13 (13%), $6M	10 (25%), $4.2M	2 (25%), $2M	
Customer Service	8 (8%), $2.1M			
Manufacturing	20 (20%), $10.4M			
Procurement	9 (10%), $1M			

Pipeline Value: $34.5m $14.7m $9.3m

FIGURE 14.2

Innovation in most organizations works like a perfume factory where a great deal of raw material must be used to extract a few drops of essence. The difference in an innovation pipeline is that the few drops that come out of the end of the pipeline may not be the best innovation. And those few innovations that do make it to market bear the cost of all of those that did not. Innovation management requires that ideas be methodically filtered at each stage of the pipeline so that only the best ultimately make it to market. Consider, for example, the high price of Pharmaceutical R&D built into the cost of drugs that are finally approved by the FDA. In this illustration, ninety-three ideas with a projected value of $34.5 million in savings and profit resulted in five ideas with a final value of $9.3 million. The question, of course, is, "Were these the right ideas or the best ideas to make it through the pipeline?"

RISE OF THE INNOVATION GENERATION

We began this book by making the case that education was central to the expansion of global enterprise—in fact, all enterprise. But when we look at how dramatically the notion of an innovation economy will change the world, we are compelled to once again return to the topic of education as we come to the end of the book.

If the great fire of innovation and the trend toward globalization in the twentieth century was sparked by the rise of higher education, its flames in the twenty-first century will be fanned by the revolution we are undergoing in primary and secondary grades, K–12.

We say this because of our firm belief that a seismic shift must occur in the development of a new set of foundational skills and capabilities at the level of the individual that will focus on problem-solving, creativity, and innovation.

The last two centuries saw the great democratization of learning across the globe. Education went from being a privilege to a right in most of the industrialized world. Yet the very thing that has allowed primary and secondary education to flourish in this time is also likely to be its greatest liability as we move into the next 100 years. Education, like so much of our story about the evolution of the organization, has been cast in the image of the factory. It has become a mass production engine of in-the-box learning. But in-the-box learning is the last thing that children thrust into a world of ever-increasing uncertainty need.

The very nature of the world these children inhabit is defined by on-demand and spontaneous interaction. Today's youngsters are connected through instant messaging, informed of world events via blogs, and immersed in an always-on world of constant interruptions. Their world is shaped by armies of one, extreme personalization (from the MP3s on their iPods to their personal Web sites), and a virtually unlimited pool of information sources.

So how does the classroom education offered today help to prepare these children for the world? In simple and blunt terms, it doesn't. Yes, of course there will be those few exceptional children who always stand out in their creativity and ability to achieve greatness in any setting. But we are afraid that for the mass of humanity being pumped through the current K–12 system, we are accomplishing the equivalent of teaching rocket engineers to use plowshares.

If all of this is coming across as much too harsh, we apologize for sounding the fire alarm. But don't confuse the inconvenience of being awoken from a sound sleep with the greater threat posed by the flames at your backside.

Are we just being ridiculously pessimistic or is there something to offer here as constructive advice? We wouldn't have gone this far in describing the problem if we didn't have some optimism to add to the discussion. What we see are a set of new skills that are just starting to make their way into the mainstream of K–12 education. These skills are all centered on a category of learning focused on creative problem solving, or CPS. Originally founded by Alex F. Osborn, CPS has been around for over sixty years in professional circles and has been taught informally in a variety of venues outside of the classroom, but it is only recently that attention is being paid to it within K–12 classrooms.

CPS, in its simplest form, offers a series of formalized tools and methods for problem-solving that foster creativity and out-of-the-box thinking. If you find yourself questioning the value of this, try answering a simple question: Can you name the tools that you use to foster creative problem-solving and innovation in your own organization?

If you are coming up short or if your list does not get past brainstorming, don't be alarmed—few people can list more than that. The fact is that most of our creative problem-solving is limited to the freeform exercise of open dialogue and brainstorming. There is nothing wrong with that other than the fact that we have all become one-trick ponies when it comes to innovation. When problems get larger we just throw more ponies at them. In our work studying the mechanics of innovation across a broad range of industries, we found that despite the high stakes involved innovation was most often more a matter of serendipity and brute force than science and planned discovery. It is not that the scientists, engineers, and knowledge workers who are involved in discovery are unable to be innovative, but rather that they have not been trained in innovation as a science.

Surprisingly enough, however, some organizations, such as the nonprofit Destination Imagination and the Creative Education Foundation, founded by Alex Osborn in 1954, have been teaching these skills to children and adults for decades. Destination Imagination has been conducting local, national, and global competitions involving millions of children from primary through university levels for the past twenty years. To observe the level of creativity and ingenuity expressed by the participants in these programs is to find new hope in the notion of an innovation economy and in a generation that may truly be able to take on the challenges of this absurdly complex new era of uncertainty.

At the risk of appearing to be parochial, our expectation is that the United States is positioned to lead the charge here and define the benchmark for innovation education in the twenty-first century by focusing on primary and secondary education and incorporating the methods of CPS into mainstream classroom learning. But the global competition will be intense and we will need to foster a new culture of creative problem-solving among children. In many ways the U.S. economy is perhaps the most susceptible to disruption because so much of our economy is based on services. Without a bridge to a leadership role in the innovation economy, we will be left in a precarious and unenviable economic predicament as we attempt to redeploy displaced workers into an already shrinking services industry.

THE COUNTERBALANCE TO UNCERTAINTY

So we've arrived at the end of our journey. Are you prepared to take it from here? Are any of us?

The next five years will represent one of the most profound periods of change and advancement in how globalization is understood and leveraged. However, with advancement comes disruption and discomfort. But if we get through this period of tumult, the outlook is extraordinary.

Note we said, *if* we get through it. We are not taking for granted the precarious position that we are in as a global society or as a nation under siege by economic and political forces that can easily disrupt the playing field. Yet we feel strongly that the shift to an economy of innovation will not only deliver new products and services, but it will also deliver new strengths in how we cooperate and develop the sort of mutual reliance and reliability we talked about earlier. This gives us profound hope for the future.

However, that future begins with the challenges we face today.

What comes next may be a quiet revolution, in contrast to the over-the-top fanfare that often accompanies most revolutions. But it will be no less revolutionary—lasting well into the next decade and offering virtually limitless opportunities for business innovation.

We began this book with a simple question: What will define us best, the factors that separate us or those that connect us? The answers will be much simpler as historians look back at our age and ask the question, What best defined the changes of the twenty-first century? How did the actions, the technologies, and the behaviors that these citizens of a past era provide the foundation for our reality? Are we better off because of their actions or in spite of them? What did they do best?

Smartsourcing, globalization, even full employment (dare we suggest we can come close to achieving it) will not be the answer we expect. Although it may be the pinnacle of arrogance to write the history books of the future now, we feel compelled to take a stab at it, both to set a compass and to enthuse action.

So what do we see?

We see a near-term future of uncertainty beyond any of our expectations. We cannot write a script for the changes that are about to take place, nor the toll they will take on us emotionally. There will be setbacks as we struggle through microclimates of high turbulence in otherwise calm seasons of progress—like flying through clear skies with no warning of the sudden turbulence that lies ahead.

Terrorism will not go away. It will haunt us at best and enrage us at worst.

The gap in the digital and economic divide will only be mitigated in localized ways. It will otherwise grow as the population increases in underdeveloped nations and as we mobilize the many social and political systems that will need to be in place to start turning this tide of potential into kinetic economic energy.

Sounds unpleasant, doesn't it? But we are anything but despondent, because we believe that the footnote we will leave as the legacy of globalization will be that of creating the counterbalance to the uncertainty of each of these trends.

Globalization will be the navigator that charts an unforeseen course through these challenges. We firmly believe that our time will be known as one in which we finally understood uncertainty and leveraged the power of humanity to harness it. And we have just begun to understand the full power of that statement.

Like some of the world's greatest cities and most valuable real estate, our greatest ideas and our most profound achievements are built on the fault lines, those precarious spots on the geological, meteorological, and political precipice, where we cannot predict the future. Yet we can build to withstand it. Globalization, extended enterprise, and smartsourcing will build structures to withstand the future. And these will also create the bridges that connect us across national and corporate interests in the creation of interdependent global interests.

In his classic treatise on capitalism, Adam Smith spoke of the invisible hand of commerce that shaped the many miniscule aspects that make a free market work.

We've always been fascinated by Adam Smith's invisible hand—the way markets and economies are driven by these invisible forces that seem to defy the prognostications of even the smartest among us. As a leader, however, you must build organizations that can withstand and thrive in the future, even if you cannot predict it. In today's climate of high uncertainty and global unrest, this difficult task of the manager and leader seems next to impossible. Or is it?

Economist Paul Romer once said that the difficulty we all have in predicting the future is that "opportunities do not add up, they multiply." In these pages we've attempted to look at many of the factors that are involved in that multiplication effect. These are opportunities to apply sound business methods, concepts, frameworks, and technologies to the complex problems we face in our organizations and our world.

From the reshaping of commerce through the use of business service platforms to the evolution of process management tools to the emergence of social networks, there is a common momentum building in how we leverage this new era of global connections in ways that we are just beginning to perceive.

These are complex times for business leaders. Risk and uncertainty have taken center stage and there they will stay. But somewhere, perhaps tallied by an invisible hand, opportunities are already multiplying. Calculate carefully and you will find a future worthy of your greatest innovations and ambitions.

INDEX